The Planning and Management of Responsible Urban Heritage Destinations in Asia

Dealing with Asian urbanization and tourism forces

Walter Jamieson
and
Richard A. Engelhardt

(G) **Goodfellow Publishers Ltd**

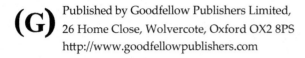

Published by Goodfellow Publishers Limited,
26 Home Close, Wolvercote, Oxford OX2 8PS
http://www.goodfellowpublishers.com

British Library Cataloguing in Publication Data: a catalogue record for this title is available from the British Library.

Library of Congress Catalog Card Number: on file.

ISBN: 978-1-911396-58-1

 Design and typesetting by P.K. McBride, www.macbride.org.uk

Cover design by Cylinder

Printed by Baker & Taylor, www.baker-taylor.com

Contents

Acknowledgments

The authors sincerely thank all of the contributors to this publication. We feel very fortunate that a significant number of experts, in conservation, tourism and planning in Asia, agreed to come together and share their experiences and lessons.

Harold Goodwin was an important part of the development of this book; he was, in fact, the initial supporter of the idea and not only provided Chapter 1 but also gave advice throughout the process.

Think City was invaluable in sharing information and knowledge from their 'work in progress' – a demonstrable model of a plan-led approach to urban regeneration in the George Town UNESCO World Heritage site. It is an inclusive urban regeneration model that widens participation and welcomes constructive criticism to make the city more liveable.

Think City's support in the development of the book and commitment to the idea of aligning development and conservation is an important contribution to the planning and management of Asian urban heritage. In particular we wish to recognize Think City's Programme Directors Neil Khor and Matt Benson not only for their contribution of Chapter 6 but their ongoing advice and direction.

Many thanks to Thanan Lilaonitkul for agreeing to share his experience in developing the valuable Bangkok case study presented in Chapter 7.

Michelle Jamieson of Green Door Solutions Ltd. played an important role in helping to coordinate the overall publication while at the same time providing substantive input.

Sarah Oliver, the research assistant on the project, not only provided much-needed support but also helped to provide a student's perspective on the book. Her time was financially supported by Green Door Solutions Ltd.

Keenan Mathura has helped us in ensuring that our graphics support our ideas and concepts.

We are indebted to Ellie Meleisea, our copy editor, who did a masterful job in bringing together diverse writing styles and provided invaluable information and suggestions for improving the book. Without her, developing the book would have been a much more difficult task.

Finally, we wish to thank Sally North, Editorial Director of Goodfellow Publishers Limited who was a constant source of advice and support throughout the process of putting this book together.

Walter Jamieson and Richard Engelhardt
Editors

Introduction

Policies that promote large-scale urban redevelopment, coupled with a lack of regulation relating to urban development and a lack of heritage protection policies, have, since the end of the Second World War, resulted in the loss of a large proportion of the distinctive tangible heritage assets in Asian cities, including historic monuments, buildings and vernacular housing. With this loss of historic built environments, long-term inhabitants have also been displaced. Concurrently, the loss of traditional inhabitants from re-developed historic spaces has resulted in the disappearance of traditional expressions and practices of intangible urban culture, expressions that once gave each city its unique, recognizable cultural identity.

The loss of heritage can also be traced to the independence struggles in certain countries, including in Bangladesh, Cambodia, India, Indonesia, the Koreas, Pakistan, Malaysia, Myanmar, Singapore, Sri Lanka, and Vietnam. This struggle later led to intentional removal of built heritage, as it was a reminder of their colonial past, and all of these countries embarked on building programmes very much influenced by ultramodern architecture, in order to showcase their new-found identity and sense of self. The post-Cultural Revolution building boom in China can be seen as a similar manifestation.

These heritage losses have created modern urban environments that are increasingly homogenous throughout Asia, and which lack the definable, recognizable cultural identities seen in Asia's traditional urban centres in the past. This distinctiveness of Asian cities was at the foundation of the strong feelings of identity and attachment that local inhabitants felt for their cities – emotions that provided for a culture of social solidarity, environmental protection and cultural stewardship. It was also this strong sense of unique identity that made Asian cities subjects of fascination and places of attraction for visitors for centuries.

Within the significant number of issues that must be addressed the planning, design and management of the rapidly-growing urban environment, heritage conservation and tourism development are two areas that have emerged as pivotal in terms of their influence on urban place-making policy and planning, as well as their overall impact on long-term urban sustainability. Hence, many forces are at work demanding that those responsible for the planning, design and management of urban areas in Asia develop more integrated, inclusive, responsible and resilient policies, strategies, practices and tools.

The adoption, in 2015, of the United Nations Sustainable Development Goals (SDGs) provided a revised context and refreshed global strategy within which the urban environment can be designed, planned and managed. Given that for the first time in the history of humankind, the majority of the population lives in cities, much interest is now focused on the development of urban areas. The SDGs identify a large number of urban-related programmes that impact on heritage conservation and tourism development, most specifically within Goal 11 for Sustainable Cities and Communities, which emphasises the need to make cities inclusive, safe, resilient and sustainable, and recognizes the relevance of international standard-setting instruments directed at protecting urban heritage (United Nations, 2015). These instruments include the *Recommendation on the Historic Urban Landscape (HUL)*, which was adopted by the United Nations Educational, Scientific and Cultural Organisation (UNESCO) in 2011 and which has since provided the foundation for the discussion of the linkages between heritage conservation and urban development (UNESCO, 2011). The HUL builds upon a number of previous international charters, including the *Convention for the Safeguarding of Intangible Cultural Heritage* (UNESCO, 2003), the *International Cultural Tourism Charter* (ICOMOS, 1999), the *Charter for the Conservation of Historic Towns and Urban Areas* (ICOMOS, 1987) and, of course, the *Convention Concerning the Protection of the World Cultural and Natural Heritage* (UNESCO, 1972).

In 1975, the importance of the tourism industry as a key player in global development was recognized with the establishment of the United Nations World Tourism Organization (UNWTO). Acknowledging the systemic relationship between culture and tourism, and the fact that they are much dependent on each other as tools for development, in 2018 the UNWTO published a report titled *Tourism and Culture Synergies*.[1] The report observes that there is now a growing number of visitors who, based on a desire to experience and learn from heritage environments, are looking for a renewed and reinvigorated authenticity. Furthermore, after a century of urban redevelopment, there is a demand for renewed 'place making' to recover the unique past of each urban space. All this interest is very much welcomed but this demand places significant pressure on not only the heritage environment but also on the residents of heritage areas. Many heritage environments are now experiencing visitation levels beyond their capacities, resulting in what has been identified as 'overtourism'.

While in the past there always seemed to be an inherent choice to be made between economic growth and urban area heritage conservation, there is now growing evidence, at least in theory, that this choice is no longer valid. This is due in part to the reality that cultural heritage conservation is an indivisible part of human rights, as stated in the 1948 *Universal Declaration of Human Rights*. Importantly, it is now widely recognised that a single-minded pursuit of growth for growth's sake, measured in percentage increases in GDP or percentage increases of visitor arrivals, is not sustainable. Certainly, these GDP or visitor arrival measures are not sufficient to assess the achievement of overall social goals such as elimination of poverty, freedom from hunger, health and longevity, universal education, gender equity and stabilization of population growth.

The intent of this book is to provide a framework for understanding urban heritage area conservation and tourism within the larger urban development context. The book examines various facets of urban heritage area conservation,

---

1   Tourism and Culture Synergies, Madrid, UNWTO, 2018

including heritage area policies, the conditions that enable heritage conservation, and planning and management responses, taking into account the broader context. This book presents and analyzes 48 case studies and examples of actual urban heritage conservation initiatives and identifies the necessary elements for an integrated and responsible approach to planning, managing and developing a policy and planning framework where heritage conservation and tourism development are essential elements of overall sustainable and responsible urban development. This publication does not seek to repeat the work of other authors and experts dealing with Asian urban areas but rather to establish the context and interface at which heritage conservation management and tourism development planning meet and merge.

The book is designed for those involved in the process of planning, managing and designing cities, developing tourism and protecting heritage resources. It presents a reality check on the state of urban heritage conservation and tourism management in Asia today.

The book is organized around eight chapters.

Chapter 1 provides a conceptual and theoretical framework for responsible urban development, with a focus on heritage and tourism. The following chapters build on this ethical setting.

Chapter 2 explores the challenges arising in the conservation and management of heritage areas in Asian cities, given the complexity of these urban areas. The analysis identifies the forces working on urban areas as well as the realities of maintaining and enhancing such areas, including those that attract large numbers of tourists.

Chapters 3, 4 and 5 offer case examples and studies that illustrate the Asian situation through diverse examples of practice in the region, representing a cross-section of issues related to heritage conservation and tourism development, as well as analytic approaches and planning, policy and design responses.

Chapter 6 focuses on a well-developed and structured urban management initiative in George Town Malaysia. The case study indicates how knowledge-based planning provides a basis for sustainable development in a number of ways, including (a) protection of heritage integrity as a common good; (b) ensuring equitable access to the city's resources, including cultural resources; (c) regulation of speculation in the property market; (d) regulation of carrying capacity limits; (e) avoiding inefficient public sector (taxpayer) investment in over-building of unnecessary and destructive infrastructure; (f) reinvestment of profits for community good (job creation, etc.); and (g) protection of livelihoods essential to the city's identity.

Chapter 7 examines Bangkok's Creative District, which has placed an emphasis on mobilizing community resources, maintaining essential tangible and intangible heritage resources and seeking investment in community infrastructure. This approach is determining a new future for an area that is quickly evolving.

The case study examines the opportunities that come with the adoption of planning mechanisms that aim to safeguard community assets while providing a level playing field and stable platform for investment that encourages the private sector to be creative and, in so doing, promotes the extension of the community's cultural continuum through expansion of authentic liveable cultural heritage experiences.

Chapter 8 recognizes that the planning, design and management of urban areas is a highly complex process requiring the participation, alignment and engagement of a wide range of stakeholders, including experts on both heritage conservation and tourism development. It is a particular challenge in the Asian context where many urban planners, policy-makers and designers do not necessarily view tourism development or heritage conservation as major components within their overall mandate, in spite of the obvious contributions both sectors give to urban place-making, with the result that either or both heritage and tourism are pushed onto the sidelines of the planning process. This chapter argues that an integrated approach to tourism and heritage conservation management is essential to sustainability.

There could not be a more appropriate time for a publication that addresses these issues with an interdisciplinary perspective. While a number of studies have dealt with these areas as independent vectors of urban management, few studies within the Asian context and within holistic urban development planning paradigms have looked at the relationship between policies to promote tourism and those that protect heritage assets. The challenge is to move the discussion to how to responsibly plan, design and manage the rate and nature of urban change to ensure success and respect carrying capacities. This will be accomplished by integrating policies on urban heritage area conservation, enabling conditions and planning and management practice responses, taking into account the larger institutional, development and economic and social environment. Throughout the book there will be a reference to the larger policy and planning context but always from the perspective of urban heritage area conservation.

References

ICOMOS (1987) *Charter for the Conservation of Historic Towns and Urban Areas.* https://www.icomos.org/charters/towns_e.pdf (Accessed 28 August 2018.)

ICOMOS (1999) *International Cultural Tourism Charter* (Managing Tourism at Places of Significance). https://www.icomos.org/en/newsletters-archives/179-articles-en-francais/ressources/charters-and-standards/162-international-cultural-tourism-charter (Accessed 28 August 2018.)

UNESCO (1972) *Convention for the Safeguarding of the World Cultural and Natural Heritage.* https://whc.unesco.org/en/conventiontext/

United Nations (2015) 'Sustainable Development Goals'. https://sustainabledevelopment.un.org/topics/sustainabledevelopmentgoals (Accessed 28 August 2018.)

UNESCO (2011) *Recommendation on the Historic Urban Landscape.* https://whc.unesco.org/uploads/activities/documents/activity-638-98.pdf (Accessed 28 August 2018.)

UNESCO (2003) *The Convention for the Safeguarding of Intangible Cultural Heritage.* http://www.unesco.org/new/en/santiago/culture/intangible-heritage/convention-intangible-cultural-heritage/ (Accessed 28 August 2018.)

UNWTO (2018) *Tourism and Culture Synergies*, Madrid: UNWTO.

About the authors

Dr. Richard A. Engelhardt, educated at Yale and Harvard universities, has advanced degrees in anthropology, history and archaeology. Since the 1980s, he has spearheaded heritage conservation efforts throughout Asia, serving in academia and with the United Nations. In 1990, he inaugurated the UNESCO Field Office in Cambodia and initiated the International Safeguarding Campaign for Angkor, in recognition of which King Norodom Sihanouk awarded him the title Commandeur de l'Ordre Royal du Cambodge. From 1994 to 2008, he was UNESCO Regional Advisor for Culture in Asia and the Pacific, and from 2008 to 2010, the UNESCO Senior Advisor for Culture. Between 2010 and 2015 he was Visiting Research Professor of Architecture Conservation at the University of Hong Kong. He is now concurrently Honorary Professor of Architecture at Southeast University, Nanjing; Honorary Professor in Architecture and Urban Planning at Tongji University, Shanghai; and UNESCO Chair Professor of the Conservation of Historic Towns and Urban Centres at the National College of Art in Pakistan. Professor Engelhardt is a Member of the Committee of Honour of the International Network for Traditional Buildings, Architecture and Urbanism (INTBAU), and was awarded the Lifetime Achievement Award by the Global Heritage Fund.

Dr. Walter Jamieson has worked to bridge and challenge the academic and consultancy worlds through creative, innovative and out-of-the-box thinking for more than 40 years. He has, through his work, made significant contributions to organisations at the international, national and local levels (ADB, UNWTO, ESCAP, UNESCO, JICA and ASEAN). His activities have included heritage, planning and tourism work in Canada, research and consultancy work in China, extensive community-based tourism work in Southeast Asia, and exploration of the power of tourism as a tool for cultural, economic and social development all over the world. He has held high positions in universities in Canada, the United States and throughout Asia, including in Thailand and Japan. His awards and recognitions include the Queen's Jubilee Medal for his contributions to heritage preservation in Canada, the Heritage Canada Lieutenant Governor's Award, and his election to the College of Fellows of the Canadian Institute of Planners. He has authored and contributed to 140 academic publications and over 150 consultancy and research projects. Recent consultancies include participation in the ASEAN Tourism Strategic Plan; the ASEAN Tourism Marketing Strategy; Myanmar Tourism Master Plan and the updated 'Greater Mekong Subregion Tourism Sector Strategy (2016-2025)'. Currently, Professor Jamieson is an Adjunct Professor at Ryerson University in Toronto, Canada; Distinguished Adjunct Professor at the Asian Institute of Technology, Bangkok, Thailand; and Chief Innovation Officer at Green Door Solutions Ltd.

Key contributors

Dr. Matt Benson, a trained geographer, is a Programme Director at Think City – a specialized urban regeneration organization established by the Malaysian government's strategic investment arm, Khazanah Nasional. Over the past 20 years he has been involved in over 250 planning and development projects in suburban, brownfield and remote settings, in Malaysia and internationally. He is an experienced analyst, strategic planner and project manager, and has led complex consultation, data collection, master planning, urban regeneration and public realm improvement projects. In his current role at Think City he leads a team of urban designers and researchers developing and piloting innovative solutions to improve the liveability of Malaysian cities.

Dr. Neil Khor is a social historian and the Founding Director of the George Town Grants Programme, Malaysia's first public grants programme for urban regeneration in the George Town UNESCO World Heritage Site. He is currently the Programme Director of Think City. Overseeing two offices, in Kuala Lumpur and Johor Bahru, he leads a multi-disciplinary team to help deliver urban regeneration projects in historic town centres. He is also the Secretary of the George Town Conservation and Development Corporation, a tripartite organisation of the Penang state government, Think City and the Aga Khan Trust for Culture. Neil has published several books on Penang highlighting the social and cultural histories of its main communities. He is an Associated Scholar at the Centre for South Asian Studies of the University of Cambridge, and the Honorary Secretary of the Malaysian Branch of the Royal Asiatic Society.

Dr. Harold Goodwin has worked on four continents with local communities, their governments and the inbound and outbound tourism industry. He is an Emeritus Professor and the Director of Responsible Tourism at the Institute of Place Management at Manchester Metropolitan University, the Managing Director of the Responsible Tourism Partnership and an advisor to the World Travel Market (WTM) on its Responsible Tourism programme at WTM London, which attracts 2000 participants each year, and on WTM Africa and Latin America and Arabian Travel Mart. He chairs the panels of judges for the World Responsible Tourism Awards and other awards in Africa and India. Professor Goodwin conducts research on tourism, local economic development, poverty reduction, conservation and responsible tourism, working with the tourism industry, local communities, governments and conservationists. He also undertakes consultancies and evaluations for companies, NGOs, governments, and international organisations. He is the Founding Director of the International Centre for Responsible Tourism (2002), which promotes the principles of the Cape Town Declaration.

Thanan Lilaonitkul is a Bangkok-based writer and one of the founding directors of the Creative District Foundation, a Thai non-profit organization that focuses on the renewal of the city at a district level, through partnerships and collaborative projects. Prior to his move to Thailand, Thanan was a biomedical engineer and researcher at Rehabilitation Institute of Chicago. Post-graduation, he became a consultant at Deloitte Consulting LLP, managing enterprise resource planning system implementation projects, and then moved on to work on the communications team in the CEO office in New York. He now channels his skills and experience toward civil society projects.

1 Responsible Tourism and the Conservation of Heritage in Asian Urban Areas

Harold Goodwin

Introduction

Fundamental to the conservation of heritage in urban areas is a planning, design, development and management process based on responsible and sustainable objectives and criteria. This chapter establishes the ethical setting required, through discussing the topics presented in Figure 1.1.

Figure 1.1: Topics in Chapter 1

Cultural heritage explored

Culture and heritage are valued worldwide. The Universal Declaration on Cultural Diversity reminds us that the "defence of cultural diversity is an ethical imperative, inseparable from respect for human dignity" (UNESCO, 2001, Article 4). This is because cultural diversity "is one of the roots of development" (ibid, Article 3).

Cultural heritage is esteemed and handed on to future generations because it contributes to local, national and international identity. While national identity is state sponsored, local identity emerges "naturally through the evolution of the history and cultural experience of the people" (Embong, 2011: 16). Cultural heritage is also valued as it is "the wellspring of creativity" (UNESCO, 2001, Article 7).

Cultural heritage is made up of both physical (movable and fixed) and intangible elements that are successfully passed from one generation to the next. Movable physical elements include handicrafts, sculptures, paintings, archaeological objects, musical instruments and furniture. Fixed cultural dimensions include "houses, factories, commercial buildings, places of worship, cemeteries, monuments and built infrastructure such as roads, railways and bridges; physically created places such as gardens, mining sites and stock routes; and other places of historical significance such as archaeological sites" (Modern Heritage Matters, 2013); as well as historic districts and townscapes.

Intangible heritage encompasses oral traditions and expressions, including language – a vehicle of intangible cultural heritage, "performing arts, social practices, rituals, festive events, knowledge and practices concerning nature and the universe" (UNESCO, n.d.), and traditional craftsmanship. Intangible heritage is important not only for the cultural manifestation itself, but also for "the wealth of knowledge and skills that is transmitted through it from one generation to the next" (ibid.). This transmission of knowledge is valuable for all social groups, both minorities and the mainstream, and in both 'developing' and 'developed' countries.

Places are given meaning, 'a sense of place', by people. It is the interaction between the place and the people who live there and visit it that makes a place significant. A place may engender multiple senses of place because places have different meanings for different people. Places therefore belong to many groups, each of which may have a different sense of place.

Decisions about which heritage resources and places to retain and not retain, and how that should be accomplished, require considering several dimensions, not only economic factors. As the Universal Declaration declares, "Market forces alone cannot guarantee the preservation and promotion of cultural diversity" (UNESCO, 2001, Article 11). Governments must therefore develop cultural policies that consider all of the dimensions, including social and environmental factors.

While some cultural heritage resources and places are considered to be worthy of designation as World Heritage sites and are protected by internationally-recognized criteria and procedures (see Chapter 4), others are of particular national or local significance (see Chapter 5). A resource's significance, the political and community objectives and the level of development determine the conservation and interpretation approaches used (see Chapter 2). The conservation of heritage buildings generally requires an ongoing use to ensure that the building can be maintained. Sometimes that use may conflict with the original cultural purposes or the spirit of the place.

Urban challenges

Given the numerous challenges facing residents of urban areas in Asia, including insufficient clean, running water; ineffective solid waste management; unafford-able housing and education; and security issues, heritage conservation is often not considered a major concern. Therefore, conservation receives insufficient financial support. A significant increase in financial resources is required to address the various challenges, including those relating to heritage conservation.

As with any other area of urban governance, various factors are involved when it comes to urban heritage conservation. These factors include: planning and management policies and plans; property interests; ownership land-use patterns; political influence on decision-making processes; economic policies and conditions; levels of expertise; bureaucratic processes; local traditions; and decision-making structures.

The act of conservation often requires cooperation between administrative realms (public, private and non-governmental) that do not always see eye to eye. Uncoordinated planning and management has negative outcomes that are exacerbated when people working in the bureaucracy do not have the necessary knowledge, skills or mindset to deal with the complexity of the issues confront-ing urban areas. The impact is greater when bureaucrats are assigned tasks that do not allow for a system-thinking approach to problem solving. This makes it difficult, if not impossible, to manage, sustainably, urban heritage conservation in tandem with other urban planning and policy issues.

The planning and management of historic urban areas presents planners, managers, policy makers and designers with challenges that defy resolution using the linear, directive planning approaches typically employed in Asia. In this narrow context, heritage conservation, if it takes place at all, is severely limited as a driver for tourism development, or for any other activity grounded in heritage resources.

Tourism takes place in other people's places

As Ringer (1998: 1) has noted, "Tourism is a cultural process as much as it is a form of economic development, and the destination of the tourist and the inhabited landscape of local culture are now inseparable to a greater degree". Furthermore, a destination is not merely a leitmotif for a geographic place. Rather, [destina-tions] are also social and cultural constructions whose meanings and values are negotiated and redefined by diverse people, and mediated by factors "often related only tangentially to a particular tourist setting" (Squire, 1998). Thus, "the visible structure of a place expresses the emotional attachments held by both its residents and visitors, as well as the means by which it is imagined, produced, contested and enforced" (Ringer, 1998: 6). Tourists from different source markets, international and domestic, contribute to the construction of a place's sense of place. The tourism industry and tourists contribute to "the less tangible aspects of a place that give it whatever special appeal it has" (Bosselman et al. 1999:19).

Tourists are attracted by the opportunity to experience other people in other places. According to a study of the motivations of holidaymakers from the United Kingdom, almost all (95%) felt that the experience of travel is just as important as value for money (Travel Daily Media, 2010). Tourists consume heritage for nostalgia and also to celebrate and recognise modernity (Picard and Wood, 1997). As Embong (2011:13) points out, the massive structures built in Asia in recent decades, such as the Petronas Twin Towers in Kuala Lumpur, the Taipei 101 Tower in Taiwan and the Shanghai World Financial Centre, are "iconic material expressions have been thrust to the fore as new cultural symbols like the proverbial show-off new kids on the block". This new 'heritage' affirms for them that these states have strong, modern economies.

The tourism industry has been described as a business of renting out "other people's environments, whether this is a coastline, a city, a mountain range, or a rainforest" (Goodwin, 2011:20). But where does the income from this 'rent' go? The primary beneficiaries of tourism are the providers of accommodation, food and transport. At heritage sites, the tourism industry uses built heritage to house hotels, restaurants and museums, which are often the primary attractions for visitors. However, when tourists visit a destination, the overall built environment, along with its cleaning and maintenance, often comes for free. Tourists can view the destination's buildings and take 'selfies' at no cost. Rarely does the entrance fee for a destination, where there is one, cover the management and maintenance cost of the visit. Furthermore, very little of the profits are reinvested in the conservation of the heritage that attracts tourists.

The impact of tourism on urban heritage areas

Politicians and policy-makers increasingly use the economic benefits of tourism to justify their decisions to preserve or conserve heritage resources. Likewise, conservationists use 'tourism potential' to make a case for conserving buildings and townscapes. Similarly, the development of urban heritage areas for tourism is often justified on the basis that tourism will generate revenue that can be used to assist in the conservation process. But although the preservation and re-use of a building for tourism may bring economic benefits while also rescuing the physical structure of a building, the introduction of tourism tends not to preserve the cultural meaning and purpose of the building.

Most tourism developments do create jobs, but how often the revenue is used to protect heritage buildings is questionable. Furthermore, tourism is often exploitative. It may bring some employment but these jobs tend to be of poor quality and with low remuneration. In addition, tourism also often contributes to the gentrification of heritage areas, changing the land value systems of those areas and displacing communities who may have lived in the areas for generations.

The negative impacts of tourism on built heritage and townscapes include:

- Loss of the spirit or sense of place, and disinheritance for communities that lose access or use.
- Loss of diversity and authenticity through reconstruction processes that homogenize a place's unique characteristics.
- Commodification of built heritage, for example, when a traditional building is converted to a hotel, bar, café or restaurant. On the other hand this may be a sustainable use, essential to a building's restoration and maintenance.
- Loss of spiritual or sacred value.
- Congestion, crowding and noise pollution.
- Litter and other physical pollution.
- Trampling and wear and tear.

One of the major challenges in urban heritage areas is how to plan for and manage tourism so that tourism is a positive force for development and does not negatively impact the tangible and intangible heritage or the people living within heritage areas.

When the impacts of tourism become serious, it is described as 'overtourism'. This is seen in destinations where both hosts and guests, locals and tourists, feel that there are too many visitors and that the quality of life in the area and/or the quality of the experience has deteriorated unacceptably (Goodwin, 2017a). Overtourism can therefore be understood as a situation in which there are significant negative impacts on the place, the residents, the working community and the visitor experience.

Many destinations dislike the label 'overtourism', so instead refer to the negative impacts of tourism as the "challenges of coping with success" (WTTC, 2017) or describe it as "inadequately managed" tourism (Responsible Tourism Partnership, 2018). While better management of supply and demand can diminish the issues, there are real physical and social limits.

Overtourism is one example of what happens when more and more seek to consume a common resource. Tourism makes extensive use of common resources in the public realm and takes advantage of, for example, public museums and galleries, which are free or merit-priced (initially for the benefit of citizens). The tourism industry enjoys free access to public goods, which are very often its core product, but these tourism commons are very vulnerable to crowding and degrading by tourism pressure (Responsible Tourism Partnership, 2018). Overtourism is thus an example of the tragedy of the commons, where the individual pursuit of self-interest and the consequent exploitation of resources in the public realm results in ruin for all (Hardin, 1968). Each tourist pursues individual self-interest in visiting a heritage place in the public realm and each person earning income from tourism pursues self-interest in profiting from tourism. When neither the tourists nor the beneficiaries of tourism are responsible for the heritage assets that the tourists visit, then those assets, the place and the peoples' experience of it becomes degraded and worthless to no-one. Therein lies the tragedy.

Overtourism is a consequence of the industry's failure to become sustainable. The industry is now bumping up against the limits to growth. In many destinations, the limits are being reached across the triple bottom line: social, economic and environmental. In such destinations, there are cultural clashes because of differences between locals and visitors in terms of social norms about behaviour; local people are displaced by holiday rentals; shops that used to meet the needs of residents are displaced by outlets catering exclusively to tourists; and "lawns are trampled to bare earth and beaches littered" (Responsible Tourism Partnership, 2018). Feeling these limits, the residents of many historic areas, including in Amsterdam, Barcelona and Venice, are increasingly voicing their opposition to tourism (Ross, 2015; Diaz, 2017; Goodwin, 2017b).

Sustainable and responsible tourism

Responsible tourism is about taking responsibility for making tourism more sustainable. It is about creating or making "better places for people to live in and for people to visit" and respecting the interests of indigenous people and local communities.

In particular, responsible tourism seeks to:

- Minimise negative economic, environmental and social impacts.
- Generate greater economic benefits for local people and enhance the well-being of host communities, and improve working conditions and access to the industry.
- Involve local people in decisions that affect their lives and life chances.
- Ensure that tourism (the industry and the consumers) makes positive contributions to the conservation of natural and cultural heritage and to the maintenance of the world's diversity.
- Provide more enjoyable, authentic, experiences for tourists through more meaningful connections with local people, and a greater understanding of local cultural, social and environmental issues.
- Provide access for people with disabilities.
- Ensure that tourism is culturally sensitive, engenders respect between tourists and hosts, and builds local pride and confidence (International Conference on Responsible Tourism in Destinations, 2002).

The issue of agency, i.e. the capacity and willingness of people to think independently and to make their own decisions, is critical to taking responsibility. It is not enough to debate the concept; it is about doing something about the issues. As Krippendorf (1987) observed, tourism is what we make it, and if we take responsibility we can change it.

Three aspects of the concept of responsibility are particularly relevant to agency:

- **Accountability**: Individuals and legal entities must be held to account for acts and omissions. For some acts and omissions there may be legal liability.

- **Capacity**: The individual or organisation must have the capacity to act, to make a difference. With opportunity comes the impetus to responsibility.

- **Responding**: Individuals and organisations are expected to respond and to make a difference. Responsibility involves entering a dialogue.

Towards a responsible conservation approach

The Universal Declaration on Cultural Diversity reaffirmed the "pre-eminence of public policy, in partnership with the private sector and civil society" (UNESCO, 2001, Article 11) as key to the preservation and promotion of cultural diversity. While in some cases, the government, local or national, can restore heritage buildings and establish museums and cultural centres, with development funds or with the support of civil society, in other cases, conservation and restoration require private sector funding and a 'new' use for the building. In either situation, success requires the appropriate regulatory frameworks, staffing, knowledge, skills and mind-set. The quality of the government's skills in planning, conservation and building control is critically important. The planning of places should be undertaken by locally-accountable experts, with advice from international experts and funding support where required.

References

Bosselman, F., Peterson, C. and McCarthy, C. (1999) *Managing Tourism Growth: Issues and applications*, Washington DC: Island Press

Embong, A. R. (2011) The question of culture, identity and globalisation: An unending debate, *Kajian Malaysia*, **29** (Suppl 1), 11-22

Diaz, A. L. (2017) Why Barcelona locals really hate tourists, *The Independent*, 9 August.

Goodwin, H. (2011) *Taking Responsibility for Tourism*, Oxford: Goodfellow Publishers.

Goodwin, H. (2017a) *The Challenge of Overtourism*, Responsible Tourism Partnership Working Paper 4, October 2017.

Goodwin (2017b) A new challenge 'overtourism', *World Travel Market Responsible Tourism Blog*, 27 September. https://news.wtm.com/a-new-challenge-overtourism/ (Accessed 14 August 2018.)

Hardin, G. (1968) The tragedy of the commons, Science, **162** (3859), 1243-1248. http://science.sciencemag.org/content/162/3859/1243 (Accessed 14 August 2018.)

International Conference on Responsible Tourism in Destinations (2002) Cape Town Declaration on Responsible Tourism, August 2002.

Krippendorf, J. (1987) *The Holiday Makers*, Oxford: Butterworth-Heinemann.

Modern Heritage Matters (2013) What is built heritage? http://modernheritage.com.au/mhm/understand_heritage/what-is-built-heritage/ (Accessed 25 July 2018.)

Picard, M. and Wood, R. E. (eds.) (1997) *Tourism, Ethnicity, and the State in Asian and Pacific Societies*, Honolulu: University of Hawaii Press.

Responsible Tourism Partnership (2018) Overtourism: Can we have too many tourists? http://responsibletourismpartnership.org/overtourism/ (Accessed 12 July 2018)

Ringer, G. (ed.) (1998) *Destinations: Cultural landscapes of tourism*, London: Routledge.

Ross, W. (2015) The death of Venice, *The Independent*, 14 May.

Squire, S. J. (1998) Rewriting languages of geography and tourism, in G. Ringer (ed.), *Destinations: Cultural landscapes of tourism*, London: Routledge, pp. 80-100.

Travel Daily Media (2010) Britons looking to travel further afield, *Travel Daily Media*, 9 April. https://www.traveldailymedia.com/britons-looking-to-travel-further-afield/ (Accessed 10 August 2018.)

UNESCO.(n. d.) What is intangible heritage? https://ich.unesco.org/en/what-is-intangible-heritage-00003 (Accessed 30 May 2018.)

UNESCO (2001) Universal Declaration on Cultural Diversity, Adopted by the 31st Session of the General Conference of UNESCO in Paris, 2 November.

WTTC (2017) *Coping with success: Managing overcrowding in tourism destinations*, McKinsey & Company and World Travel & Tourism Council.

2 Challenges in Conserving and Managing Heritage in Asian Urban Areas

Walter Jamieson and Richard Engelhardt

Introduction

This chapter builds on the ethical setting presented in Chapter 1. It discusses the challenges facing residents in Asian urban areas and provides an overview of the context in which urban planning, design and management in Asia occurs. Based on this analysis, the chapter then examines the problematic nature of the interface between heritage conservation and the planning, design and management of urban areas, including the impact of tourism in heritage environments. This discussion will provide the context for the case studies and examples that follow in Chapters 3, 4 and 5.

The chapter is organised around key ideas as seen in Figure 2.1.

Figure 2.1: Organisational framework

The state of Asian urban areas

Urban areas in Asia vary in size and include metropolitan areas, regional towns and large cities, as well as portions of cities, such as historic districts. They also differ in terms of geography, economic conditions, political systems and cultural and social systems. Given these differences, it is difficult to generalise about them. However, Asian urban areas have certain similarities, one of which is that their populations are growing at unparalleled rates (see Figure 2.2). Also, the populations of these fast-growing and rapidly-expanding urban areas are demanding infrastructure development at a pace that is often far beyond local economic, financial and human capacities. Such urban areas often have poorly-developed urban management structures and weak decision-making systems, however. Furthermore, these cities have planning and governance approaches that are neither comprehensive nor robust enough to deal with the growth and complexity of the urban situation. In the very largest cities, the limits of liveability have been reached and they are unsustainable in their current form.

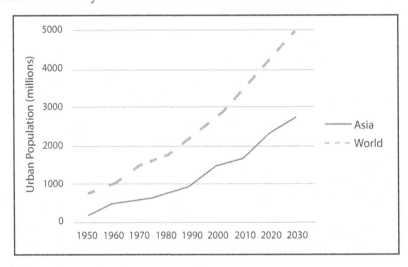

Figure 2.2: Growth in urban population and projections (Source: Adapted from Johnson et al, 2013)

In many Asian cities the percentage of the population living below the locally-acknowledged poverty line is as high as 40% (Jamieson, 2009). Measuring poverty in urban areas is more complex than simply using the traditional US$1 a day baseline, however. While some urban residents may have higher incomes, the lack of basic services and the high cost of rent, transport, healthcare, education and other essentials make living conditions difficult and make it impossible for many residents to make ends meet. Most urban slum dwellers do not have access to clean water, sanitation, social services, decent housing, schooling or steady jobs, and live trapped in situations that contribute to poor levels of health and well-being. As well as limited access to social services, they lack basic rights, are often exploited and have no power to influence their futures. In the urban slums of sprawling cities like Manila and Mumbai, generation after generation are born, grow up and start families themselves without ever escaping poverty.

In such circumstances, the diversion of scarce resources to heritage conservation, or to the development of high-end facilities for visitors, is an unimaginable and unacceptable luxury. Thus, heritage conservation, while fundamental to a community's identity and cultural continuity, may constitute an impossible short-term investment, even if it makes good economic sense in the long-term. On the other side of the equation, if the redevelopment of an historic area for the purposes of accommodating visitors[1] is predicated on the 'gentrification' of the area and displacement of its long-term inhabitants, then the net effect is socially unconscionable and politically very unwise.

Addressing urban challenges

Accommodating population growth and renewing and expanding infrastructure are ongoing challenges for urban planners and city managers worldwide. Over the past five decades numerous meetings have been held at the international, regional and national levels to identify workable and sustainable solutions to these challenges.

Key meetings and their outcomes include:

- The United Nations Conference on the Human Environment, held in Stockholm, Sweden, in 1972. The conference resulted in the Stockholm Declaration.

- The UN Conference on Human Settlements (HABITAT I), held in Vancouver, Canada, in 1976. It resulted in the Vancouver Declaration on Human Settlements and the Vancouver Action Plan.

- The Second UN Conference on Human Settlements (HABITAT II), held in Istanbul, Turkey, in 1996. This meeting resulted in the Istanbul Declaration on Human Settlements (the 'Habitat Agenda'), a global plan of action.

- The UN Conference on Housing and Sustainable Urban Development (HABITAT III), held in Quito, Ecuador, in 2016. This resulted in the New Urban Agenda (NUA), a guideline for urban development for the following 20 years.

The 'HABITAT' conferences are described in more detail below.

HABITAT I

The United Nations Conference on Human Settlements (HABITAT I) held in 1976, articulated two major challenges relating to managing the urban condition: (i) how to halt the deterioration of degrading infrastructure and building stock and (ii) how to ensure and enhance the liveability of cities, equitably, for all sectors of

---

1 The term 'visitor' is used here to describe all individuals and groups that visit a city, including people from the city itself. Tourists can be seen as a subset of visitors.

the population. The Vancouver Declaration called for action at both the national and international levels to address unacceptable urban living conditions, which were 'likely to be aggravated by inequitable economic growth and uncontrolled urbanization' (UN Conference on Human Settlements, 1976). The Vancouver Action Plan was an ambitious document, with 64 recommendations, in six sections: settlement policies and strategies; settlement planning; shelter, infrastructure and services; land; public participation; and institutions and management. Following the HABITAT I meeting, the UN General Assembly created the UN Centre for Human Settlements, which later merged with other organisations to become the United Nations Human Settlements Programme (UN-Habitat).

Key initiatives that followed HABITAT I included:

- The Healthy Cities Programme, which was launched by the World Health Organization in 1986 to develop health-enhancing public policies that would create physical and social environments to strengthen community action for health and well-being.

- The Urban Management Programme (UMP), which was a collaborative initiative of UN-Habitat, the United Nations Development Programme (UNDP) and the World Bank that sought, between 1986 and 2006, to develop and apply urban management knowledge in the fields of participatory urban governance, alleviation of urban poverty and urban environmental management.

- The Regional Network of Local Authorities for the Management of Human Settlements (CITYNET), established in 1987, which links municipal governments, community-based organisations and research centres that together seek to create the conditions and mechanisms necessary for communities to plan and manage sustainable and resilient cities.

- The Sustainable Cities Programme (SCP), which is a joint venture by UN-Habitat and the United Nations Environment Programme (UNEP). It was established in the early 1990s and seeks to strengthen the capacity of municipal authorities so as to improve urban planning and management, and manage natural resources sustainably.

- Localizing Agenda 21 (LA21), which is a capacity building programme that seeks to enable local authorities to develop and implement Agenda 21[2] programmes within their communities.

HABITAT II

At the Second UN Conference on Human Settlements (HABITAT II), held in 1996, an important step was taken to bring universities, non-governmental organisations (NGOs) and the private sector into a dialogue, in recognition of their significant contributions to programme planning, implementation and resourcing. This set the stage for a new paradigm of cooperation between (a) top-down approaches

2 Agenda 21 is an action plan for achieving sustainable development. It was the key outcome of the UN Conference on Environment and Development, held in Rio de Janeiro, Brazil, in 1992.

of government-led planning and financing, and (b) bottom-up actions driven by community activism and private sector investment. The results of HABITAT II were incorporated into the Istanbul Declaration on Human Settlements and its Global Plan of Action (UN Conference on Human Settlements, 1996). The plan of action sought to stop the deterioration of shelter and living conditions and to sustainably improve the living environments of all.

Key initiatives that followed HABITAT II included:

- The Urban Governance Initiative (TUGI), which is a UNDP endeavour that built on the Urban Management Programme for Asia and the Pacific. The TUGI, launched in 1998, promoted good urban governance through institutional capacity building, policy advisory services and improved governance methods, and thereby assisted local governments in making Asia-Pacific cities more liveable.

- The World Urban Forum (WUF), which was established in 2001 by UN-Habitat to examine one of the most serious issues facing the world today: rapid urbanisation and its impact on communities, cities, economies, climate change and policies.

- The Culture for Sustainable Urban Development Initiative, which was initiated by the United Nations Educational, Scientific and Cultural Organization (UNESCO) in 2015, in recognition that safeguarding cultural heritage and promoting the diversity of cultural expressions is a key tool for realizing sustainable urban development. As part of the initiative, UNESCO launched the Global Report on Culture for Sustainable Urban Development, which presents the situation, trends, threats and opportunities in regional contexts, and offers a global synopsis of initiatives relating to urban heritage safeguarding, conservation and management, and the promotion of culture and creative industries.

HABITAT III

The UN Conference on Housing and Sustainable Urban Development (HABITAT III) took place in 2016. It brought together government representatives of the Member States and other stakeholders, including civil society organisations, foundations, professionals, researchers, women and youth groups, trade unions and the private sector. Taking place 20 years after HABITAT II, the participants of HABITAT III recognised that cities were being managed with out-dated models and systems that urgently needed to be revised, and that action was required to deal with the challenges of the 21st century, particularly the issue of rapidly-increasing urbanisation. The key outcome of HABITAT III was the New Urban Agenda, which serves as a guideline for urban development within the framework of the 2030 United Nations Sustainable Development Goals.

In response to HABITAT III, the ninth World Urban Forum (WUF9), which was convened in 2018 in Kuala Lumpur, Malaysia, focused on the implementation of the New Urban Agenda.

The New Urban Agenda

This guide promotes a new model of urban development, one that integrates all aspects of sustainable development to promote equity, well-being and shared prosperity. It was conceived as a 'roadmap' to addressing the spatial and infrastructural challenges attendant upon rapid urban growth, and to tackling the related social challenges, including migration to cities, increasing poverty, rising socio-economic inequality, diminished and unequal access to basic human services, changes in family patterns, loss of social cohesion, and rising crime rates and other security issues.

Recognising that cities develop depending on how we structure them and on how their growth is managed, the New Urban Agenda offers a 'paradigm shift' in city planning and management. It argues that urbanisation need not be negative and that when urbanisation is well-managed, cities can be a source of solutions to the challenges we face (UN-Habitat, 2016).

The New Urban Agenda rests on five guiding principles for strategy and policy-making: (i) protect and promote human rights and the rule of law; (ii) ensure equitable urban development; (iii) empower civil society and expand democratic participation; (iv) protect and promote environmental sustainability; and (v) promote and support innovation and learning (UN-Habitat, 2016).

The New Urban Agenda identifies several levers of change. The nine that relate to heritage conservation are as follows:

- Establish national urban policies.
- Develop urban legislation and systems of governance.
- Harness the urban economy, creating opportunities and improving existing working conditions for all.
- Strengthen municipal finance.
- Improve territorial planning and urban design.
- Ensure universal access to quality basic services.
- Provide adequate housing for all.
- Strengthen gender equality and empower women.
- Place culture at the heart of sustainable urban development (UN-Habitat, 2016).

The tension between heritage conservation and urban development in Asian cities

The disconnect between historic Asian urban planning precedents and contemporary practice

2

In Asia, sustainable development was once linked with cultural heritage conservation and this connection was enshrined in the traditional practice of urban design and management (Engelhardt, 2001, 2012). Indeed, for more than 2000 years, Asian urban planning, whether derived from the South Asian (Indian) tradition or East Asian (Chinese) tradition, emphasised long-term sustainability, based on the maintenance of a community's culture.

Briefly stated (and recognizing the danger of over-simplification), the South Asian tradition views the Earth as a reflection, albeit an imperfect one, of the cosmos, with Mt. Meru, home of the gods, at its centre. The direct implication of this concept for urban planning is that the more accurately the Earth can be made to conform to the heavenly template, the more long-lived and sustainable the Earth will become.

The East Asian tradition is a more intimate, personal one, but is based on similar concepts. Under this approach, harmony, tranquillity, peace and well-being can be achieved by humankind only through achieving a carefully-planned and well-maintained balance between the natural setting of a place and humankind's interventions in place making and therefore, by implication, in city-building. When this balance is not achieved, the heavens – that is to say the natural order of the universe – will react forcefully, even violently and ruthlessly, to restore the balance.

Significantly, these concepts were codified into what can be described as the earliest 'planning manuals' in the South and East Asian regions. For example, in China, the *I Ching* (Book of Changes) written around the middle of the 6th century BC, but incorporating much older ideas, laid out a geometric structure that was adapted as the morphological basis of many urban settlement plans in China and elsewhere in East Asia. In India, the principles for laying out reflections of cosmic patterns in the built environment, referred to collectively as the Vastu Shastra, were standard components of all Indian builders' manuals from at least the 3rd century CE.

With the introduction in the 20th century of modern Western-derived systems of professional education in architecture and the related urban planning disciplines, traditional knowledge in sustainable urban design was sidelined, ignored, gradually forgotten and eventually replaced by templates transferred directly from Western urban planning practice, with its post-war emphasis on the twin pillars of (i) inner city re-development (urban renewal) and (ii) suburban expansion to deal with the issue of rapid urban growth.

Both of these pillars have within them an unspoken assumption that 'old' equals 'bad' or 'irrelevant' and therefore that heritage conservation is an impediment to urban renewal and growth. The result has been that the long-evolved built heritage of most of Asia's urban areas has been summarily destroyed and replaced by contemporary constructions without reference to what preceded them, or left to fall into dilapidation and disrepair, with consequent loss of economic value, thus 'proving' that heritage assets are of diminishing relevance and little practical use.

Conservation standards that are changing the urban planning paradigm

The Venice and Washington Charters

The paradigm of urban planning that undervalues historic forms was not without critics, however. Voices have long championed conservation. Indeed, the prescient 1964 International Charter for the Conservation and Restoration of Monuments and Sites (the Venice Charter) called for safeguarding historic buildings for their value as 'works of art' and as 'historical evidence' (Second International Congress of Architects and Technicians of Historic Monuments, 1964). These voices became louder following the 1972 United Nations Conference on the Human Environment and the adoption of the 1972 Convention for the Protection of the World Cultural and Natural Heritage, known widely as the World Heritage Convention (UNESCO, 1972).

Since 1972, international standards of conservation practice have proliferated and have been codified in UNESCO conventions, recommendations and guidelines as well as those of the International Council on Monuments and Sites (ICOMOS)[3] and the International Centre for the Study of the Preservation and Restoration of Cultural Property (ICCROM).[4]

In the area of urban historic area conservation practice, the 1987 ICOMOS Charter for the Conservation of Historic Towns and Urban Areas, known also as the Washington Charter (ICOMOS, 1987), has a fundamental standard-setting function. This charter was later augmented by the UNESCO Recommendation on the Historic Urban Landscape, which was implemented to assist in integrating conservation policies and practices into the wider goals of urban development (UNESCO, 2011).

The Burra Charter

Supplementing these international standard-setting instruments, ICOMOS and other organisations have established regional and national charters of conservation best practice, which have been extremely important in the formation of national conservation standards. In this regard, the provisions of the Australia

---

3 ICOMOS is a non-governmental professional association that works for the conservation and protection of cultural heritage.

4 ICCROM is an inter-governmental organisation established by UNESCO in 1956 that is dedicated to the preservation of cultural heritage worldwide through training, information, research, cooperation and advocacy.

ICOMOS Charter for the Conservation of Places of Cultural Significance (known as the Burra Charter) are significant. The Burra Charter, first adopted in 1979 and since updated, established guidelines for the preservation of a 'sense of place' (ICOMOS, 1979), a sensibility that has particular resonance for Asian populations with their multi-generational attachment to place of origin.

The Burra Charter principles were summarised by Walker (1996) as follows:

- Places of cultural significance should be conserved and safeguarded. This is because they enrich our lives. They do this by helping us understand the past and contributing to the richness of the present environment. Investment in the cultural assets of a community is of value to future generations.
- The cultural significance of a place is embodied in its physical material (fabric), its setting, its contents, and its meaning to people through associations with the place.
- To understand the cultural significance of a place, and issues affecting its future, it is necessary to collect and analyse information before making decisions.

The Burra Charter seeks to ensure that people involved in the conservation of heritage places fulfil the following obligations:

- Understand the place and its cultural significance, including its meaning to people, before making decisions about its future.
- Involve the communities associated with the place in its present and future stewardship.
- Care for the culturally significant fabric of a place together with, and not disassociated from, other significant attributes, including intangible cultural values and associations.
- Care for the place's setting.
- Provide an appropriate use for the place.
- Provide security for the place.
- Use available local and traditional expertise to inform safeguarding and management practices.
- Make records of the place and changes to it, and the reasons for decisions and actions.
- Interpret and present the place in a manner that conveys its significance (Walker, 1996).

The Nara Document on Authenticity

A turning point in understanding the value of intangible heritage came in 1994 at the ICOMOS Conference on Authenticity, convened in the World Heritage city of Nara, Japan. The conference aimed to provide professional guidance as to how safeguarding living heritage could be systematically mainstreamed into modern urban and territorial planning practice. The resulting Nara Document on Authenticity (ICOMOS, 1994) was later incorporated into the Operational

Guidelines for the Implementation of the 1972 Convention for the Protection of the World Cultural and Natural Heritage (UNESCO, 2017), which today sets the standard for heritage conservation practices that are conscious and respectful of local cultural values.

It is now evident that safeguarding heritage is fundamental to the preservation of the cultural identity of any place. In this context, the conservation of local, national and regional cultural resources can be understood as being fundamental to sustainable and equitable social and economic development.

Threats to Asia's urban heritage

Recognition of the link between culture and development has special relevance in Asia where the region's built heritage arose from a longstanding interaction between the natural geographical setting and local cultures. This built heritage serves as the setting for continuing intangible expressions of cultural traditions.

Cultural heritage assets are passed from the communities that first created them and have cared for them on to subsequent generations. During this transmission, the tangible fabric inevitably evolves, but the essential qualities that made these assets identifiable as 'authentic' heritage are retained and are recognised as such by the community. Unfortunately, this authenticity faces ongoing threats, particularly in Asia where the explosive growth of urban populations has made urban redevelopment an economic, social and political priority.

Finding a balance between urban development and heritage conservation requires, in the first instance, an understanding of the threats to heritage and the sources of these threats. Armed with this understanding, it is possible to negotiate solutions acceptable to all stakeholders. Such solutions will safeguard the physical fabric of urban heritage and also ensure continued commitment to the underlying values embodied in the traditional cultural practices that have animated and sustained historic districts across generations.

As noted in the Hoi An Protocols for Best Conservation Practice in Asia (Engelhardt and Rogers, 2009, p. 3), urban development and modernisation have too often resulted in negative consequences for the historic urban environment. These negative impacts include:

- Dismemberment of heritage sites, with resultant loss of integrity.
- Deterioration of the fabric of the region's built environment to the point where it can no longer adequately support the human uses for which it is intended.
- Replacement of original components with counterfeit and non-indigenous technologies and materials.
- Loss of the sense of place of the region's heritage sites, through inappropriate reconstruction processes that homogenise their unique characteristics.
- Expropriation of heritage from the traditions of community use by inappropriate development of heritage resources as tourism 'commodities'.

Along with inappropriate urban redevelopment, factors that threaten Asia's built and intangible heritage include: climate change and environmental degradation; industrialisation and globalisation of the economies of the region; rural-to-urban migration; rapid population growth; overtourism and tourism that commodifies culture; and the attrition of the traditional socio-cultural fabric. Collectively, these factors erode the value of the region's urban heritage as a source of identity and a resource for development.

Challenges facing urban planners

When it comes to efforts to conserve urban heritage in Asia, urban planners face three types of challenges: threats to heritage, governance issues and development pressures, as shown in Figure 2.3.

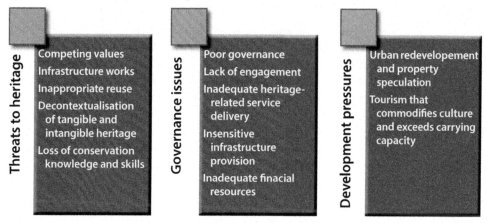

Figure 2.3: Urban heritage conservation challenges

Each of the challenges listed in Figure 2.3 are explained below.

Competing values

In many communities in Asia, the custodians of important heritage sites are of ethnicities, religions and cultures that are different from those of the current power-holding majority. It is not unusual, for example, for Islamic nations in Asia to have within their borders valuable Hindu and Buddhist sites. Similarly, many cities in Asia have multiple cultures, which meet, mix and sometimes merge. This diversity is a source of creativity and underpins development. But when there is a hierarchy of competing values, tensions can arise, leading to the destruction of heritage structures and the loss of related intangible heritage. The 1994 Nara Document on Authenticity reminds us to respect other cultures and all aspects of belief systems, so as to preserve cultural diversity (ICOMOS, 1994). It is therefore incumbent on urban planners to protect the heritage of all cultures, with equitable ethical standards and rigorous professional practice.

Infrastructure and other engineering works

Redevelopment and infrastructure works impact heritage resources both directly and indirectly. Directly by damaging and destroying fabric and indirectly by degrading settings and environmental buffer zones. Such works change visual envelopes and destroy symbolic connections between places and their settings, and often alter drainage and hydrology, thereby increasing erosion and sedimentation, and augmenting the risk of landslides. Such engineering works are often seen in the redevelopment of historic buildings into higher-density occupancies. The expansion of road networks and other major infrastructure works associated with modern mass transportation systems have the greatest impact. Such works have a devastating effect on historic structures, visual urban landscapes and underground archaeological sites.

Inappropriate reuse

All too often, conservation and adaptive reuse projects compromise aspects of authenticity of a heritage property, such as the original use (e.g. the conversion of a religious building into a baror restaurant), spatial layout (e.g. the construction of high-rise buildings within a low-rise historic precinct) and traditional materials (e.g. replacing traditional lime-based renders with cement-based renders). Such interventions inevitably have negative impacts on the intangible heritage values that give a place its distinctive character, including the spirit of place. The spirit of place conveys the cultural essence of a site, encompassing the meanings of a place accrued overtime and through its past and present uses. Expressed through tangible built heritage, the spirit of a place resides in its authenticity, the retention of which is essential to heritage conservation.

De-contextualisation of tangible and intangible heritage

When historic neighbourhoods are cordoned off as 'heritage districts', the cultural values embodies in the built heritage are de-contextualised. Thus, such districts are reduced to being theme parks, while their historic structures are degraded to the status of ornaments. Similarly, expressions of intangible heritage are de-contextualised when taken out of their traditional settings. Dinner-dance performances, for example, reduce traditional expressions of art and ritual to nothing more than trivial consumption. De-contextualisation is a very serious, even fatal, threat to cultural heritage because the detachment of a cultural space, practice or expression from its original setting within the community negates the very purpose, authenticity and significance of these expressions. De-contextualisation is one of the more significant errors made by the urban planning profession, whether as a well-intentioned attempt to safeguard and showcase heritage or an ill-informed response to the presumed 'demands' of a prospective clientele.

Loss of conservation knowledge and skills

Successful conservation of heritage structures depends on the inter-generational transmission of precision skills related to construction. However, the use of Western construction concepts, techniques and materials, which has accelerated in response to rapid urbanisation in Asia, has resulted in the decline and, in some cases, the disappearance of traditional building crafts, artisan skills and materials production. While traditional craft workshops still exist in some rural areas, the traditional master-apprentice teaching system has, for the most part, disappeared from urban centres. Accordingly, the authentic conservation of heritage is difficult to achieve. Unfortunately, the modern professional education system for architects and urban planners has not compensated for the disappearance of traditional modes of skill transmission. Training (in traditional skills) for conservation professionals and site managers, if it exists at all, is short-term, anecdotal and case-based, and is therefore unable to develop the skilled professional capacity required. It is therefore not surprising that heritage conservation efforts are often unsuccessful and unsustainable in the long term.

Poor governance and lack of capacity

In most parts of Asia, the political and bureaucratic structures, often the legacy of colonial regimes, are ill-suited to dealing with the complexity of managing rapidly-expanding urban areas while maintaining their cultural significance. Governance challenges include: uncertainty, corruption, bureaucratic bottlenecks, inadequate human capacity and unwillingness to change.

As a result of these governance issues, urban administrations often lack: adequate historical data to make evidence-based decisions, access to sufficient financial resources to implement decisions, skilled human resources to manage the complexity of implementation, and institutional impact evaluation mechanisms. Many countries in Asia lack national systems of development-oriented administration and their city managers have poorly-developed capacity to cope with the challenges facing them relating to heritage conservation, especially as concerns technical issues.

These administrative issues lead to inadequate urban planning and design due to factors such as inadequate laws and a lack of enforcement; a lack of design guidelines to protect the authenticity and integrity of heritage areas; poor human resource policies and programmes; inadequate implementation of policies and plans; and poorly-coordinated sectoral planning. Even where a city's administration has a heritage planning and design function, in many cases the strategies informing planning and design are borrowed from textbook models and are ill-suited to dealing with the actual issues facing a specific city. They also do not take into account the limited capacity of a city to bring about significant changes. While heritage-retention strategies and conservation plans are often produced, few plans are implemented and the planning and design process therefore has little impact on the development trajectory of the city.

Lack of engagement

Engagement processes in urban development projects, if they exist at all, tend to be poorly structured and are administered arbitrarily. Very often those most affected by urban development, the poor and underprivileged, are not given a voice in the engagement process, especially as concerns the redevelopment of their familial homes and businesses.

Inadequate service delivery

With explosive urban growth comes increasing complexity in the systems to deliver urban services, within a political climate of rising expectations and escalating demand for these services. Services of particular concern to heritage conservation include housing, transportation, solid waste management, water supply, electricity and safety and security. The speed of population growth combined with lack of governance and administrative competence is such that in many urban areas of Asia these services are not available to residents of poorer areas, which are often heritage districts.

Insensitive infrastructure provision

Service delivery requires the provision of adequate infrastructure, a major challenge in urban management in Asia today. As well as the need to replace deteriorated and obsolete infrastructure of all kinds, it is also necessary to build and expand new infrastructure to meet the requirements and demands of an exponentially increasing urban population. And in historic cities with heritage assets to showcase, this infrastructure must also meet the needs of large numbers of visitors. But the efficient provision of infrastructure requires adequate finance and coordination between the various stakeholders, including government departments. Such coordination is essential because infrastructure issues often cut across several domains of administrative responsibility. For example, traffic congestion is not only a matter for the transport department but also for the health and labour departments, as the pollution produced by traffic negatively affects the health and productivity of the urban work force. Matters are further complicated when issues of private property and development 'rights' are involved. Furthermore, heritage areas face particular issues because very often the insensitive development of infrastructure, especially roads, can seriously diminish the authenticity of a historic setting.

Inadequate financial resources

In parts of Asia where tax revenue is low but public infrastructure and service provision costs are high, there is always an administrative budget shortfall at the local government level. To cover the costs of expanding infrastructure and services, revenue generation becomes a basic, and often overwhelming, concern of all local government units. Replacement of heritage structures often offers a profitable income stream. In such contexts, heritage conservation is relegated to the back seat.

Urban redevelopment pressures and property speculation

The socio-economic pressures forcing the continuous renewal of the fabric of Asia's towns and cities have combined to threaten cultural heritage at a scale never seen before. Recognising the threats, there are calls from many quarters to find ways to incorporate heritage conservation into urban planning models. On the surface, these exhortations do not seem unrealistic: historic structures are often well-constructed, composed of sturdy high-quality materials and are sometimes carefully maintained. However, the real threat to heritage fabric is not the fact of urban renewal per se. Rather, the most serious threat is uncontrolled speculation in property values in historic inner-city areas, prior to their redevelopment.

Tourism that commodifies culture and exceeds carrying capacity

When tourism turns local culture into 'products' and exploits culture in ways that do not meet the socio-cultural and economic needs of local residents, and when it exceeds the local carrying capacity, it constitutes a threat to heritage, both built and intangible, and diminishes the quality of life of residents. This issue will be discussed in further detail below, while the concept of carrying capacity will be expanded in Chapter 8.

The heritage conservation and tourism interface

Given the significance of negative dimensions of tourism in heritage conservation areas and the potential positive dimensions of tourism as part of the conservation effort, it is important to better understand the links between tourism and the overall conservation of urban heritage areas. This discussion is particularly important given the issue of overtourism introduced in Chapter 1.

There can be no underestimating the power of tourism, given the scale and influence of the industry globally as listed below. The percentages are global averages, so in some countries these percentages can be much higher, with tourism often being a major driver of GDP, employment and exports. This is particularly the case in island nations and developing countries. For example, in the Seychelles 62% of GDP derives from tourism, in Cabo Verde 43% and in Mauritius 27% (UNCTD, quoted in UNWTO, 2018a, p. 27).

The UNWTO (2018b) has identified the following dimensions of international tourism:

- 1.322 billion international arrivals in 2017
- 10.2% of the world's GDP derives (directly and indirectly) from tourism
- 9.6% of global employment is related, directly and indirectly, to tourism
- 30% of exports in services globally are related to tourism

Tourism is often pursued in heritage areas because it promises economic benefits to local communities and governments. Indeed, one of the rationales for tourism in such areas is that the quality of life of the residents will be improved by income generated by heritage tourism activities. The importance of such tourism is recognised by international charters, declarations and the tourism industry, which tout the benefits of tourism within a heritage conservation framework (jobs, financial resources, public support for conservation activities, opportunities for investment, etc.). While tourism may contribute to GDP, the promised benefits for residents have not always eventuated.

Many stakeholders – including community development professionals, poverty reduction organisations and heritage advocates – are deeply sceptical that there are any real benefits for heritage conservation or local communities in the tourism development paradigm as presently constructed. Indeed, little of the income from tourism is reinvested in heritage conservation – in fact, just the opposite; local governments must often provide funding to offset damage to built heritage by tourists. Many sceptics argue that even the employment created by expansion of tourism is often not accessible for locals, with new jobs filled by economic migrants. Furthermore, residents in heritage districts find themselves priced out and displaced from their traditional abodes, and therefore from their long-standing cultural traditions and intangible heritage. Thus, tourism has often led to a reduction in residents' quality of life. For residents who lose not only their livelihoods, but also their homes and traditions, tourism is perceived as their nemesis. Hence the backlash against tourism by inhabitants of heritage districts (De Vries, 2018; Massola and Rosa, 2018; BBC News, 2018).

Moreover, tourism can damage cultural heritage when that heritage is promoted as a kind of 'product'; that is, when it is presented through a simplistic replication of cultural forms. For example, when the same dances are performed over and over again, repeated night after night for changing audiences of tourists. The result is standardised, modified and commodified cultural assets, resulting in a serious loss of authenticity and meaning.

Issues also arise because, too often planners, in their zeal to 'redevelop' the physical fabric of historic communities to improve physical conditions and to make heritage areas palatable as tourist 'products', do not consider the cultural and emotional needs of local residents. This process of redevelopment and commodification leads to the trivialisation of the physical fabric of heritage resources and their intangible aspects, making it impossible for these assets to maintain, regenerate or augment their original value to the community.

This type of 'product' is created for tourists because the packaging and presentation of heritage is usually carried out by those whose job is 'promotion and sales' and not by traditional custodians and knowledgeable experts responsible for the safeguarding of cultural heritage value. The root cause of the unsustainable exploitation of historic urban districts is a short-sighted tourism promotion policy that is motivated by an economic model that seeks the quickest profit extraction with the smallest amount of investment, without regard for the impact or sustainability of tourism.

As well as inflicting damage on heritage and residents, ill-conceived tourism development together with a lack of understanding of how to manage urban heritage sustainably has also resulted in increasingly truncated and desultory visitor experiences. Many tourists report being disappointed with the crowds and noise, and are seeking higher quality options (Kakissis, 2018).

The heritage tourism strategy based on tourism 'products' displays a lack of understanding of the nature of cultural tourists and their motivations when visiting urban heritage areas. These tourists can often make up a significant proportion of the visitors to a historic area. They are typically motivated to travel because they wish to gain inter-cultural knowledge through first-hand experience of authentic places, where they can participate in sustained interaction with unfamiliar cultural communities, their customs, life ways and cultural practices. Cultural tourists seek value-laden meaning in their interactions; values which are dependent on the possibility of experiencing authentic cultural heritage. They do not seek a naively-construed, re-constructed or simulated 'culture tourism product'. While a significant number of visitors will visit heritage areas for non-culture related motivations, such as shopping, restaurants or for taking the ubiquitous 'selfie', they are often also able to appreciate cultural aspects, particularly when appropriate interpretation is provided. Moreover, in a globalised world, with countries becoming more and more alike, these visitors, while not focused on 'culture', are increasingly seeking something different from the norm, not a standard 'product'.

Heritage tourism is growing, particularly in urban areas. According to World Travel Monitor, city trips doubled between 2011 and 2016 to reach 26% of all holidays in 2016 (GTP, 2017), and such trips are likely to continue to grow. Several countries in Asia, including Cambodia, Laos and Vietnam, have experienced huge surges in tourism in recent decades, and tourist numbers in these countries are expected to continue to rise (Smith, 2018). Given the lack of appropriate tourism development and absence of sustainable heritage management in many Asian urban areas, growing interest in historic cities is expected to exacerbate the problems caused by present levels of visitation.

Heritage tourism in urban areas can be a positive force, however, when local government units are able to manage both tourism and heritage, and ensure that the financing of tourism expansion provides genuine employment and business opportunities for local residents, while at the same time safeguarding the heritage assets and cultural traditions that attract visitors to the city. The various stakeholders must increase the resources directed towards (i) conserving heritage, (ii) raising awareness of tangible and intangible heritage and the importance that these play in the overall well-being of a city and (iii) helping heritage advocates and residents to tell their stories.

Given that tourism was until recently seen largely as only a private sector activity, governments, the private sector and donors, including development banks, often worked from a position that market forces would suffice to develop a responsible tourism environment. However, this assumption was based on an incorrect understanding of heritage resources as infinite and renewable. It has now become evident that market forces alone cannot be relied upon to provide responsible direction and structure to tourism development in historic urban environments. Since heritage resources, like other public goods, are finite and irreplaceable components of the common wealth of a community, and are essential assets for the long-term viability of communities, it is important for all stakeholders to recognise that there are limits to tourism in heritage areas and that it is necessary to manage tourism as a supply-driven not demand-driven activity.

Towards sustainable urban heritage conservation

It is within the context of the urban challenges discussed above that both tourism development and heritage conservation occur. The combination of rapid urbanisation, severe urban challenges, poorly developed heritage tourism experiences and high numbers of visitors threatens not only heritage structures but also the authenticity (and therefore the perceived value) of heritage. The scale of this threat is only beginning to be understood in the Asian urban context.

The magnitude and momentum of the urban challenges are such that heritage conservation will require significant amounts of funding. It is necessary to explore creative financing, public-private partnerships, micro-lending and mechanisms for achieving cost efficiencies. It is important to also tap directly into the revenue-generating power and increasing profitability of the tourist sector which, to date, has not been proportionally or equitably captured by local government units. Indeed, tourism development must finance the cost of its own infrastructure requirements and its voracious demand for local services.

The significant challenge of planning for and managing the surviving pockets of heritage in urban areas in Asia presents policy-makers, conservation advocates, and local community stakeholders with a so-called 'wicked problem'.[5] This is because those who hold the financial purse strings of development often have no interest in resolving the issues or, if they have interest, have no ability to do so. Indeed, the greatest obstacle to responsible, equitable, sustainable planning and management of heritage areas and historic districts is the unchecked power and influence wielded by property owners and corporate development interests. This is an underlying structural problem, related to larger economic and political issues of social inequalities and ineffective governance. As it is not possible to address these issues in the short term, urban planners and heritage managers in historic cities should focus on ways to deal with the rate of (inevitable) change caused by ongoing urban development and seek to achieve sustainable conservation through value-added cultural asset management.

Heritage can be conserved when there is a well-defined and broad-based consensus on what constitutes a city's heritage assets – in terms of both historic physical fabric and traditional cultural practices; and when there are enforced regulatory controls to safeguard that heritage, along with adequate access to small-scale finance and incentives to retain and conserve heritage. What is needed is greater public understanding of the value of heritage assets and how conservation contributes to sustainable asset management, along with better localisation of management responsibility over heritage resources, so that a negotiated solution, reconciling the differing values of the various local stakeholders, can be reached

---

5 'Wicked problems' are ones for which there is no clear 'stopping rule' – you cannot say for sure when the problem has been solved. Working on it further might well bring forth a better solution. There is no single right answer and every attempt can matter because it affects the things people depend upon. (http://lexicon.ft.com/Term?term=wicked-problem)

and implemented.

In preserving the identity manifested in the tangible and intangible heritage of cities, urban area planners must work in close consultation and cooperation with heritage experts, tourism industry stakeholders and also with members of the local community. The best outcomes are seen when custodianship of heritage sites remains in the hands of traditional owners, who are empowered and assisted to carry out necessary conservation and assume responsibility for heritage asset management.

Chapters 3, 4 and 5 contain short case studies providing examples of both successful and not-so-successful practice. These and the following longer case studies, in Chapters 6 and 7, include examples of comprehensive management processes that have dealt with the challenge of integrated heritage conservation and urban development, including the promotion of cultural tourism. Chapter 8 explains the paradigm shift required to ensure the co-management of urban heritage area conservation and cultural tourism development. The ongoing analysis will be carried out from the perspective of local area heritage conservation policies, planning practices and approaches.

References

BBC News (2018) Cape Town anger over slave quarter gentrification, 5 August. https://www.bbc.com/news/world-africa-44777755 (Accessed 28 August 2018.)

De Vries, J. (2018) My Amsterdam is being un-created by mass tourism, *The Guardian*, 8 August.

Engelhardt, R. (2001) 'Landscapes of Heaven Transposed on Earth: Achieving an Ethos to Guide the Conservation of Cultural Landscapes in Asia and the Pacific', Keynote Address to Asian Places in the New Millennium, *38th IFLA World Congress*, 26–29 June, Singapore.

Engelhardt, R. A. and Rogers, P. R. (2009) *Hoi An Protocols for Best Conservation Practice in Asia: Professional Guidelines for Assuring and Preserving the Authenticity of Heritage Sites in the Context of the Cultures of Asia*, Bangkok: UNESCO.

Engelhardt, R.A. (2012) The Hoi An Protocols for best conservation practice in Asia: Application to the safeguarding of Asian cultural landscapes, in K. Taylor and J. Lennon(eds.), *Managing Cultural Landscapes*, New York: Routledge.

GTP (2017) IPK's World Travel Monitor: Global Travel Trends 2016/2017 at ITB Berlin 2017, Greek Travel Pages: Headlines.

ICOMOS (1979) Charter for the Conservation of Places of Cultural Significance. https://australia.icomos.org/publications/charters/ (Accessed 10 July 2018.)

ICOMOS (1987) Charter for the Conservation of Historic Towns and Urban Areas. http://www.getty.edu/conservation/publications_resources/research_resources/charters/charter40.html (Accessed 10 July 2018.)

ICOMOS (1994) Nara Document on Authenticity, Nara Conference on Authenticity in Relation to the World Heritage Convention, Nara, Japan, 1-6 November.

International Monetary Fund (2017) The March of the Cities, http://www.imf.org/external/pubs/ft/fandd/2007/09/picture.htm (Accessed 28 August 2018.)

Johnson, C., Adelekan, I., & Bosher, L. (2013). Private sector investment decisions in building and construction: increasing managing and transferring risks. https://www.researchgate.net/publication/298022705_Private_sector_investment_decisions_in_building_and_construction_increasing_managing_and_transferring_risks

Jamieson, W. (2009) *Managing Tourism in Metropolitan Areas - An Asian Perspective,* Madrid: United Nations World Tourism Organization.

Kakissis, J. (2018) In Amsterdam, even the tourists say there are too many tourists, NPR, 7 August.

Massola, J. and Rosa, A. (2018) China's tourism boom prompts fears that Bali is being 'sold cheap', *Brisbane Times,* 26 August.

Second International Congress of Architects and Technicians of Historic Monuments (1964) International Charter for the Conservation and Restoration of Monuments and Sites (The Venice Charter 1964). https://www.icomos.org/charters/venice_e.pdf (Accessed 28 August 2018.)

Smith, O. (2018) Revealed: The countries that rely most on your money, *The Telegraph,* 22 March. https://www.telegraph.co.uk/travel/maps-and-graphics/Mapped-The-countries-that-rely-most-on-your-money/ (Accessed 11 July 2018.)

United Nations Conference on Human Settlements (1976) The Vancouver Action Plan. http://www.un-documents.net/van-plan.htm (Accessed 7 July 2018.)

United Nations Conference on Human Settlements (1996) Istanbul Declaration on Human Settlements: The Habitat Agenda. https://unhabitat.org/wp-content/uploads/2014/07/The-Habitat-Agenda-Istanbul-Declaration-on-Human-Settlements-20061.pdf (Accessed 7 July 2018.)

UNESCO (1972) World Heritage Convention, https://whc.unesco.org/en/convention/ (Accessed 10 July 2018.)

UNESCO (2011) Recommendation on the Historic Urban Landscape. https://whc.unesco.org/en/hul/ (Accessed 10 July 2018.)

UNESCO (2017) Operational Guidelines for the Implementation of the World Heritage Convention. https://whc.unesco.org/en/guidelines/ (Accessed 10 July 2018.)

UN-Habitat (2016) *New Urban Agenda,* New York: United Nations.

UNWTO (2018a) *Tourism for Development, Volume 1: Key Areas For Action,* Madrid: UNWTO.

UNWTO (2018b) *Tourism for Development, Volume 2: Success Stories,* Madrid: UNWTO.

Walker, M. (1996) *Understanding the Burra Charter: A simple guide to the principles of heritage conservation in Australia,* Canberra: Australia ICOMOS.

3 Managing Urban Heritage Areas in the Context of Sustainable Tourism: Heritage Conservation

There has been very little documentation of the Asian experience in planning and managing urban heritage areas, especially those experiencing tourism pressures. In order to better understand the challenges in these areas, 47 case examples have been authored by experienced practitioners who have worked in Asia over the past two decades in the areas of heritage conservation and/or cultural heritage tourism. The issues discussed in the case examples are those that the practitioners have identified as being of particular relevance to the heritage and sustainable tourism debate. Combined, these case examples provide geographic breadth and longitudinal depth, offering a comprehensive and credible body of data.

In this chapter the case examples relate to heritage, which encompasses issues such as authenticity, integrity, heritage impact, historic urban landscapes, intangible heritage, tangible heritage and World Heritage sites.

The post-earthquake revitalization of Kotagede Heritage District, Yogyakarta, Indonesia

Laretna T. Adishakti, architect and lecturer, Center for Heritage Conservation, Department of Architecture and Planning, Faculty of Engineering, Universitas Gadjah Mada

Keywords: Indonesia, geography, cultural heritage, revitalization, heritage impact

The people of Yogyakarta Special Territory and Central Java, Indonesia, have experienced difficult times since an earthquake measuring 5.9 on the Richter scale struck them on 27 May 2006. At least 6000 died, many more were injured and many lost their homes. Furthermore, much of the unique tangible and intangible cultural heritage in these areas was lost or damaged. The tangible heritage affected by the earthquake included some parts of the World Heritage Prambanan Temple, Yogyakarta Palace Complex, Baluwerti Fortress, Tamansari Water Castle and Kotagede Heritage District. The earthquake also seriously disrupted core activities of local industries, including the traditional sterling silver, batik, pottery, wood and ikat crafts practised in the southern part of Yogyakarta City and Bantul Regency. Most of the artisans lost the resources to continue their work.

As a result of the earthquake, Kotagede Heritage District, one of Yogyakarta's older areas, which contains the remains of the Old Mataram Kingdom Kotagede, is now seriously endangered. Many traditional houses, unique *kalang* houses and artisans' *kampong* (villages), were destroyed by the earthquake. Their owners, deprived of the necessary means and resources for restoration, might not be able to restore their houses in traditional forms.

Figure 3.1: Omah (House) Universitas Gadjah Mada in Kotagede in 2018

Local institutions launched several responses, including the Comprehensive Revitalization Program (CRP), initiated by Pusaka Jogja Bangkit! (Jogja Heritage Revival!) and implemented in collaboration with the Jogja Heritage Society, the Center for Heritage Conservation of Universitas Gadjah Mada (UGM), the Indonesian Heritage Trust, ICOMOS Indonesia and others, along with the local community. The CRP vision was to revive the Kotagede Heritage District to improve socio-cultural life and the environment to a state better than that existing prior to the earthquake, as well as create community capacity to manage the restored cultural heritage independently and ensure the restored cultural heritage has a positive economic and cultural impact on the community.

Many international organizations have supported the CRP, including the Japan International Cooperation Agency (JICA), which implemented the Community Empowerment Program (CEP) to build the capacity of local people to actively engage in the reconstruction process (2006-2007); the Royal Netherlands Embassy in Jakarta, which financially supported the reconstruction of some traditional houses (2007); Universitas Gadjah Mada, which bought a damaged traditional wooden house, which was then rebuilt by JICA and Total Indonesie and converted into Omah UGM (UGM House), the office of the university's Center for Heritage Movement (2007); the UNESCO Bangkok and Jakarta offices, which assisted the Jogja Heritage Society (JHS) and the Kotagede Heritage District Local Organization (OPKP) in the publication of the *Homeowner's Conservation Manual for Kotagede Heritage District*, with the support of the Kingdom of Saudi Arabia (2007); and a collaboration between Universitas Gadjah Mada and Exxon Mobile to conduct the Kotagede 'Economic Revival Post Earthquake through Craft' initiative (2007-2008). In addition, many individuals have supported the heritage emergency response.

The programmes that were part of the first stage (2006-2009) of the Kotagede CRP were initiated by heritage advocates, academics and organizations, supported by philanthropies. The next stage (2009-2011) was organized by the Government of the Republic of Indonesia and was supported by donors from various countries. Recently, initiatives to conserve traditional houses and adapt them for re-use for social, cultural and economic development so as to make Kotagede more livable, have been carried out by individuals.

Kotagede has become one of the most important heritage areas in Yogyakarta. Based on the experiences with the Kotagede Heritage District post-disaster programme, and those in other regions in Indonesia, heritage-related disaster risk management was included as one of the eight instruments listed in Indonesia's Charter for Heritage Cities Conservation in 2013.

Bibliography

Adishakti, L. T. (2008) Community empowerment program on the revitalization of Kotagede Heritage District, Indonesia post earthquake, in T. Kidokoro, J. Okata, S. Matsumura and N. Shima (eds.), *Vulnerable Cities: Realities, Innovations and Strategies*. Tokyo: Springer, pp. 241-256.

Adishakti, L. T. (2009) *Reconstruction process in Kotagede Heritage District, Yogyakarta, Indonesia*. Yogyakarta: Jogja Heritage Society.

Adishakti, L. T. (2011) Bunka Dinamism to Saigai ni Chokumen suru Isan Toshi Yogyakarta (Yogyakarta heritage city facing culture dynamics and disaster challenges), *Kankyou to Kongai (Research on Environmental Disruption)*, **40** (3).

Indonesian Heritage Trust (2013) *Charter for Indonesian Heritage Cities Conservation*, ICOMOS Indonesia, Indonesian Network for Heritage Cities, Ministry of Public Works, Ministry of Social Welfare, Jakarta

Rahmi, D. H. and Handayani, T. (2009) *Post-disaster Conservation Manual for Kotagede Heritage District, Yogyakarta, Indonesia*, Yogyakarta: Jogja Heritage Society.

UNESCO Office Jakarta and Regional Bureau for Science in Asia and the Pacific; UNESCO Office Bangkok and Regional Bureau for Education in Asia and the Pacific; and Jogja Heritage Society (2007) *Homeowner's Conservation Manual: Kotagede Heritage District, Yogyakarta, Indonesia*, Jakarta and Bangkok: UNESCO.

Passing the torch

Frances B. Affandy, Board of Advisors, Bandung Society for Heritage Conservation

Keywords: Indonesia, geography, conservation, urban planning, heritage initiative, community development

The Bandung Society for Heritage Conservation is the oldest grassroots heritage initiative in modern Indonesia. It was formed in 1987, during the Orde Baru era under President Soeharto, by a group of 13 Bandung residents who recognized the potential that good heritage management would have on the city they loved.

The group included architects, academics from three local universities, the president and several staff of a local hotel (the largest taxpayer in the city), the editor of the local newspaper, the director of the largest astrophysical observatory in Southeast Asia, several anthropologists interested in local culture, and the director of the national geological museum.

This group met twice a month at the hotel. After several months discussing the directions that might be taken, and agreeing on a name, they set their mission:

The Society believes that the identity of Bandung, which derives from its unique culture and heritage, is the city's most important preserve, and therefore needs to be strengthened and enhanced.

The definitions of 'identity', 'unique culture', 'heritage' and 'strengthened and enhanced' purposely cast a wide and imprecise net, so the society could discover, along the way, where it might function most effectively. Eventually, the built environment of Bandung became the focus, as public agencies were already engaged in environmental issues and local cultural affairs. This focus on historic sites and monuments in the city was also stimulated by the increased threats these sites and monuments faced at the time. Property development was booming following the Indonesian government's decision to deregulate banking, which had spurred the growth of private banking institutions and had increased credit opportunities.

In 1988, the society staged its first exhibition and seminar using locally-raised funds, and invited city officials and the public to view historic pictures of Bandung and to discuss heritage conservation, community development plans, tourism potential, education initiatives and other topics. ICOMOS Friends from the US and Singapore attended, along with a beloved former Minister of Tourism. The local newspaper reported on the three-day exhibition and the related events.

Over the following years, the society became well known and widely supported. Its meetings attracted over 100 attendees each month, including many architecture students, who formed the backbone of inventory and research projects for the society. Moreover, city fathers invited society officers to participate in discussions on planning and development matters.

Not everything went the society's way, however. Although some lobbying efforts (mostly to save buildings from demolition) were successful, others were not. Old sites and monuments were under siege by developers, most of which were from outside the community, particularly from Jakarta.

The society had an all-volunteer board made up of a president, secretary-treasurer and three vice presidents, one for each of the three areas of interest: the built environment, socio-cultural heritage and the natural environment. The working group had four sections: a membership and volunteers committee, an education and outreach (planning and organizing monthly meetings) section, a fundraising section, and a lobbying section. The nine officers of the group were all volunteers.

The society set term limits of three years with one possible three-year extension, but these limits were not respected. Attempts were made to hold elections, but no one wanted to run. As a volunteer group at a very dynamic period in the city's growth, the first president of the society was in office for ten years. Eventually, the president asked to be replaced due to failing health, and a paid executive director was hired to handle day-to-day affairs. Five years later, a younger, prominent and popular board member assumed the presidency. She held office for the next ten years. Board members saw no turnover at all.

By 2011 the original board members were beginning to retire and the issue of leadership renewal became an urgent concern. Many active younger members had joined the society, but none expressed interest in running for office.

The board decided that each member would identify a younger person to 'shadow' his/her board responsibility, and eventually take over the position. This initiative was trialled for two years but was a failure. Economic pressures forced younger members to concentrate their efforts on their livelihoods, limiting their volunteer time. More importantly, however, the younger 'shadow board' members would not contradict their seniors, and in many cases would not even offer suggestions at board meetings. It was seen as unseemly for a young person to contradict an elder or even engage in a discussion.

Cultural norms were constraining efforts to renew the society. This is reflected in the use of wayang (puppet theatre) as a working metaphor in Bandung. It features the all-powerful dalang who controls the puppets and flow of events. Furthermore, the concept of president for life is strong in Bandung. It is a common concept in Asia, whether it be for a company, institution, organization or an entire country. This stems partly from traditions of filial piety and partly from the fact that democratic practices are not yet fully acculturated. Democratic tools such as elections are still not widely practiced in the Western sense.

In view of the situation, the entire board decided to stage a walk-out; quit en masse. An upside-down coup!

This was a shocking manoeuvre. Young members vigorously disagreed with the decision, but the alternative was that the society would disband. Accordingly, the younger members took over running the society, by default. As of 2018, some three years later, these capable individuals remain in office, but elections have yet to be held.

The original mission of the society has not changed and the society continues to this day to pursue good heritage conservation initiatives for the sake of the city the residents love.

The historic centre of Macao: Morphing into another shopping district

Professor John Ap, Institute for Tourism Studies, Macao

Keywords: China, geography, tourism, authenticity, World Heritage Site, gentrification

The historic centre of Macao spans eight squares and comprises 22 principal buildings. When inscribed as a World Heritage site by UNESCO in 2005, it was described as "the oldest, the most complete and consolidated array of European architectural legacy standing intact on Chinese territory today" (World Heritage Committee, 2005).

Inscription as a World Heritage site was seen as a means to boost tourism. This has certainly been the case. Between 2005 and 2017 tourist arrivals to Macao increased from 8.7 million to 32.6 million. The large number of tourists, along with the transformation of Macao into the world's leading gambling destination, has had unintended negative impacts on the historic centre. These include crowding, congestion, greater commercialisation and the gentrification of retail establishments close to major heritage sites.

A key concern has been the gentrification of retailing in and around the Ruins of Saint Paul and Senado Square-St Dominic's Church precinct, with many local traditional and independent establishments replaced by non-local stores, including international brand stores. A study of ground-level shop frontage in May 2018 revealed that local independent stores represented only around one third of the establishments, and that many traditional uses have disappeared (see Tables 3.1 and 3.2). Furthermore, of the 25 remaining local independent stores, 12 are owned by three major local bakeries, which have multiple store locations.

Table 3.1: Commercial establishments in or near the major heritage sites of Macao's historic centre (n=70)

Feature	Senado Square - Saint Dominic's Church Precinct	Rua do St. Paulo	Total
Length of street frontage	130 m	150m	280 m
No. of local independent establishments	3 (14%)	22 (45%)	25 (36%)
No. of non-local establishments	18 (86%)	27 (55%)	45 (64%)
Total no. of commercial establishments	21 (100%)	49 (100%)	70 (100%)

While the tangible elements of the historic area are now protected, the intangible elements and traditional uses have diminished, and the site's authenticity has been compromised.

Table 3.2: Types of commercial establishments (n=70)

Establishment type	Senado Square - Saint Dominic's Church Precinct	Rua do St. Paulo	Total
Bakery, snacks and refreshments	1 (4.5%)	24 (49%)	25 (36%)
Pharmacy, cosmetics and perfumery	6 (29%)	8 (16%)	14 (20%)
Clothing, handbags, accessories and shoes	6 (29%)	5 (10%)	11 (16%)
Watches and jewellery	5 (24%)	3 (6%)	8 (11.5%)
Sports	0	5 (10%)	5 (7%)
Chinese furniture	0	2 (4%)	2 (3%)
Money changer	1 (4.5%)	1 (2%)	2 (3%)
Restaurant	1 (4.5%)	0	1 (1.5%)
Electrical	1 (4.5%)	0	1 (1.5%)
Optical	0	1 (2%)	1 (1.5%)
Total	21 (100%)	49 (99%*)	70 (100%)

*does not add to 100% due to rounding

As Bitner (1992) noted, the physical environment can influence behaviour and 'create an image' (p. 57). In view of this, as tourists primarily seek memorable experiences when travelling, one asks whether the Macao historic centre is offering a heritage experience or a shopping experience.

Key questions that need to be answered are:

- Must increasing numbers of tourists inevitably result in increased commercialisation and gentrification of heritage areas?
- What can be done to minimise commercialisation of heritage areas to avoid them becoming shopping centres?

- Is it reasonable to expect property owners to forgo economic income in order to prevent the loss of authenticity or traditional uses?

- Should heritage managers focus on crafting and managing the image of a heritage resource, and delivering memorable, authentic experiences for visitors?

Unless the issues implied in the above questions are addressed, the historic centre of Macao may inevitably morph into yet another shopping area and eventually lose its original appeal as a 'must see' attraction.

References

Bitner, M. J. (1992) Servicescapes: The impact of physical surroundings on customers and employees, *Journal of Marketing*, **56**, 57-71.

World Heritage Committee (2005). Opening of the 29th Session of the World Heritage Committee. http://www.wh.mo/applicationProccess/E/detail/5151 (Accessed 28 June 2018.)

Surviving the Taj Mahal

Amita Baig, Heritage Management Consultant

Keywords: India, geography, tourism, urban planning, historc urban landscape, World Heritage Site, cultural heritage

Agra is the hub for four World Heritage sites: the Taj Mahal, Agra Fort, Fatehpur Sikri and the Keoladeo National Park. Once the capital of the Mughal Empire and one of the most prosperous cities in the world, Agra was reportedly "larger in population than London and busier than all of Constantinople" and as "the emporium of the traffic of the world". Its eminence is now a distant memory. Today it is a small town that has yet to address the issues that come with being at the heart of India's tourism traffic.

The once cosmopolitan city of Agra was in many ways doomed by the Taj Mahal. In 1648, almost as soon as he had completed the monument, Shah Jahan began the construction of his new capital at Delhi and when he moved there so did the nobility and all the attendant patronage. Agra's robust economy, with its metal, leather, carpet, stone and inlay industries, was set adrift, along with the local workers and the merchants from Turkey, Persia and beyond.

Agra never recovered its primacy and the city began to decay, with its monuments becoming shabby or, worse, misused. The once sacred and magnificent centres of Mughal power became mere housing for the occupying British garrison, and the Mughal riverfront city became a small mofussil (rural) town.

Over the past century, noteworthy efforts have been made to protect Agra's monuments. The Archaeological Survey of India, which shifted from being a British to an Indian institution, is charged with protecting the heritage of Agra.

But there is much heritage outside their domain and indeed, it would seem, outside the public imagination. This is the city's multi-layered heritage: the homes of the nobility, traders and merchants; the bathhouses, libraries and markets. This cultural legacy has floundered in the changes wrought on the city. Settlements were once defined by occupation or trade, which made a legible city fabric. Today, although much of the city still functions within this, the cohesion and interdependence of these communities has been lost.

The most recent dislocation to affect Agra's cultural heritage was the Supreme Court decision of 1996 that ordered all factories in Agra to close so as to preserve the pristine white marble of the Taj Mahal. Over 450 small scale factories closed overnight, rendering some 1.5 million people jobless. Forced out of their work places, Agra's residents, who had evolved with the loss of their Mughal patrons, the transformation of the city into an insignificant garrison town, the conversion of their skill sets from makers of swords for Shah Jahan to makers of trunks for the British Army and later the local market, were yet again disempowered.

Figure 3.2: Taj Mahal (Source: Rahul Mehrotra)

The 20 years following the landmark court decision were challenging. And the situation is unlikely to improve. As of 2018, the economy is stagnant and tourism is a large scale consumer of Agra's limited resources. A new expressway into Agra largely serves the Taj Mahal and a strip of hotels on the road to the Taj, and has excluded the community and the wider city from their potential share of tourism revenue. The monument itself is now overexploited and the public has turned its back on this historic city, one of India's richest in heritage.

A dynamic new vision for Agra is essential for its residents and its heritage. With a resident population of 1.7 million and over 6 million visitors a year, there is a critical need to ensure both the city and the Taj will survive; they cannot survive in isolation.

In recent decades many reports have been commissioned, but action has yet to be taken; governments lack the commitment to invest in transformative change. One such report was prepared by the Centre for Urban and Regional Excellence (CURE). According to this report, Agra has 432 slum communities of which 168 lie alongside monuments. For these communities, potable drinking water, sanitation and public health remain elusive, while the monument gardens are lush and green. It is a gulf that must be reconciled to secure the future of the citizens and their heritage.

Historic buildings and areas lost within the old town of Agra must be brought back into the public domain. As most of these are either encroached upon or illegally tenanted, a major rehabilitation and resettlement plan is needed as well as plans for adaptive re-use. Furthermore, a robust tourism development plan is needed to bring a swathe of exceptional monuments such as I'timad ud Daulah's Tomb, Ram Bagh and Sikandra within the tourism ambit.

Moreover, the left bank of the river, flanked by factories closed by the court order needs a comprehensive revitalisation scheme. These buildings could be re-used as malls and multiplexes, serving Agra's communities. Equally, Taj Ganj requires new vision and a robust and creative plan that will revive the quarter, serve the local residents and meet contemporary demands.

It is essential to construct an urban environment that works both for citizens and tourists; one that is as contemporary as it is historic. In order to be sustainable, we must address our historic sites and cities in the broadest and most inclusive terms.

Bibliography

Baig, A. and Mehrotra, R. (2017) *Taj Mahal: Multiple narratives*, New Delhi: Om Books.

Edensor, T. (1998) *Tourists at the Taj: Performance and meaning at a symbolic site*, London: Routledge.

Harkness, T. and Sinha, A. (2004) Taj Heritage Corridor: Intersections between history and culture on the Yamuna riverfront, *Places*, **16** (2), 62.

Taj Mahal Conservation Collaborative (2001) Briefing document, Unpublished.

Taj Mahal Conservation Collaborative (2003) Site management plan Unpublished.

Tillotson, G. (2008) *Taj Mahal*, Cambridge: Harvard University Press.

A heritage area for Honolulu: A wonderful but premature idea

William Chapman, Interim Dean, School of Architecture, University of Hawai'i at Mānoa

Keywords: Hawaii, geography, tourism, historic urban landscape, preservation, urban planning

In 2008, a coalition of civic leaders, preservationists, historians, architects, planners and tourism specialists united to produce a blueprint for Honolulu's future as a tourism magnet – seeking to complement and to some degree offset Hawai'i's traditional focus on 'sun, sea and sand'. Directed (with the hope of future funding) at the U.S. National Park Service's Heritage Area Program, the emphasis of the Hawai'i Capital National Heritage Area (HCNHA) plan was on urban Honolulu and the surrounding ahupua'a (a traditional Hawaiian land division stretching from the ocean to the mountains behind).

Although in 2008 Honolulu had already lost much of its historic built heritage, the coalition and the team responsible for refining the plan believed that the strong associative character of the metropolitan area, along with a number of key buildings from the late 19th and early 20th centuries could help to underscore the special qualities of the essentially colonial city. Unfortunately, some property owners and – ironically – a few representatives from the Native Hawaiian community saw the proposal as yet another layer of federal bureaucracy and as a surreptitious effort to interfere with the administration of Hawaiian Homelands included within its boundaries. As a result, the proposal came to a halt. Nothing concrete has been done since to resurrect the plan.

As the originators of the HCNHA idea recognised, Honolulu is a fascinating historic city. Founded in the early part of the 19th century as a haven for seal hunters and whalers, by the end of the century the city had grown to be a significant Pacific port. What made Honolulu unique was its ancient origins as a sacred site for Hawaiians, home to sacred springs and several important *heiau* (Hawaiian temples).

With the rise of commerce, the political centre of the Hawaiian kingdom shifted to Honolulu (from the former capital of Lahaina on the island of Maui). And with the overthrow of the Hawaiian Queen Liliuokalani in 1893 and the absorption of Hawai'i as a territory of the United States in 1900, Honolulu grew in stature as an important centre for the agriculture industry and a regional hub for banking, insurance, manufacturing and medicine. It also became home to an outstanding collection of Beaux Arts, Neoclassical, Spanish Colonial Revival, and Hawai'i Regionalist architecture, making it one of the most elegant cities in the Pacific. At the same time, the city retained special qualities of traditional Hawaiian life: from lei sellers to local food to language. In addition, the city possessed a rich heritage of Asian immigrant life, including Chinese temples and restaurants, Japanese cinemas and Filipino music venues, much of it centred in 'Chinatown', a

30-block commercial and residential area adjacent to the central business district. There was once also a large 'Japan Town', now lost to public housing projects.

Much changed with statehood in 1959. Along with a tourism boom, statehood led to investment in resort hotels, highways and downtown skyscrapers. It also encouraged suburban growth and the loss of a residential urban population. Some former residents were attracted to newer homes at the periphery and some were forced out by an aggressive urban renewal programme. Fortunately, a few stalwart preservationists fought to save a remnant of the old Chinatown (by that point reduced to 13 blocks). The preservationists formed non-profit organisations to advocate for and save some of the key older buildings, notably Iolani Palace, home of Hawai'i's last monarchs, and several other buildings associated with Hawaiian royalty. The creation of a special Capitol District centred on the 1964-period state capitol building, and other sites from the monarchy and territorial periods, later helped redefine the urban core, as did the introduction and enhancement of several downtown parks.

Figure 3.3: Iolani Palace, built in 1882 for King Kalakaua, Hawaii's then sovereign. The palace is one of the island's principal cultural attractions.

Despite the overall sanitizing of the city centre and the loss of residents, Honolulu retained pockets of genuine interest. These included some of the earliest commercial buildings, fine examples of early 20th-century Beaux Arts and Spanish Colonial Revival Style architecture, a few industrial sites, several old theatres, an early missionary station, and several historic schools and churches. Some sites were associated with significant events, from labour uprisings to coronations. Other places were connected with important Hawaiian leaders of the 19th century and with tales and myths of ancient times. Often mere echoes, these places nonetheless conveyed a sense of history and place that many preservation advocates wanted to formally recognise and support.

Despite the pushback on the HCNHA plan, there have been numerous – and hopeful – small steps towards actualizing parts of that plan. The Hawai'i Community Development Authority, working with a grant from the Save America Fund (also administered by the National Park Service), has supplied a large number of interpretive signs in the old commercial areas along Merchant Street and Fort Street. Moreover, considerable private investment in Chinatown has meant that the area has finally begun to realize its potential as an alternative gathering spot for both tourists and locals. Furthermore, there is increasing recognition of the special historic character of the downtown area, including a new appreciation for the modernist-period buildings that once took so much away from the historic core.

More remains to be done, including enhancing both museum-based and street-based exhibitions and performances that speak of Honolulu's history; expanding existing walking tours, both commercial and non-profit (the local chapter of the American Institute of Architects has weekly walking tours focused on downtown buildings); and increasing the promotion of urban Honolulu by the Hawai'i Tourism Authority. A visitor centre and museum, both envisioned in the HCNHA plan, would also do much to help visitors and local residents to re-envision the city as a place of cultural and historical significance. These may all be small steps, but together they can help to return a 'sense of place' to Hawai'i's only large city and tie it to its broader heritage context in the Pacific.

Phnom Penh: Opportunities lost and gained

William Chapman. Interim Dean, School of Architecture, University of Hawai'i at Mānoa

Keywords: Cambodia, geography, urban planning, historic urban landscape, preservation, built environment

Following Cambodia's truly horrific civil war of the 1970s, Phnom Penh was well situated to emerge as a vibrant and – paradoxically – well-preserved city. Indeed, Phnom Penh had every promise of retaining the moniker, the 'Paris of the East', an appellation also assigned to other cities in Asia, though certainly well deserved by Phnom Penh. The lack of the kinds of development that had characterized other Southeast Asian cities, namely Bangkok, Kuala Lumpur and Jakarta – featuring high-rise construction based on essentially the United States' model – had never been put in place in the old French colonial capital and ancient Cambodian city. What existed in the 1980s and 1990s was a surprisingly intact low-rise urban construct, with well-preserved rows of shop houses, grand colonial buildings of the late 19th and early 20th centuries and a striking collection of modernist structures associated with the so-called 'Golden Age' of post-1953 independence. Several significant Buddhist temples and the chedi-ornamented Wat Phnom gave evidence of the city's ancient past, and a bold Beaux Arts-inspired urban plan, reminiscent of metropolitan France, provided essential linkages within the sprawling urban area.

In 1997, a non-governmental advisory group called the Atelier Parisien d'Urbanisme, working closely with the Ministry of Culture and Phnom Penh's newly re-established planning department, published a comprehensive plan for Phnom Penh's redevelopment. It envisioned a future city much like, in fact, Paris. Calling for height limits of six to eight storeys, depending on the area, and wholeheartedly emphasizing the retention of key historic buildings and sites (as well as respecting the traditional architectural building block of many Southeast Asian cities: the shop house), the 'Atelier' plan offered an alternative to the kind of market-driven development experienced in most other Asian cities. At the same time, key investments, including the resurrection of Phnom Penh's Hotel Le Royal, as well as the re-use of many colonial era building as restaurants, hotels and company offices, promised a future in which historic preservation (conservation) would dominate decisions about tenure, development and land use.

Unfortunately, a number of forces coalesced in the early 2000s to change this trajectory. Initiated in part by Prime Minister Hun Sen, decision-making shifted gears toward more intensive development. The time was indeed ripe for this change. Land values had increased exponentially, leading to an influx of capital from outside, principally from China, Malaysia and Thailand. In addition, the city had seen a rise in expertise in the form of architects and engineers – both foreigners and Cambodians who had trained abroad and in the country's own resuscitated institutions.

By the end of the decade, Phnom Penh's building boom was in full swing: a new multi-storey mall pushed up against the historic central market and rows of shop houses had fallen to developers' new schemes. In 2010 the city could claim over 600 high-rise buildings, with many more either in the planning stages or under construction. The opening in 2014 of the 38-story Vattanac Tower, the vision of Khmer tycoon Chun Leang, led to even more grandiose schemes, including that of the Cambodian-owned Thai Boon Roong Group, which is investing 2 billion dollars to build a twin tower fully 108 metres taller that the Petronas Towers in Kuala Lumpur.

While it appears that the attempt to save Phnom Penh as a city of human scale and preserved heritage is lost, there remain, as with other cities in the region, opportunities for cultural appreciation and for preserving at least some pockets of heritage. As of 2018, it appeared that the central market and surrounding square might be preserved, as well as the former governmental centre in the northern section of the old city, near Wat Phnom. Prior investments, such as that in the grand Hotel Le Royal, appeared safe, as did some of the key buildings of the resurgent 1950s. It is hoped that George Groslier's magnificent national museum and architect Vann Molyvann's independence monument will endure, but other key buildings from the colonial period, including the Royal University of Fine Arts and the famous residential block known as the White Building (built in 1963 in frank emulation of Le Corbusier's Ville Radieuse), are clearly on the chopping block.

Figure 3.4: Exterior of Hotel Le Royal

Figure 3.5: Vann Molyvann Monument

Phnom Penh is a city that demonstrates that heritage is often at the front line of development. Visitors to Phnom Penh in the 1990s came largely to see historic sites, witness the resurrection of ancient traditions of music and dance, visit the museum and sample Cambodia's rich cuisine. A manager at Hotel Le Royal feels that this is a diminishing niche, however. He is right in many ways. The 2000s saw Phnom Penh ushering in a new age of investment and new kinds of tourism, from business travellers to sex tourists. It is safe to say the majority of travellers to Phnom Penh today have less interest in heritage sites and more interest in shopping, making deals and staying in luxury surroundings.

There remain opportunities, however. The midcentury architecture of Vann Molyvann and his contemporaries has attracted a special audience, resulting in both regular tour groups and new publications. Furthermore, planning authorities now recognise the importance of signature historic buildings. Moreover, heritage diehards remain, including a substantial population that see in the buildings of the past an intangible romanticism, and Cambodian activists and entrepreneurs who wish to build on their city's rich legacy of architecture and culture. We can only hope that new wealth will translate into worthy heritage projects and that the appeal of history will not die altogether.

Restoring the identity of the Bukchon heritage area of Seoul

Cho, In-Souk, Architect / Principal, Co-Director of UIA Work Program Heritage and Cultural Identity, DaaRee Architect & Associates, Seoul, Republic of Korea

Keywords: South Korea, geography, historic urban landscape, governance, tourism, commercialization, displacement

The Bukchon ('northern village') neighbourhood of Seoul, located between Gyeongbokgung Palace and Changdeokgung Palace, is a showcase of the layers of 20th-century urban history. Traditional wooden houses (*hanok*) and winding alleyways represent the 1930s to 1950s; markets, commercial strips and two-storey houses represent the 1960s to 1980s; concrete and masonry residential buildings represent the 1990s to 2000s; and new galleries and cafes represent the present.

Various changes have occurred in Bukchon over the past two decades, including to the village landscape, the size of the existing hanok, the height and the scale of the architecture, the real estate market value and the neighbourhood's relationship with the surroundings. Many of these changes stem from an ordinance enacted by the Seoul metropolitan government in 1999 to provide technical support and subsidies for improving public facilities and purchasing hanoks in Bukchon. This ordinance allowed people to design, repair and maintain hanok residences and ensure their sustainability. However, this led to Bukchon becoming commercialised due to gentrification and land value inflation, leading to the displacement of the original residents.

Several other factors have altered the identity and reduced the authenticity of Bukchon. A key factor is that the name of this residential area was changed to 'Bukchon Hanok Village'. This change appears to have been a misguided attempt by the Seoul metropolitan government to make Bukchon appear more like a heritage site. However, as a result, visitors look for a hanok village in the middle of Bukchon. In other words, a residential area of Seoul is viewed by tourists as a sightseeing spot. Sightseeing facilities such as an observation deck encourage this perception. Commercial tour companies now offer Bukchon Hanok Village tours from each hotel in Seoul, and guides with loudspeakers show tourists through the Bukchon residential alleyways at all hours, destroying the local ambience and reducing the quality of life of the residents.

The first step in restoring the identity of this residential area would be to change the name from 'Bukchon Hanok Village' back to 'Bukchon'. The second would be to stop advertising this residential district as a tourist destination. In addition, the use of loudspeakers in the neighbourhood should be prohibited and sightseeing facilities should be removed. The removal of the elements not suitable for a residential area would enable Bukchon to recover its ambiance and the residents to improve their quality of life.

Addressing this issue also requires that the Seoul metropolitan government gain an understanding of the authenticity of the hanok and the identity of the hanok residential area. Furthermore, ordinances must be enacted to prevent further drastic changes to the residential landscape, the size of the hanok and the real estate market. This requires reviewing and revising existing unit district plans. Rational regulations that take into consideration the relationship with the surroundings, the height and the size of the houses, and the maintenance of the hanok landscape should be made. Moreover, commercial facilities should not be permitted.

It is also necessary to actively review the establishment of a dedicated organization to provide practical support for the repair and maintenance of hanok, so residents can incorporate modern conveniences into their homes, which will aid in ensuring the sustainability of the hanok residential area. In addition, the Hanok Committee must apply strict consultation standards, and identify a supervisory and architectural organization that can conduct on-the-spot inspections during repair work on hanok.

It is imperative that insurance companies (perhaps supported by a government initiative) provide insurance, particularly fire insurance, for hanok. This will allow banks to provide mortgage finance, which will enable more residents of hanok to protect these historic buildings. Also, it is necessary to carry out campaigns to raise residents' awareness and to strictly regulate restaurant garbage.

Bibliography

Cho, I. (2008) A stroll around the Bukchon Village, Enticing charms of old Korean wooden houses, *Korean Heritage*, **1** (1).

Cho, I. (2009) '우아한한옥주거지로거듭나기', 시대정신년가을호

http://sdjs.co.kr/read.php?quarterId=SD200903&num=325 (Accessed 25 July 2018.)

Conservation of Mumbai's community housing, Mumbai, India

Vikas Dilawari, VikasDilawari Architects, Mumbai

Keywords: India, geography, conservation, governance, redevelopment, government policy

Introduction

Heritage conservation in India is limited mostly to monuments and landmarks, leaving the larger part of the heritage fabric on unstable ground, with little or no governmental support. Government policies relating to heritage structures lack consideration of the quality of life of the residents and the needs of the city, and have resulted in insensitive development and redevelopment.

The majority of the lived-in heritage structures of Mumbai are tenanted properties governed by the Rent Control Act, which was introduced to protect tenants from astronomical increases in rents after World War II. The rents have therefore remained stagnant for nearly 70 years, and the buildings have been left to decay. Thus, the Act has been detrimental to the city's traditional housing fabric. A drastic change in government policies is needed regarding rental housing.

Recognizing the crumbling state of these housing units, the government invited private builders and developers to redevelop them. However, these companies have tended to increase the sizes of the buildings and add free parking areas, which have placed an excessive load on the city's fragile infrastructure. This has interfered with the urban design and planning that functioned effectively for a century and has also altered the formerly well-woven socio-economic fabric.

The GZRF Trust

The Parsi community in Mumbai is an affluent one and it has addressed housing issues in a sensitive manner. This Zoroastrian community nurtures and promotes communal living and supports a building typology that is built according to the needs of the inhabitants and that is climate responsive. In the late 19th century, the community established the Garib Zoroastrian Rehethan Fund (GZRF) Trust, which restored the Cama Building (c.1898) and its flanking Murzban Colony ensemble. The first buildings in the Murzban Colony to be restored were the Sethna, Gamadiya, Patel and Dadyseth buildings off Wadia Street. These were followed by the Lal Chimney Compound, which included the Modi, Cooper, Wadia, Dadachandji and Talukdar buildings. The third set of buildings to be restored is that in Gilder Lane.

Case study

This case study examines the skilful conservation of about a dozen buildings belonging to the Parsi Community: the Lal Chimney Complex, the Sethna building and the Gilder Lane buildings. All three complexes are owned by the GZRF. These conservation efforts demonstrate that it is better to conserve than to redevelop, as conservation allows one to retain not only built heritage but also the socio-cultural ethos and lifestyle of the generations that grew up in these buildings. Furthermore, conservation does not further burden the fragile infrastructure of the city. Conservation also promotes a revival of dying crafts and develops a sense of pride in the community.

The conservation approach was practical. Although substantial repairs were undertaken, there was minimum intervention in terms of materials, so as to retain the authenticity of the buildings and to also make the repairs economical. The original aesthetics and uses were restored, thus returning the buildings to the residents, who have a sentimental bond with these structures.

Prior to the conservation effort, the buildings were dilapidated, with leaking roofs and rotten floors. The buildings had to be vacated for the works, so the tenants were moved into empty flats in another colony. Complete roof works were undertaken to make the buildings watertight and the floor slabs were replaced. The rotted timber members were spliced and repaired with new wood, and steel beams were installed to strengthen the structures. The exterior skin of the buildings was retained. All insensitive accretions altering the cultural significance of the fabric were removed, along with all ill-informed repairs, and attempts were made to restore the original form, using like to like materials. However, the interiors were upgraded using contemporary finish materials as per the preferences and needs of the respective residents. Thus, modern day functions were incorporated without compromising the heritage character of the structure.

The Trust employed traditional skilled labour wherever possible, and sought to sensitize and educate civil contractors about heritage properties and the concept of skilled repairs.

(Left) **Figure 3.6:** The Cama Building of Murzaban Colony post-restoration

(Right) **Figure 3.7:** The Lal Chimney Compound post-restoration

Conclusion

With some funding and professional attention, the lifespan of these tenanted buildings has been prolonged and they are no longer seen as a hindrance to development. Instead, they are viewed as enriching the fabric of the city.

The conservation of the GZRF buildings is an example for the city to emulate as it illustrates the effectiveness of one of the basic principles of conservation: minimum intervention. It also illustrates that it is possible to conserve precious heritage and give it new lease on life in an economical way. Economical conservation is essential if it is to become a mass movement.

This approach demonstrates to decision-makers that a better result can be achieved, and an economical one, if we repair buildings rather than reconstruct them. It is hoped that the government and other community trusts learn from such projects and that policy-makers develop policies that support repair and conservation rather than reconstruction and redevelopment.

Heritage and real estate: Conflicts of interest in Ho Chi Minh, Vietnam

Tim Doling, historian and freelance consultant

Keywords: Vietnam, geography, heritage impact, built heritage, tourism, urban planning

In recent years, Ho Chi Minh (formerly Saigon) has experienced rapid economic growth, which, while improving the lives of many, has impacted heavily on the city's built heritage. Recognizing the negative impact, a land use master plan for 2025, approved in March 2008, resolved that "the historic core of the city in Districts 1 and 3 should be protected" (Hồ Chí Minh City People's Committee et al., 2007). However, in spite of the plan, the authorities approved the construction of new high-rise office, retail and residential projects in the low-rise city centre, leading to the destruction of many existing historic buildings, including the former Chamber of Commerce (1867) and Grands Magasins Charner (1924).

While in many other parts of Asia the boom in high-end property construction has stalled, the 'emerging market' of Vietnam, and in particular of Ho Chi Minh, is still touted as a real estate 'hot spot' (Zhen, 2017), which poses a threat to the buildings and streetscapes that once gained the city its reputation as the 'Pearl of the Orient'.

A recent example of heritage destruction was the demolition of the Ba Son Shipyard to build a 60-storey residential complex (Vinhomes, 2016). Built in the early 1790s, the Ba Son Shipyard became a French naval arsenal in 1864, and was subsequently equipped with workshops, ateliers, dry docks, cranes and slipways. In the early 20th century it became the headquarters of the French 'naval forces of the Oriental Seas' and it continued to function right up to 2015 as both a naval shipyard and a commercial enterprise.

In the lead-up to the decommissioning of Ba Son as part of a plan to relocate ship repair and construction downriver to Cái Mép-ThịVải, it was recognized that the compound housed many fine examples of French industrial architecture dating back to the 1880s. On 28 June 2013, the Hồ Chí Minh City People's Committee approved the *Regulation on management of urban space and architecture in the existing centre of Hồ Chí Minh City*, which expressly provided for the preservation of Ba Son's most important structures (depots, workshops, offices and dry docks) and stated that "new development must respect and at the same time harmonize with these historic structures" (Quyếtđịnh, 2013). This idea was endorsed publicly by several prominent Vietnamese government heritage specialists, who argued publicly that "the cultural and historical relics of Ba Son Shipyard, large dry dock and related works should be listed as a national heritage site" (Sàigòn Giải Phóng, 2012). Furthermore, travel and tourism practitioners voiced the hope that the old Ba Son buildings might one day be repurposed as a world-class maritime heritage and leisure complex. However, apart from a workshop building associated with revolutionary hero Tôn Đức Thắng, that had been listed in 1993 as a national monument, the shipyards were demolished.

Developers in Vietnam wield considerable power and influence, which invariably outweigh those of the handful of dedicated culture officials responsible for protecting the city's remaining old structures. The task of the latter is hampered by the fact that, with few exceptions, only temples, pagodas and revolutionary sites are currently afforded heritage status, leaving other historic buildings without legal protection. With the concept of a civil society still in its infancy, efforts by individual members of the local community to raise awareness of the value of built heritage carry little weight.

Realistically, in an environment where property speculation remains rife and developers seek swift returns on their investments, arguments based on longer-term regeneration have limited impact. However, it is increasingly recognised that built heritage not only has aesthetic value and a key role in reaffirming citizens' sense of identity, but can also bring considerable economic benefits, particularly through tourism. Thus, the systematic destruction of built heritage – the very thing which attracts high-paying and longer-staying cultural tourists – may yet elicit official concern.

The local community is actively engaged in efforts to protect their heritage. A Facebook group Đài Quan sát Di sản Sài Gòn / Saigon Heritage Observatory (facebook.com/groups/SaigonHO) – set up in 2014 by a group of concerned locals to educate the public about the value of heritage – has attracted a large membership, and the Héritage GO mobile app (heritagego.org), developed in 2016, is seeking to crowdsource the conservation of surviving old buildings. However, the local authorities make the decisions, so the need to engage them remains paramount. Efforts are currently being made to develop partnerships with state tourism agencies, and also with the city's foreign consular missions, with a view to sharing other countries' experiences of heritage conservation, including the effectiveness of incentive programmes such as Transfer of Development Rights (TDR).

References

Ho Chi Minh City People's Committee, Urban Planning Institute of Ho Chi Minh, and Nikken Sekkei (2007) *Study on the Adjustment of the HCMC Master Plan up to 2025, Final Report*. Ho Chi Minh: HCMC People's Committee.

Quyếtđịnh 3457/QĐ-UBND 'Vềduyệt Quychếquảnlýkhônggian, kiếntrúccảnhquanđôthị Khutrungtâmhiệnhữu Thànhphố Hồ Chí Minh (930ha)', 28 June 2013. http://www.congbao.hochiminhcity.gov.vn/ (Accessed 25 July 2018.)

Sàigòn Giải Phóng (2012) Cầngiữnguyêntrạng di tíchtạikhu Ba Son, PhápLuật, 23 August; 'Cầnbảotồn di tíchtrongkhuvực Ba Son', 3 January 2013.

Vinhomes (2016) 'Vinhomes to transform Ba Son Shipyard into mega development', *Saigoneer*, 18 March. en.vinhomesgoldenriverapartment.co (Accessed 25 July 2018.)

Zhen, S. (2017) Vietnam quickly becoming Asia's latest property hotspot, *South China Morning Post*, 6 June.

Upgrading of roads to spread tourism benefits in the world heritage city of Vigan, Philippines

Ricardo Laurel Favis, Former Programme Specialist for Culture, UNESCO Bangkok Office

Keywords: Philippines, geography, tourism, World Heritage Site, urban planning

Established in the 16th century, Vigan is the least damaged example in Asia of a planned Hispanic colonial town. Its architecture reflects a fusion of cultural elements of the Philippines and China along with those of Mexico and Europe to create a culture and cityscape unique in East and Southeast Asia. Inscribed as a World Heritage Site in 1999, Vigan was recognized by UNESCO in 2011 as a model of best practice in World Heritage site management, achieved with relatively limited resources.

Since its inscription as a World Heritage Site in 1999, Vigan has become one of the country's top destinations. Tourism activities, shops and service providers are concentrated along the main historic street, Calle Mena Crisologo, which is a cobblestoned pedestrian zone, where only horse-drawn carriages are allowed. Visitors seldom visit the adjacent roads, where a considerable number of ancestral houses are located. Several houses at the northeast end of Plaridel Street are used as hardware stores and warehouses, with heavy trucks parked on the street.

Recognizing the need to reduce the tourism pressure on Mena Crisologo Street and spread the economic benefits of tourism to other parts of the historic core, the Department of Public Works and Highways, in close collaboration with the city government and concerned homeowners, has begun upgrading Calle Plaridel and Calle V. De Los Reyes, which run parallel to Calle Mena Crisologo, and the roads around Plaza Burgos and Plaza Salcedo where the architectural dominants of religious and civil buildings are located. The upgrading works include: improvement of drainage, repair of sewerage and water lines, laying locally-sourced limestone cobblestones on the roads, provision of appropriate street lighting and furniture, and enhancement of Plaza Burgos.

The owners of the hardware stores and warehouses along Plaridel Street have committed to maintaining only their showrooms; they will move their warehouses and heavy trucks outside the historic core. Only light motorized vehicles will be allowed to pass through these streets, and several roads will eventually be pedestrian-only. At the same time, a number of ancestral houses along Mena Crisologo Street are being restored, compelling souvenir shops and tourism service providers in this street to relocate elsewhere.

Upgrading the roads within the historic core is expected to bring multiple benefits, including lengthening the stays of tourists, providing adequate space for new businesses and, more importantly, encouraging homeowners in the core zone to restore their ancestral houses for adaptive re-use. The road project is a significant step forward in the development of Vigan as a major tourist destination.

Figure 3.8: Mena Crisologo Street, the main historic road where tourist and economic activities are concentrated (Source: City Government of Vigan).

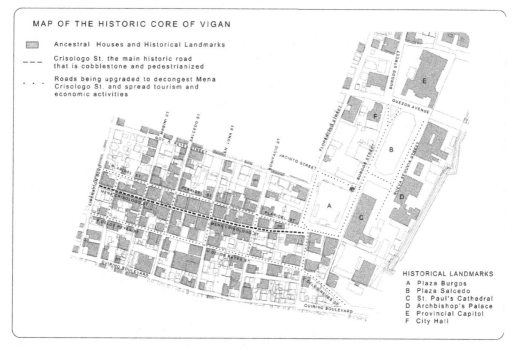

Figure 3.9: Map of the historic core zone of the World Heritage City of Vigan (Source: City Government of Vigan).

Revitalization of Mei Ho House, Hong Kong

Desmond Hui, Professor, Hang Seng Management College

Keywords: China, geography, conservation, heritage impact, revitalization, public housing, built heritage

Mei Ho House is an example from an innovative scheme with a bottom-up approach that provides non-profit organizations with an open invitation to come up with sustainable and meaningful plans for revitalizing specific historic buildings under public ownership.

Mei Ho House is the only remaining block of the first type of public housing design in Hong Kong. The decision to revitalize the building fabric and to maintain and interpret it is testimony to the importance of public housing in the city's history. Thematically, Mei Ho House contributes to the city's collective memory of early city development and the social transformation of Hong Kong. The building has been revitalized as a hostel, thus maintaining the original housing function. The revitalization process has thereby also taken into account the social network of past residents in the building, thus conserving not only physical heritage but also the intangible network.

Figure 3.10: Mei Ho House pre-revitalization (Source: Hong Kong Youth Hostels Association).

Figure 3.11: Mei Ho House post-revitalization (Source: Hong Kong Youth Hostels Association).

The Mei Ho House Heritage space (which takes up two half-floors of one wing of the building) presents the heritage history and experience for public education and enjoyment, and possibly offers reflections for future heritage conservation efforts and directions in Hong Kong.

Japan Heritage: Unveiling forgotten histories and stories

Dr. Nobuko Inaba, Professor, World Heritage Studies, Graduate School of Comprehensive Human Sciences, University of Tsukuba

Keywords: Japan, geography, heritage impact, tourism, governance, tangible heritage, revitalization

Facing an aging society and a declining population, local governments in Japan are seeking new means of economic revitalisation. In support of such efforts, the central government is encouraging local governments and agencies to develop decentralized planning policies, laws and programmes to enhance historical landscapes and resources. Such programmes include using heritage resources to encourage tourism and to assist young people to move to rural areas. Following a period of confrontation between tourism infrastructure development and urban conservation, we may now have reached a stage at which we can devise wise approaches to economic revitalisation through heritage tourism.

As part of this effort, the Agency for Cultural Affairs launched a new programme called 'Japan Heritage' in 2015. This is a list of local histories and stories nominated by municipalities, connecting heritage properties and sites, both protected and non-protected, tangible and intangible. The agency is planning to list approximately 100 narratives by 2020, the year of the Tokyo Olympics. This is not for protection per se, but for recognition, aiming to encourage independent and voluntary revitalisation, and outreach tools based on heritage resources.

As of May 2018, 64 narratives had been listed under the brand 'Japan Heritage'. While many have concerns regarding the effects the 'Japan Heritage' programme will have on the character of their communities, the programme is becoming more and more popular, and many municipalities are preparing nominations. The 'Japan Heritage' emblem is helping its popularity.

The agency selects narratives annually, and seeks charming stories, while also looking for vision and strategy, and inter-departmental or inter-municipal networks. Single municipalities' narratives are also selected, but broader networks of multiple municipalities (even those separated geographically) more clearly reflect the unique character of the programme.

One interesting example is a network of 38 rural port towns on the Japan Sea coastline that once flourished as suppliers of seafood to the cities in central Japan, and which imported rich merchandise from the cities. These towns declined economically after a major change in the system of distribution of seafood, and subsequently faded into history. Because of the fragile character of port town facilities, they do not possess strong visible monumental evidence so their tangible heritage did not enjoy legal protection. The narratives of the network of towns provide a means of safeguarding the heritage of each.

While the programme is unveiling forgotten histories, the challenge is how these communities can develop innovative projects on their own initiative. Supported by the national assembly, this programme may give rise to an exciting vision of heritage recognition systems for the cities and towns of Japan.

Discovery of long-lost heritage sites, Jaipur, Rajasthan

Abha Narain Lambah, Principal Architect, Abha Narain Lambah Conservation Architects and Historic Building Consultants

Keywords: India, geography, urban planning, heritage impact, historic urban landscape, World Heritage Site

Founded in 1727 by Maharaj Jai Singh II, the 'Pink City' of Jaipur in Rajasthan is among the most famous historic sites in India. It is home to the World Heritage site of Jantar Mantar and iconic monuments such as Hawa Mahal and Isar Lat. In accordance with the ancient architectural treatise, the Vastu Shastra, the city was planned in a grid pattern and divided into nine chaupar (squares), with the two most significant intersections at Badi Chaupar (Badi Square) and Choti Chaupar (Choti Square).

In recent decades, the inner city has suffered from heavy vehicular traffic, which has diminished the quality of life of the residents and reduced access by pedestrians to market places. Recognizing this issue, the Chief Minister of Rajasthan, Vasundhara Raje Scindia, initiated a project to build an underground metro line that would pass under the walled city and connect various sites within it. During the construction of the metro, heritage consultants were appointed to document each historic streetscape along the planned metro line; assess the impact of the underground metro on the city's heritage; and monitor vibrations and movements caused by the tunnelling, however minor, to ensure minimal impact.

Archival research by the consultants revealed two old black and white photographs from the 1870s showing what seemed to be a water tank and step well in the centre of the Choti Chaupar. These had since disappeared; a traffic roundabout and municipal park had been in place at the site for decades.

This archival find was a revelation; the team realised that long lost archaeological sites and step wells may be hidden under the city's two main chaupar. This was reported to the Chief Minister and she decided to save the step wells, even if it meant relocating the metro stations that had been planned at the centre of the roundabouts.

An excavation by experienced archaeologists revealed step wells and fountains in local stone and stucco, with marble water spouts carved in the shape of cow heads, as well as traditional qanat (underground tunnels) that had once channelled water from the hills far away.

During the metro construction, each stone piece of the wells and fountains was carefully numbered and stacked for anastylosis. In 2018, following the completion of the metro stations, the process of replacing each piece began. When this is complete, commuters will be able to alight from the metro and make their way to the restored step wells through an archaeological gallery. Residents and visitors alike will thus be able to appreciate yet another facet of Jaipur's rich heritage.

Respecting the cultural layers: Hanoi, Vietnam

William Logan, PhD, FASSA, Professor Emeritus, Deakin University

Keywords: Vietnam, geography, World Heritage Site, urban planning, urban heritage management, restoration

Very few cities are created in a single time period; instead, they are built up over considerable time, with each period part of a city's evolutionary history. The resultant layering is an essential part of a city's urban heritage, contributing to its richness and unique identity.

Underlying the notion of the Historic Urban Landscape (UNESCO, 2011) is the acknowledgment that contemporary cities possess striking cultural and social plurality and contain a modern layer as well as earlier layers. Sensitive urban heritage management respects a city's cultural layering. This does not mean freezing a city as it currently exists or as it existed at some time in the past. Rather, urban heritage management should protect the layers and also allow for new uses and meaning to emerge within the community. In this way, the city is managed as a living landscape, responding to the changing needs and aspirations of its occupants.

In some cities, however, efforts are being made to return historic centres to some halcyon period in the past. Sometimes governments want this for ideological or nation-building reasons, but it is usually done to make places attractive to tourists. This idea seems to be based on the view that visitors are unable to cope with cultural complexity.

When the Imperial Citadel of Thang Long - Hanoi was inscribed on the World Heritage list in 2010, the Statement of Outstanding Universal Value (OUV) focused on three features, namely: the citadel's longevity, its continuity as a seat of power and the presence of a layered record of vestiges. In conserving the site for current and future generations, with its Outstanding Universal Value intact, it is critically important that the values underlying these three elements are respected and form the basis of site management.

In 2013 the Vietnamese media reported, however, that a detailed plan had been submitted to "restore and preserve" the citadel site (Dan Tri International, 2013) and that the planners had been requested to ensure the restored citadel looked "as much as possible as it looked originally". Thus, the multi-layered citadel was to be reinterpreted and remodelled to emphasize the period of King Ly Thai To, whose reign, from 1009 to 1028, is seen as the beginning of the independent Vietnamese state (Logan, 2014). Accordingly, some of the citadel's surface structures – including French colonial elements and some of the more recent Vietnamese military buildings – have in fact been demolished since the inscription. The fact that that there are many important relics of dynasties since the Ly, and that the citadel has evolved over more than 1,300 years, has been overlooked. The layering component of the site, one of the reasons it was inscribed on the World Heritage list, has thus been ignored.

Failure to respect the OUV effectively puts World Heritage sites on the slippery slope towards World Heritage in Danger listing or even de-listing. If States Parties to the World Heritage Convention want the World Heritage 'brand', they need to follow the World Heritage system rules that go with it.

Figure 3.12: Ly Thai To statue, Hanoi.

References

Dan Tri International (2013) Hanoi mulling over restoration of Thang Long Imperial Citadel, Dtinews. http://dtinews.vn/en/news/019004/30268/hanoi-mulling-over-restoration-of-thang-long-imperial-citadel-.html (Accessed 8 March 2018).

Logan, W. (2014) Making the most of heritage in Hanoi, Vietnam, *Historic Environment*, **26** (3), 62-72.

UNESCO (2011) Declaration on the Conservation of Historic Urban Landscapes. http://whc.unesco.org/document/6812 (Accessed 6 March 2018).

From appreciation to conservation

Moe Moe Lwin, Director, Yangon Heritage Trust

Keywords: Myanmar, geography, governance, built heritage, stakeholder engagement, cultural heritage

The Yangon Heritage Trust (YHT), a non-profit organization that aims to protect and promote urban cultural and built heritage, has implemented multiple projects since its inauguration in 2012. Two such projects have been particularly successful.

One is the Blue Plaque project, which involves installing blue plaques on selected buildings in Yangon in recognition of their high heritage significance and considering their high-visibility to pedestrian traffic. The first plaque was installed at the City Hall, one of the most important buildings in Yangon given its unique architecture and landmark location in the city centre. As of 2018, the YHT has installed 22 plaques across Yangon, including those owned by the government, religious institutions and residents. So far, the oldest building recognized with a blue plaque is the Armenian Church, built in 1867. The project has been generously sponsored by the Royal Philips Foundation.

To implement this project, the YHT garnered the full support of the Yangon regional government and municipal authorities, as well as the collaboration of the various government agencies that own the selected buildings. The project has generated a great deal of publicity, with wide media coverage and attention from the authorities at both the union and regional levels. Each installation ceremony is attended by representatives of the government and local societies, and relevant stakeholders, including alumni (in the case of heritage school buildings), health care professionals (in the case of Yangon General Hospital building), and the judiciary (in the case of the Supreme Court building). The ceremonies have brought together the various parties and provided opportunities to discuss the heritage buildings and current issues, and to address those issues.

The project has become one of the most effective and visible means of celebrating Yangon's rich history. It has raised public appreciation of our city's built heritage and has been effective in the YHT's heritage conservation advocacy efforts with government and other stakeholders. It has also been a means of enhancing the tourism potential of the city.

The second very successful project launched so far by the YHT, is the free walking tour of Yangon, which has been held every other weekend since 2014. These guided tours are conducted by YHT's volunteers and experienced guides, and are aimed at local residents, so are conducted in the Burmese language. It has become so popular that the sign-up list, limited to 30 participants, fills within minutes once posted on social media. Many young people, including professional tour guides, are interested in joining the tour. This project has increased awareness of the valuable built and cultural heritage in the downtown area, and how these are linked to the city's history and also to its future prosperity.

Figure 3.13: Ribbon-cutting ceremony at the instillation at the Commemorative Blue Plaque at Yangon Regional High Court (Formerly High Court)

Figure 3.14: One of the YHT's walking tours for local residents. The tours are free-of-charge and offered twice a month, except during the monsoon season.

Working with Church Heritage Resources

Victorino Mapa Manalo

Keywords: Philippines, geography, tourism, conservation, cultural mapping, community engagement, heritage resources

Introduction

Recognizing that the heritage resources of the Roman Catholic Church in the Philippines offer enormous potential for generating income for both the Church and for local residents through heritage tourism, a community group launched a project in Lawig Province to tap this potential.

Lawig is one of the least affluent provinces of the country. Its residents have long needed to leave their homes to seek employment or to trade elsewhere. Many towns in the northern section of the neighbouring island of Mindanao host inhabitants who originally came from Lawig. The province is known for its many well-preserved churches that date from the later Spanish Colonial period (16th to 19th centuries). Lawig Province also has fine beaches and other natural features that attract tourists.

The project was implemented between 2006 and 2010 in the town of Pook, a small coastal municipality. The main compound of the Roman Catholic parish of Pook has a beautiful setting, overlooking the sea. The main church mostly dates to the 19th century, though its bell tower was built in the 20th century. The priests' residence (*convento*) dates to the early 18th century. Across from the convento is a late 18th century watch tower.

Project goals

The main aim of the project was to boost the tourism potential of Pook, through developing the pilgrimage prospects of church structures in a sustainable manner, so as to provide steady employment for local residents. The project sought to train the residents of Pook in skills that would be in demand in the province's growing tourism industry and hoped to revitalize local crafts, such as jewellery making. Furthermore, by restoring and repurposing some of the church facilities, the project hoped to show the public that heritage resources can be used to generate income for the church and the community, and are therefore worth preserving. This was in light of past activities that had sought to raise funds, but were contrary to heritage conservation practices.

The project was funded by a private donor from Manila, a member of a prominent family. The donor worked closely with the parish priest.

Project description

The project began with consultations and planning, which were carried out with the residents and parish officers. Furthermore, cultural mapping was carried out among Pook's smaller villages. In addition, a World Heritage Education and Education for Sustainable Development workshop was held with selected community leaders and educators.

A plan was prepared and the following activities were implemented. A management company was set up by the donor to pay for the development of the compound in return for operating the place as a heritage tourism and pilgrimage tourism site for a number of years. The company entered into an agreement with the Roman Catholic Diocese of Lawig (the site owner). This agreement was signed by the Bishop. In addition, the management company agreed to hire local personnel to run the site. Designers were called in to design the visitor facilities in the Church compound, and residents were challenged to use local images and even stories as sources for design. In addition, the donor paid for the repair of the convent roof. The project then restored and developed certain sections of the Pook compound for re-use. These included the dining room in the convent, a nearby air-conditioned room, an outdoor facility and a new kitchen. These were set up as venues that could be rented for events. A souvenir shop was also established, along with a café and a gallery/museum.

The convento personnel were trained in how to cook and serve local food in a restaurant setting. Consultants were then requested to design menus for dinners, which were then held in the convent dining room, a beautiful space. The menu featured local dishes. The public could book seats for the dinners through the parish offices. Sometimes performances were held along with the dinners. Visitors could also join a paid guided tour.

A large pilgrimage event, held with support from the donor, showed that many people would come to Pook, as it was quite accessible.

Discussion points

While the project succeeded in many ways, a number of issues arose. The use of an old stage from the 1950s to hold performances using the back of the church as backdrop was not well received by certain members of the community. Shortly after the project was fully launched, a group of about ten parishioners sent a letter to the Bishop protesting what they considered an inappropriate use of church facilities. Rumours soon spread that the Archdiocese had been given a loan by donor, with the Church properties as collateral. It was also said that the donor was digging for gold (treasure hunting). Despite attempts at dialogue, the rumours persisted. This is a common rumour in the Philippines. At one point, a treasure hunter was even given permission from highly placed officials to dig up a heritage area in Manila so as to provide 'evidence' of such motivations and create confusion. While the rumour was absurd, many local residents believed it because they could not understand why the donor was being so altruistic. Although many, if not most residents, went along with the project they were still quite concerned when the rumours spread.

Part of the problem was that many residents were not aware that the church compound and structures are treated under Philippine law as private property owned by the local Archdiocese as a private corporation, with the Bishop as its head. The residents were under the impression that the compound and structures were somehow communally owned.

Another issue was that, although the donor sought to help the local community, the repurposing of sacred church property was disorientating to residents. A lesson learned through the project that such repurposing requires thorough planning and intensive community consultations. A good communication plan, one that addresses community concerns, is vital.

Despite the many problems it faced, the project showed that church heritage structures can be successfully developed as resources for the church and for local residents.

Conserving Pulau Ubin for heritage, national identity and tourism, Singapore

Chin-Ee Ong, Lecturer, Department of Geography, National University of Singapore

Keywords: Singapore, geography, tourism, conservation, urban planning, cultural mapping, urbanization

The city-state of Singapore is one of the most urbanised and most intensely-planned places on the planet (Neo, 2007). A former British colony, the Southeast Asian state inherited a set of British-planned old town areas and ethnic clusters, around the hub of commerce: the Singapore River. Post-independence, Singapore underwent massive land use changes, as swamp and coastal areas were paved over, knolls levelled and forests cleared for the construction of factories, public housing and other facilities, all linked by a network of roads. Rural residents were resettled from *kampong* (village) houses into concrete high-rise flats, resulting in the loss of the village way of life. Very little remains in Singapore's islands in terms of their original land use. Singapore has also lost much of its mangroves and the associated biodiversity.

In such a context, Palau Ubin (known also as Ubin) is exceptional. Ubin is an island in Singapore's territorial waters that has thus far remained isolated from the intense urbanisation that has occurred on the main island of Singapore. Ubin has also not experienced the conversion to petrochemical, heavy industrial, military and landfill functions seen in the other islands ('Jurong Island', Pulau Tekong, Pulau Brani and Pulau Semakau).

Figure 3.15: Chinese opera or 'wayang' stage at the heart of Ubin's network of villages.

Figure 3.16: Bicycle rental-dominates the main town commerce area, illustrating the island's recreation and tourism dependent economy.

Its significance lies in its combination of natural and cultural assets – a living kampong nestled in a mangrove-fringed natural landscape. The island's economy was once fuelled by lucrative granite mining and in the 1960s the quarries supported several thousand villagers on the island. Aquaculture, vegetable and fruit farming also contributed to the village economy. Since the 1980s, however, the island has been predominately a leisure and tourism destination. The island draws visitors because of its natural beauty and rustic charm.

In spite of the island's dependence on tourism, in 2001 the government announced plans to develop part of the natural sandy beach at the eastern end of Ubin into a military facility. At the time, the beach, Chek Jawa, was an undiscovered gem known only to a handful of nature lovers (The Straits Times, 2001). The threats to the beach galvanised a nature conservation movement on the island, and in 2002 civil society groups succeeded in persuading the government to instead create a wetland reserve on the site. The success of the Chek Jawa movement prompted further efforts to protect and rehabilitate other natural sites, including mangroves and other flora and fauna on the island.

In 2017, following cultural mapping of the island by the Singapore Heritage Society, the National Parks Board of Singapore announced plans to conserve the kampong houses on the island (Channel NewsAsia, 2017). The Singapore Heritage Society had found that Ubin was the only substantial and living kampong remaining in Singapore. This was evidenced by various factors including, for instance, the intact calendar of religious events of the island's Taoist temple. This signalled a community that was still close-knit. Ubin's kampong are essential in illustrating how Singapore's village life once was.

While conservation efforts have had great success, conserving Ubin still has its share of challenges. A key issue is that the resident population is declining and ageing. Furthermore, livelihoods on the island are currently overly-reliant on the tourism industry. This means that while the island's economy does well on weekends and days of fair weather, with surges in visitor numbers on such days, the economy experiences a sharp drop on weekdays and rainy days.

Another challenge has been in conserving kampong houses given the short leases of the land on which houses stand. These short leases discourage occupants from investing in such houses and finding appropriate new uses for them. Moreover, as in most places of cultural and heritage significance that receive visitors, there are issues relating to tourist intrusion, over-commercialisation and gentrification that threaten the rustic village life that attracts visitors to Ubin.

References

Channel News Asia (2017) More Pulau Ubin kampong houses to be restored, , 16 July. https://www.channelnewsasia.com/news/singapore/more-pulau-ubin-kampong-houses-to-be-restored-9035732 (Accessed 8 May 2018)

Neo, H. (2007) Challenging the Developmental State: Nature Conservation in Singapore, *Asia Pacific Viewpoint*, **48**(2): 186-99.

The Straits Times (2001) Chek Jawa's natural beach should be preserved, 16 July.

Conflict between contemporary design and traditional culture in Macao

Francisco Vizeu Pinheiro, PhD, Assistant Professor, University of St. Joseph, Macao

Keywords: China, geography, authenticity, historic urban landscape, rehabilitation, urban growth

Introduction

Macao, a former Portuguese enclave only 32 square kilometres (sq km) in size, is one of the smallest territories in the world. It is experiencing rapid urban growth and has a high population density, reaching in some areas 54,000 inhabitants per sq km. Following the 1999 handover of the Portuguese administration and the 2002 liberalization of the gaming industry, Macao overtook Las Vegas in profitability and has become the world's centre for gaming (Al, 2018). As a consequence of Macao's consequent economic success, the population grew from 437,455 in 1999 to 644,900 in 2017, and during that period the number of visitors jumped from 7.4 million to approximately 31 million.

With the growth in population, residential towers mushroomed everywhere in the city, including in the historical centre, where many old buildings were replaced with modern structures in styles that had no relationship to Macao's history and identity. At the same time many old squares came to be used as car parks. In this context, a movement arose for the rehabilitation of the old squares so as to preserve the cultural identity of these spaces.

The successful rehabilitation of Senate Square

The first successful rehabilitation project was in Senate Square, which was converted in 1993 for exclusive pedestrian use. The square's conversion into a pedestrian zone helped revitalize the area and attracted further tourists to the historic centre, with the square becoming a key landmark of Macao. The rehabilitation design used traditional Portuguese urban elements, including black and white cobblestones arranged in wave patterns (Cabral and Jackson, 1999).

A minimalist interpretation of vernacular values

Before the Senate Square urban intervention, which was widely considered a success, a minimalist rehabilitation design was undertaken in another popular square, known locally as *Yapo Jing* (阿婆井), which means 'old lady's well'. The Portuguese translation of the name was *Largo do Lilau* ('old lady's fountain') and the square is today known as Lilau Square. The square's fountain features a stone lion framed by a portico.

Heavy rain caused the fountain to collapse in 1933 and again in 1943, so the square was converted into a car park. In 1986, the government's cultural institute decided to revive the memories and the legends associated with the place. Given that the original configuration was unknown, the authorities decided to restore the site in "a plastic modern language, of somber lines and minimalist" (Durao et al., 1997). Accordingly, they erected the fountain using parallele piped granite stone with two faucets intending to represent the Portuguese and Chinese memories associated with the place. This minimalist approach, which can be traced to the Venice Charter (1965), uses a 'contemporary stamp' to avoid 'conjectural' reconstructions. This approach is used not only in squares, but also in the adaptive re-use of old buildings, preserving only the façade. The appearance of the restored fountain was controversial, however. A *Macao Today* (今天澳門) newspaper article contested that the minimalist fountain was ignorant of and disrespectful to Chinese culture and beliefs because it looked like a tombstone (Macao Today, 2009). Most of the locals and visitors rejected the minimalist design. The findings of a public survey in 2009 indicated that 89% of the public believed that the design of the square should reflect local history and culture and 86% preferred a classic design based on community memories and traditions. The square was subsequently redesigned, with red cobblestones laid in curves to represent water flowing from the fountain.

Figure 3.17: Drawing for restoring the memory of the Chinese well and the Portuguese fountain. The red cobblestones represent water.

Conclusion

The battle for authenticity continues, particularly in the context of rapid development inspired by global models that often erase local traditions and urban practices. Authenticity does not mean replica, but the use of local traditions in the design and construction of a place, inspired by community traditions, as recognized by the 2008 ICOMOS draft, which declared a need for rethinking the 'spirit' of a place and finding a new conceptual vocabulary that better reflects the mix of values and the tangible and intangible heritage 'according to their practices of memory'. Urban rehabilitation is not always a peaceful exercise, aesthetics cannot be divorced from local cultural interpretations. Neither 'authentic' nor 'contemporary' can be accepted as the true or the only possible design solution. Cultural identity, like the human DNA, can only be kept alive if traditional practices are kept alive, as in the cases of Senate Square and Lilau Square.

References

AI, S. (ed.) (2018) *Macau and the Casino Complex*. Reno, NV: University of Nevada Press.

Cabral, F C. and Jackson, A. (1999) *Jardins e Arte Paisagistica em Macau*, Macau: Cathy Hilborn Feng.

Durao, L., Parreira, M., and Kio, C. C. (1997) *Na afirmacao de uma identidade*, Catalog, Instituto Cultural de Macau, Macao: Hong Long Printing.

Government of Macao Special Administrative Region Documentation and Information Centre (1999) *Yearbook of Statistics*, Macao: Government Printing Bureau.

Government of Macao Special Administrative Region Information Bureau (2017) *Macao Year Book*. Macao: Government Printing Bureau.

Macao Today (2009) Yapojing mubei zu longquan xie'e zhiji, 16 April.

The eroding heritage interpretation potential of Vientiane, Lao PDR

Rik Ponne, Freelance heritage and tourism specialist, Vientiane, Lao PDR

Keywords: Lao PDR, geography, heritage impact, historic urban landscape, commercialization, development

Vientiane, the capital of Lao PDR, has had a long and turbulent history. Between the 15th and 18th centuries it was the royal seat of the vast and powerful Lane Xang Kingdom, which covered areas far beyond the country's present boundaries, while in the early 19th century the city saw near total destruction by the Siamese. Reconstruction, during the century of French colonial rule and three decades following independence in 1953, is reflected in the buildings of Vientiane, which are in the styles of the various global powers that have exerted influence over the country, including the USA and the Soviet Union. Thus, Vientiane exhibits a complex, layered, urban heritage landscape, illustrating the history of the city and of Lao PDR in general.

Since around the turn of the 21st century, however, as a result of poor governance and a lack of heritage-sensitive development controls and legal protection, many of Vientiane's historic buildings and natural wetlands have been replaced with shopping malls, international hotels and even whole new neighbourhoods. Many of these developments are financed by investors from countries in the Asian region, such as China and Vietnam, and it has been suggested that deals are being made outside of the regular decision-making processes. The changes are often presented as being good for tourism, but they are rapidly eroding the integrity of the city's heritage landscape, thus reducing its 'readability' and impairing its interpretation potential, for both residents and visitors alike.

The case of the Pakpasak villa illustrates the trend. A study in 2013 of this villa, which was, at the time, one of the oldest remaining colonial buildings (dated 1905) in Vientiane, revealed the existence of archaeological remains at the site. These remains were identified as possible foundations of a bastion, which old maps suggest was part of the Lane Xang era city wall. The villa is also significant in that it was once the home of Prince Souphanouvong, the first president of the Lao PDR. In spite of a project by Pakpasak Technical College to convert the villa into a restaurant and create a heritage information room narrating the stories associated with the site, a Chinese investor bought the site and razed the building, and with it a component of the city's rich history. While a grand hotel was planned for the site, that plan did not materialize, as is often the case with these types of projects. As of 2018, the fence surrounding the site featured pictures of a complex of townhouses.

The discoveries about the villa demonstrate the great potential that Vientiane's heritage buildings offer in terms of understanding the history of the city. Unless heritage structures are protected, this potential will soon be lost forever.

Figure 3.18: The French-colonial villa on the Pakpasak site at the time of the condition assessment in March 2013. Excavated walls thought to belong to a Lane Xang-era bastion are visible in the foreground.

Assessing the impact of the proposed metro, Pune, India

Komal Potdar, Conservation Architect, Archaeological Survey of India, New Delhi

Keywords: India, geography, historic urban landscape, governance, heritage impact, historic monuments, urban development

In 2006, India's Ministry of Urban Development adopted a policy to construct metro systems in every city with a population of more than 2 million. In early 2010, Pune Municipal Corporation (PMC) approved a plan to build a metro rail system in Pune. The metro system is expected to improve connectivity (Mohan, 2008). The proposed metro system has two corridors covering a total of 30 kilometres, partly underground and partly elevated.

The proposed metro system has raised many concerns, however. Citizen groups and experts have questioned various aspects of the plan, including the alignment and chosen route, the social and economic costs of constructing the rail, the impact of an elevated metro on the city's skyline, the required infrastructure upgrades and the impact of the routes on historic monuments (Parisar, 2010).

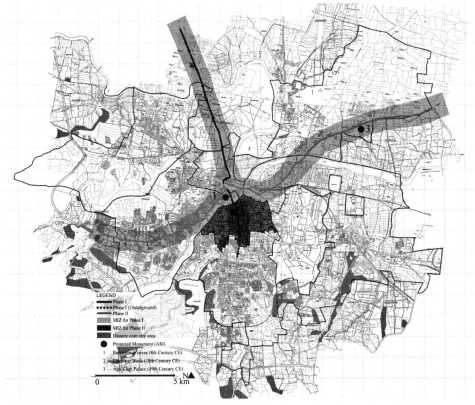

Figure 3.19: Proposed metro rail alignment in Pune city, showing metro lines, proposed metro influence zone, historic core city area and protected monuments within the Pune city boundary.

One issue is the decision, in 2015, by the Government of Maharashtra to increase the floor area ratio (FAR) to 4 (from the present 1.3) in the metro influence zone (MIZ), comprising a strip of 500 metres on either side of the railways, irrespective of the historic fabric and the type of metro rail (underground or elevated). This is intended to generate funds and is expected to bring about densification along the metro corridors and increase land value in the MIZ, leading to the renewal of old and dilapidated areas of the city (DMRC, November 2015).

Three protected monuments under the responsibility of the Archaeological Survey of India (ASI) will be affected by the planned metro. These are Pataleshwar Caves (8th Century), Shaniwar Wada (18th Century) and Aga Khan Palace (19th Century). Furthermore, almost half (45%) of the 246 listed (Grade 1, 2 and 3) heritage properties regulated by the Heritage Conservation Committee of the PMC will be affected.

3

MAPPING OF HERITAGE COMPONENTS (PROTECTED, REGULATED AND NON-PROTECTED)

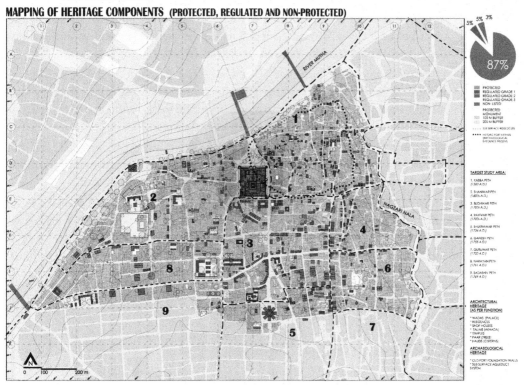

Figure 3.20: Heritage monuments in the core city.

To safeguard this historic urban landscape, the following recommendations are offered.

■ As per the Ancient Monuments and Archaeological Sites and Remains Act (Amendment) 2010, the protected monuments should have a buffer around them of 100 metres as a prohibited zone and 200 metres as a regulated zone, in which development activities are controlled, so as to protect the historic integrity and authenticity of the monuments. Proposed developments around these zones must address issues relating to archaeological, visual and other impacts.

- Schemes such as Transfer Development Rights (TDR), incentive schemes and tax-waivers for historic house owners and tenants need to be developed to safeguard local heritage and retain the sense of place.

- Financial models for generating funds for construction and densification in the MIZ need to be thoroughly scrutinized for impacts on the urban fabric, aesthetics and carrying capacity of the city. Furthermore, given that most large forced dislocations of people do not occur in conditions of armed conflict or genocide but in routine, everyday evictions to make way for development projects (Rajgopal, 2001), the plans should not lead to dislocation of traditional populations and occupations (Ghadge, 2013) or gentrification.

- The blanket rule of 4 FAR in the MIZ may be highly detrimental to the historic skyline and integrity of the historic core area. Hence, instead of proposing a blanket FAR, it is recommended that station nodes be established in commercial areas and transit oriented developments.

- A study should be conducted to assess what damage could be caused to historic structures due to metro vibrations, and the authorities should take preventive and remedial measures or realign the route of the metro away from nationally protected monuments to prevent damage.

- As in any city, a comprehensive mobility plan should be created and the authorities should examine the potential for upgrading neglected and under-funded public transport services such as buses and suburban rail.

This case of Pune city highlights the need for urban development projects to be designed in conjunction with the community and with experts in the conservation of historic core city areas and in heritage management. The absence of such consultation is likely to be detrimental to the historic fabric and the sense of place of the city.

References

Delhi Metro Rail Corporation (DMRC) (2015) *Final detailed project report for Pune metro rail project*, Pune: Pune Municipal Corporation.

Ghadge, R. (2013) *Shanghaization of Mumbai: Visions, displacements, contestations*, PhD thesis, University of Illinois.

Mohan, D. (2008) Mythologies, metro rail systems and future urban transport, *Economic and Political Weekly*, **43**, 41-53.

Parisar (2010) *The City and the Metro*, National round-table. Pune: Pune Metro Jagruti Abhiyan and Pune Technical Coalition.

Rajgopal, B. (2001). The Violence of Development. *The Washington Post*, 8 August.

Further reading

Janwani, MCCIA (2013) Detailed report for proposal of underground metro rail in Pune, unpublished.

Oh K., Jeong. Y., Lee, D-K. Lee, W. and Choi, J. (2005) Determining development density using the urban carrying capacity assessment system, *Landscape and Urban Planning*, **73**(1), 1-15.

Potdar K. (2015) Heritage impact assessment for Pune metro rail project in historic urban landscape of Pune city, unpublished thesis, School of Planning and Architecture, New Delhi.

Pune Municipal Corporation (PMC) (2008) *Comprehensive Mobility Plan for Pune City*, Pune: Pune Municipal Corporation.

3

Co-curating with communities: A digital storytelling project

Dr. Ester van Steekelenburg, Founder and Director, iDiscover and Urban Discovery

Keywords: geography, authenticity, heritage impact, living heritage

Loss of authenticity

Across Asia, from Beijing to Bangkok and beyond, old buildings are being demolished to make place for skyscrapers and shopping malls: structures that often have very little architectural or cultural reference to the local setting. The obsession of Asia's older generation with Western-style architecture as a symbol of progress, the absolute dominance of real estate developers and the dismal status of creative professional occupations in Asian society have led in recent years to the loss of authenticity, and at a speed that is unprecedented. Furthermore, gentrification and 'disneyfication' are driving the original residents and businesses out of historic centres. What remains are overcrowded streets, with more tourists than locals.

As a result, we all know cities that are changed beyond recognition. Local residents have begun to accept the new reality and, worse, forget what once made their homes so unique. As collective memory slips away, people lose pride in their own histories and lose their sense of belonging. If they forget it, who will remember their story?

Using technology for co-curating with local communities

Meanwhile, we are witnessing an increasing demand for authenticity. People want to live, shop, drink and eat in places that they can relate to, and travellers want to feel like a local and stay in neighbourhoods with character.

The iDiscover project responds to this demand and to the need to restore a collective identity among local residents. It provides a digital platform for locals to curate their own 'living heritage' trails and share this heritage with the world, building critical awareness and opening people's eyes to the value of living heritage.

We work with over 60 partners in neighbourhoods in Asia where heritage is at risk. It is an experimental partnership whereby residents become 'curators' of trails, their own 'pop-up museums'. Our partners are creative collectives, heritage enthusiasts, university students, photographers, writers and artists. Heritage routes are paths linking their favourite places and stories.

A heritage trail of this kind includes more than just temples and monuments, it is about living heritage: the people, trades, legends and eateries that make each neighbourhood unique, such as Mr. Mak whose workshop has been making bamboo steam baskets for generations, Mrs. Lam whose dumplings sell out by noon every day and Kevin who grew up here, studied overseas and now makes slow-brewed coffee in the neighbourhood from locally-sourced beans.

iDiscover provides the platform and facilitates the process to ensure quality content, accurate translation and an efficient marketing machinery. To reach a wide audience, the trails are packaged in the form of a savvy storytelling app – equipped with a GPS map – as well as an illustrated map created by a local designer. The APPXMAP packages are distributed through local hotels and independent retailers, but also internationally through online channels and a worldwide distribution network.

Figure 3.21: Young Bangkok travellers visiting Lampang.

Creating change

The concept is a playful, positive and easily replicable format that taps into a fast-growing and dynamic community of young creative entrepreneurs, hotel operators and urban professionals in Asian cities, who are increasingly aware and vocal about their city's identity slipping away.

We believe this project will motivate both long-time residents and newcomers to care more about maintaining the uniqueness of place. We also believe it will create opportunities for people to travel responsibly and respectfully, and will encourage heritage enthusiasts to visit the sites, giving them a deeper understanding of the places.

Heritage at risk from economic development in Najaf, Iraq

Robert Travers, International consultant specialising in cultural heritage and tourism management

Keywords: Iraq, geography, tourism, conservation, built heritage

Southern Iraq is not on everyone's list of tourism destinations, but it is nevertheless a rapidly growing pilgrimage tourism site that is seeing extensive cultural revival. A focus on economic development has put the region's rich built heritage at risk, however.

The Holy City of Najaf contains some of the most magnificent and sacred shrines of the Shia branch of Islam. Najaf was built around Imam Ali, who was proclaimed Caliph in 656 CE (Common era) and who was assassinated in 661. The great Imam Ali mosque and shrine, with its 42-metre high golden dome and twin gilded minarets, was built around his grave in 786 CE by the Abbasid Caliph, Huran al-Rasdid (Al-Kubaisy, 2009).

The city developed a densely-packed form surrounding the Imam Ali Mosque, with buildings of considerable beauty and richness. Walls, rising from the empty desert, once enclosed about half a square kilometre of the city, encompassing mosques, madrassa, *husseiniya* (prayer halls), libraries, *khan* (market places) and the houses of merchants and pilgrims, many of which were of superb quality and some of which survive today. The traditional houses have inner, shaded courtyards surrounded by rooms with *diwan* (guest) and *haram* (family) divisions. Some of the grander houses include private mausoleums, decorated with elaborate Islamic designs.

In the 20th century, the city underwent considerable changes. The city's walls were demolished in 1938 to make way for an inner ring road. Then in the 1950s, six axial roads were driven inwards towards the shrine in the 1950s. Property values spiralled beyond the reach of local people, and today traditional uses are ending as investors and modernity move in.

In 2008, an international airport was opened in Najaf, and in 2013 the government announced its intention to build a larger international airport near Karbala to serve both holy cities. With easier access, visitor numbers to Najaf have grown steadily and are estimated in the millions (UNWTO, 2011).

While the Imam Ali Mosque is the main attraction of Najaf, the city also serves as a halting point on the overland pilgrimage to Mecca. Hundreds of visitors come daily to Najaf's Great Cemetery for funeral ceremonies. Religious study is also an important reason for travel to Najaf, drawing long-staying visitors from all over the Shia world to the famous Kufa University, and to learn from the city's many spiritual teachers. Pilgrims usually also visit the Holy City of Karbala (shrine of Husayn ibn 'Alī), about 80 kilometres away.

Figure 3.22: Interior of Imam Ali Mosque in Najaf.

While the city's mosques and Imam Ali's house in Kufa are cared for, and some important buildings, such as Khan al Shielan, are being restored, there is little appreciation for most old vernacular buildings. Today, the central icon of the golden dome is partially hidden by high-rise buildings. Wealthier residents now prefer to live outside the old city. Poor social conditions in the historic centre have resulted in many old houses being let and sublet to multiple tenants, leading to rapid deterioration due to lack of maintenance. The inner city residential fabric is in danger of being seen as redundant for modern use.

While UNESCO (2012) observed that tourism can sometimes be a force for conservation, this does not appear to be the case in Najaf. Despite Najaf's high tourist numbers, the city has engaged in minimal heritage conservation. The case of Najaf illustrates that the conservation of heritage always involves subjective choices as to what is valuable and worth keeping, and what is not. It is clear it will be quite a challenge to change mindsets regarding the value of old buildings in Najaf.

Figure 3.23: The Imam Ali Mosque extension under construction.

References

Al-Kubaisy, F. (2009) *Najaf: The architectural and urban heritage of Iraq's holiest city*. Bahrain: BookSurge.

UNESCO (2012) Decisions adopted by the World Heritage Committee at its 36th session (Saint Petersburg, 24 June – 6 July 2012) WHC-12/36.COM/19

UNWTO (2011) *Religious tourism in Asia and the Pacific*, Madrid: World Tourism Organization.

Further reading

N. P. and Erasmus (2015) In Shia Muslims' holiest site, a new openness to other faiths. *The Economist*, 5 December.

Mervin, S., Gleave, R. and Chatelard, G. (eds.) (2017) *Najaf: Portrait of a holy city,* Paris: UNESCO.

Pew Forum on Religion and Public Life (2009) *Mapping the Global Muslim Population*, Washington DC: Pew Research Center.

UNESCO (2015) UNESCO's action in Iraq since 2003, *World Heritage: Special issue on Iraq*, pp 8-11. Paris: UNESCO.

Tiger Balm Garden: The changing fortunes of Singapore's pioneer cultural theme park

Yeo Kang Shua, Assistant Professor of Architectural History, Theory and Criticism, and *Hokkien Huay Kuan, Endowed Professorship, Architecture and Sustainable Design, Singapore University of Technology and Design*

Keywords: Singapore, geography, tourism, redevelopment, heritage impact, commercialization

Singapore's Tiger Balm Garden, also known as Haw Par Villa, was commissioned by overseas Chinese tycoon Aw Boon Haw and built in 1937 (Brandel and Turbeville, 1998). What began as a rich man's pleasure garden (Huang and Hong, 2007), filled with sculptures and tableaus depicting Chinese folklore, moral stories and virtues, morphed into a free public attraction. The garden thus served as an advertising platform for the Aw family's pharmaceutical topical ointment, Tiger Balm (Yeoh and Teo, 1996).

The Aw family constructed a similar garden with the same name in Hong Kong in 1935, but in 2004 it was demolished for redevelopment into a residential building (Commissioner for Heritage's Office, 2018).

Until 1985, Singapore's Tiger Balm Garden, like that in Hong Kong, was popular with generations of local visitors, who had fond memories of their visits. It was once not uncommon for Singaporeans to have photographs of the garden in their family albums.

In 1985, the land upon which the garden stands was acquired by the state, and the sculptures and tableaus were donated with the land under the condition that the name of Haw Par and the family memorials within the grounds be retained (The Straits Times, 1985 and 1990a). The government then redeveloped the garden and reopened it in 1990 as Haw Par Villa Dragon World, a 'high-technology' commercial Chinese mythological theme park (Huang and Hong, 2007; Yeoh and Teo, 1996; The Straits Times, 1990b). However, this commercial tourist site incurred massive losses and folded in 2001.

It was doomed right from the start. By the 1990s Singapore had many other competing forms of entertainment, and the scenes in the garden no longer appealed to young Singaporeans or to foreign tourists (Teo and Lim, 2003). While the garden still charmed older generations of Singaporeans, the conversion of the site into a commercial venture, with hefty entrance fees, was off-putting, as they had enjoyed the park for free in the past (Teo and Yeoh, 1997).

In 2001, the garden resumed operations as a free public park. Then in 2005 another attempt was made at revitalizing the garden with the opening of the Hua Song Museum, displaying artefacts of the Chinese diaspora in Singapore (The Business Times, 2002; The Straits Times, 2002 and 2008; Huang and Hong, 2007).

This endeavour also failed, however, with the museum closing in 2012 (Singapore Tourism Board, 2012). The failed attempts showed that the commodification of the garden was not the way forward, particularly given the general lack of appreciation for heritage.

Even with the rise in heritage awareness in Singapore in recent years, the garden today receives few visitors. Conceivably, the key to retaining the living memory of the Tiger Balm Garden and maintaining its relevance lie in the provision of heritage interpretation, narrative and programming to visitors at a personal level (The Straits Times, 2017).

Bibliography

Brandel, J. and Turbeville, T. (1998) *Tiger Balm Gardens: A Chinese billionaire's fantasy environments*, Hong Kong: Aw Boon Haw Foundation.

Commissioner for Heritage's Office (2018) Haw Par Mansion: Background. https://www.heritage.gov.hk/en/hpm/background.htm (Accessed 29 March 2018.)

Huang, J. and Hong, L. (2007) Chinese diasporic culture and national identity: The taming of the Tiger Balm Gardens in Singapore, *Modern Asian Studies*, 41 (1), 41–76.

Singapore Tourism Board *(2012)* Story of Chinese migrants lives on, *Singapore Government News,* 24 March.

Teo, P. and Lim, H. L. (2003) Global and local interactions in touris', *Annals of Tourism Research*, **30** (2), 287–306.

Teo, P. and Yeoh, B. S. A. (1997) Remaking local heritage for tourism, *Annals of Tourism Research*, **24** (1), 192–213.

The Business Times (2002). Overseas Chinese exhibition centre planned, 27 March, p. 9.

The Straits Times (1985) Haw Par Villa acquired, 10 February, p. 16.

The Straits Times (1990a) The saga behind the Villa, 20 September, p. 3.

The Straits Times (1990b) Old themes, new style, 20 September, p.3.

The Straits Times (2002) Exhibition centre to connect with Chinese diaspora, 27 March, p.8.

The Straits Times (2008) New life for Haw Par Villa?, 20 October, p. 30.

The Straits Times (2017) To hell and back, (Life Weekend), 27 October, p. D3.

Yeoh, B. S. A. and Teo, P. (1996) From Tiger Balm Gardens to Dragon World: Philanthropy and profit in the making of Singapore's first cultural theme park, *Geografiska Annaler, Series B, Human Geography*, **78** (1), 27–42.

4 Managing Urban Heritage Areas in the Context of Sustainable Tourism: Tourism

In this chapter, the case examples relate to tourism, which encompasses tourism planning, visitor management, carrying capacity, destination management, marketing, interpretation, visitor experience and product development.

Issues arising from the growth of tourism in Hoi An, Vietnam

Mark Chang, Associate professor, Showa Women's University

Keywords: Vietnam, geography, tourism, World Heritage Site, heritage impact, preservation, community engagement

Almost two decades have passed since Hoi An, a historic port town located in the central region of Vietnam, was inscribed on the World Heritage List. During this time, Hoi An has undergone a major transformation from a quiet old town into a bustling tourism centre.

It goes without saying that in order to preserve a heritage site like Hoi An, local efforts are very important. Fortunately, the preservation effort is being guided by the local community, under the leadership of the Hoi An People's Committee. An important guiding tool for the community has been the *Hoi An Protocols for Best Conservation Practice in Asia* (Engelhardt and Rogers, 2009).

While Hoi An's preservation efforts have been successful overall, the town, like other World Heritage sites, has seen its heritage compromised by immense and rapid growth in tourism.

In the early 1990s, Hoi An had only about 4,000 tourists annually. But following Hoi An's inscription as a World Heritage Site in 1999, the number of tourists rose enormously. By 2007 the annual number of tourists had exceeded one million and in 2017 had exceeded three million.

This large number of tourists has brought significant changes to the town. As of 2017, the tourist-related shops (such as souvenir shops and restaurants) accounted for about 70% of the total buildings in the historic quarter of Hoi An. This is at variance with the Hoi An Protocols, which advises as follows: "Do not allow tourist shops and facilities to dominate the historical precinct" (Engelhardt and Rogers, 2009, p. 34).

Another major change brought about by large numbers of tourists is in the make-up of the residents. The growth in the tourism industry has attracted many Vietnamese from outside of Hoi An and outside of the historic quarter. Accordingly, the majority of the shop tenants and shop assistants are not from the historic quarter and they do not reside there. As is often the case in heritage sites, newcomers prioritise the pursuit of commercial opportunities rather than heritage preservation. Therefore, local heritage has been compromised. The Hoi An Protocols warned us of this, noting that "too often the 'packaging and presentation' of heritage is carried out by the tourism industry for the benefit of its members and not by those responsible for the safeguarding of cultural heritage", thus trivializing and compromising both the physical fabric of the heritage and its intangible aspects (Engelhardt and Rogers, 2009, p. 13). We need to take time to reflect on this warning.

References

Engelhardt, R. A. and Rogers, P. R. (2009) *Hoi An Protocols for Best Conservation Practice in Asia*, Bangkok: UNESCO.

Compromised integrity in Malacca, Malaysia

Jo Chua, Heritage Conservationist

Keywords: Malaysia, geography, tourism, heritage impact, conservation, World Heritage Site, displacement

Malacca is a city of many layers. Kingdoms, international trade and colonial rule endowed this former entrepot with a charm like no other. Its melting-pot architecture, culture and townscape have long drawn tourists and have earned it the honour of UNESCO World Heritage site status.

Sadly, it has proven difficult to reconcile conservation and tourism in Malacca. Key elements of the community's daily life have been replaced with souvenir shops, cafes and other tourist attractions. The Jonker Walk Night Market, conceived as a vehicle for 'revitalisation' of the town, have turned Jonker Street, once a residential area, into a tangle of congestion three nights a week. Residents and traditional trades have been displaced from the core zone. Once an artery of the barter trade, the Malacca River has been closed off from the sea and turned over to the lucrative cruise industry. What has resulted is a hollowing out of the pre-existing community of Malacca and its transformation into little more than a halfway house for tourists passing through.

Figure 4.1: A Hindu religious festival participated by Chinese believers passing in front of a centuries-old mosque.

Key to this is the attitude taken towards tourism and heritage management in Malacca. Far from promoting the townscape, cultural and religious practices of the townsfolk, the focus has mainly been on increasing tourism numbers – the chief metric used in newspaper reports. Little regard has been paid to the city's physical and social capacity to accommodate tourists. Meanwhile, capital appreciation brought on by Malacca's World Heritage status has made it much easier for landowners to evict tenants. Unbridled development and selective enforcement of heritage guidelines have also led to questionable projects, such as a Hard Rock Cafe in the heart of the town. The net result has been a gradual, and worrying, erosion of Malacca's heritage value. This can hardly be called sustainable tourism.

In the face of such grim realities, there are yet glimmers of hope. Cultural and religious practices, such as processions, have managed to demonstrate resilience despite encroaching tourism. Families and clan associations have set up local museums, emphasising the intangible cultural heritage that is so lacking in state museums. Furthermore, private and community organisations have taken the initiative in conservation and restoration efforts.

Nevertheless, more needs to be done, and fast. Better management, enforcement and engagement with stakeholders are crucial for safeguarding Malacca's built and cultural heritage. Moreover, Malacca's heritage must be managed by people who understand and appreciate heritage, and who strive to strike the right balance between the economics of tourism and its social impact.

In this vividly cosmopolitan city, a shopkeeper recently remarked, 'Malacca is not a town, not a city. It is something more, it is Malaysia's history'. Unless something is done, Malacca risks losing that unique status.

Depopulation and tourism: restoring heritage in Iya Valley, Japan

Alex Kerr, Author and Japanologist

Keywords: Japan, geography, tourism, conservation, population decline, over-tourism

Population decline in rural areas is a problem affecting many parts of the world. It has been seen in deserted villages in Italy, Scotland, mid-west America, Russia and also in China, where the flow of youth to the big cities has merged with the time-bomb of the 'one child policy'.

When it comes to population decline, Japan is the hardest hit, with the most rapid drop in population and the world's largest elderly population per capita. In 2017, Japan lost 352,000 people, which is akin to half the population of the Thai city of Chiang Mai vanishing in just one year. This decline has not happened all over Japan, however. Large cities like Tokyo have stable or growing populations. It is in small towns and villages where the decline is stark; the smaller the town, the faster the drop.

Some villages in Japan are headed towards collapse and are referred to as *genkai shuraku* (villages at the edge of extinction). In such villages, over half the population is over 65 years old. A 2014 Japanese bestseller titled *Extinction of the Countryside* predicted that almost 900 towns and villages would disappear by 2040.

One lesson being learned worldwide is that in some cases it is futile to fight the emptying of villages. People die and people leave. In many cases, the population decline is unstoppable. It is, however, possible to work with it and find creative solutions to conserving heritage and maintaining the quality of life of the remaining residents. For example, Kamiyama, a town on the island of Shikoku, adopted the slogan, 'creative depopulation' and set about 'recycling' old houses and land in ways that were impossible when local communities were intact. Demography expert Peter Matanle uses the term 'depopulation dividend' to describe this approach. Such 'recycling' brings new life into abandoned villages by creating venues for outsiders to visit, and businesses that generate jobs and that support people who would like to move there. A major type of business in such villages is tourism. It is the saving grace of many countryside villages, and it has already rescued many sites in Tuscany, Provence and England's Lake District.

Japan has seen an unexpected but truly explosive growth in inbound tourism in recent decades, with tourist numbers rising from 5 million in 2003 to 8.2 million in 2012 and then leaping to 28 million in 2017. Japan is aiming for 40 million tourists by the Tokyo Olympics in 2020, and the expectation is that tourist numbers will exceed that. In this lies an opportunity.

This rapid growth in tourism also presents a danger, however. 'Over-tourism' is now an issue worldwide, as excessive numbers of tourists degrade the quality of life of residents in popular tourist places. It is likely to become a major issue in Japan because policy-makers have tended to encourage 'big bus' and 'big cruise' tourism, that is, large numbers of tourists. There are ways, however, to accrue the economic benefits of tourism for small towns and villages without bringing in excessive numbers of tourists.

In Japan, tourism offers exciting opportunities for small rural villages with declining populations. A case in point is East Iya village. The population of East Iya dropped from around 4,500 in 1973 to around 1,100 in the mid-2000s. In 2007, most residents were 70 years old or older, and there were almost no young people or children. Iya was a genkai shuraku, hurtling towards extinction. Today, thanks to a sustainable tourism initiative, the situation is turning around.

The village is located in Iya Valley, a steep and remote part of the island of Shikoku. Iya, with its precipitous slopes, is described by some as the 'Tibet of Japan', and appeals to many travelers. The hills are rich with abandoned houses, some centuries old, with huge blackened beams and wide wooden floors. When made comfortable, these houses offer tourists an opportunity to experience a taste of rural life of a bygone era, in untouched surroundings.

Figure 4.2: Restored Chiiori Alliance house in the Iya Valley.

Recognizing the potential of these structures, in 2007 the local government began supporting a project by the Chiiori Alliance to restore nine houses in Iya Valley. The project not only restored the thatched roofs and floors of the houses using original and natural materials, but also installed modern comforts. The Chiiori Alliance now rents the houses to tourists and, in spite of the remote location, the houses have had a surprisingly high occupancy. It turned out that not only foreigners, but also the Japanese were starved for this type of experience.

Because of the high quality and unique character of the houses, visitors are willing to spend more than they would at a normal guesthouse. In 2017, about 3000 people stayed in the nine Iya houses. The income earned was equivalent to about 70,000 day trippers in big buses. However, unlike with 'big bus' tourism, nearly all the income stayed in Iya.

As of 2018, the Chiiori Alliance employs six people full time, plus local cleaners. Four of the six full-time employees are young people who moved to Iya – a most unusual phenomenon as it had been a long time since anyone young moved there. Moreover, the influx of tourists had boosted the earnings of nearby restaurants, the local taxi company and other businesses.

Iya's nine houses are a small operation, but they show how tourism can help declining villages. It is a way to prevent rural decay: bringing in income and new residents, while keeping houses lived in and fields in use. Following the success of the Iya project, Chiiori Alliance restored another dozen houses in other towns around Japan, with similar results.

Not every town will survive. But, riding the wave of inbound tourism, Japan has the opportunity to save, here and there, precious remnants of rural life and cultural heritage.

Gentrify and they will come?

Khoo Salma Nasution, City Councilor, City Council of Penang Island

Keywords: Malaysia, geography, tourism, World Heritage Site, governance, gentrification

The historic city of George Town developed during colonial times and, originally, most of the shop houses were either residential or 'mixed use', with people living above the shops. In Armenian Street in the 1990s, I was the only newcomer in an old low-income neighbourhood. It was common to see several families living in a shop house, sharing the common areas and kitchen. A sundry shop was at one corner of the street, a coffee shop at another. Hawker stalls huddled around bends in the street, luring people out onto the street. Deliveries were made on cycle carts.

Today, in 2018, much has changed. The heritage buildings are relatively well-preserved – not so much as a result of conservation efforts by the Penang Heritage Trust but rather because the majority of the pre-WWII premises were tenanted, and the tenants did little to change the buildings. The tenants were protected by the Rent Control Act and a pro-tenant rent tribunal. After the repeal of Rent Control in 2000, rising rents led to more than half the original inhabitants being evicted. Some former residents of the core drifted into low-cost high rises in the periphery of the city, where housing security was better assured.

World Heritage listing in 2008 coincided with the advent of budget travel in the region and new social media trends in travel promotion. George Town saw a surge of foreign tourists, followed by domestic visitors, whose holiday choices were curtailed by the weak Malaysian ringgit.

With no federal funds for tourism development, the Penang state government introduced an annual arts festival and the 'Marking George Town' programme to attract new investors and tourists. The rest was done by journalists and social media – images of George Town architecture, cultural traditions and food helped to sell real estate and encourage tourism. Armenian Street, in the core zone of the World Heritage area, became ground zero of a street art craze.

Despite modest rentals for commercial spaces and even lower rents for residential spaces, the prices of heritage shop houses escalated. Singaporeans, Australians and others rushed to buy properties in the core of George Town, starting another wave of evictions. According to the George Town World Heritage site population and land use change surveys, undertaken in 2009 and 2013, the number of residents declined from 10,159 to 9,425 over these four years, while the number of households declined from 2,533 to 2,302. The surveys portrayed a low-income and left-behind aging population, as well as an increase in migrant workers, living in cramped quarters.

The Penang Island city council (MBPP), the statutory body for planning approvals and enforcement, has the main role in implementing heritage guidelines. However, it is still operating with the planning wisdom of the 1970s, which rezoned the city centre as 'commercial', anticipating the demographic shift to high rises in the suburbs. With the proliferation of cars and motorbikes in recent decades, the suburb-city work commute has become a traffic nightmare. Despite this, most residents remain in the suburbs.

From 2010, the state agency, George Town World Heritage Incorporated (tasked with 'managing and monitoring'), and the grant-giving federal agency, Think City (with a mission to 'rejuvenate'), began to engage stakeholders in revitalising the World Heritage area. One major change was that the Armenian Street park, once a 'thieves market' and hangout for vagrants, was gentrified in a Think City flagship project. Subsequently, with the property market upswing, more legacy properties were sold for handsome prices.

Although a minimum price bar was imposed by the state government on foreigners buying landed property in Penang, this has barely impacted purchases by foreigners and overseas Malaysians earning in stronger currencies. In a context of weak monitoring and enforcement, heritage buildings were often illegally and cheaply converted into boutique hotels and eateries, sparking the emergence of an alert group, George Town Heritage Action. Many investors who bought and renovated heritage properties in the proper fashion were disappointed with the returns on their investments, however.

Figure 4.3: Street performance of a lion dance along rope walk (Source: Think City)

As the state prioritized quantity rather than quality of tourists, its events and interventions pandered to the whims of mass tourism. Consequently, big tour buses would get stuck in Armenian Street. Lack of control over noise nuisance meant residents had to tolerate loud music until the early hours of the morning, or give up and leave. A sustainable tourism vision – to upgrade the industry to attract longer-staying, higher-spending but lower impact forms of tourism – is long overdue.

Gentrification by arts festivals and street art attracted young entrepreneurs willing to pay high rents to start hipster cafes and fancy shops, but the seasonal nature of tourism and the lack of an affluent local population meant that only a few of these outlets could be sustained. The low-income population able to provide essential services, and used to a sharing economy, now lived elsewhere, and they simply could not afford to move back in. Migrant workers have partly filled the shortfall, but the social gaps have translated into inflated prices and a less than robust local economy.

Figure 4.4: Chinese youth orchestra in front of the Penang Teochew Temple, Chulia Street (Source: Think City)

Ten years after World Heritage listing, some policy-makers are beginning to realise that it is residents we need. The World Heritage area, core and buffer, contains about 4000 houses, but many are vacant. This large number of vacant properties means that there is a great potential to repopulate this historic city centre. Real gentrification by the middle-class is highly unlikely, however, given the gritty street activities, smelly drains and lack of car parks.

Only the creation or restoration of affordable housing can provide an entry point for people who want to live and work in the historic city centre. The city government could well consider strategies for introducing affordable housing in the city centre – creating funding and incentives, enacting modern tenancy laws, nurturing existing housing trusts and working with cooperative owners to create tenant apartments. It might even be worth reintroducing the tried and tested arrangement of 'living above the shop', if it means restoring a community that can call George Town its home. A medium-term priority would be to reduce flood risk and renew the decaying heritage infrastructure, including the clogged drains and derelict sewage system, while also levelling the over-tarred roads, which displace rainwater into historic buildings.

Managing over-tourism: generating a master plan for the historic centre of Macau

Rui Leão, Architect, Chair of Docomomo Macau Research Centre

Keywords: China, geography, tourism, urban planning, heritage impact, stakeholder engagement, over-tourism

Macau's unsustainable tourism

Macau, as a city of tourism and gambling, receives millions of tourists every year. In 2015, over 30 million tourists visited Macau; an excessive number for such a small city. This influx of daily visitors into a relatively small historic centre with the typical limitations of a small town must be managed for the sake of the city's residents and heritage structures alike.

Why is the inner harbour forgotten?

The heritage trail, from the Ruins of St. Paul's to the Senado Square, has become the main route for tourists, but Rua dos Ervanários and the old town beyond it, which are also rich in heritage, have so far failed to attract tourists. The Docomomo Macau Research Centre decided to identify why this was the case. It also examined, in detail, the impact tourism was having on the property market and the condition of the historic centre.

A new approach through dialogue

Through dialogue with residents, shop owners and representatives of *kai fong* (neighbourhood associations), the researchers gained an understanding of the critical issues at stake. The stakeholders who were consulted identified the key issue as the fact that the Rua dos Ervanários and Rua da Tercena served to interrupt the continuity of the pedestrian route through the historic centre of Macau. In particular, a drop of three metres along the perimeter of the main tourist trail and a road with heavy traffic at the lower end of this drop was deterring tourists from continuing along the route.

Following research into the government's policies and the methods of managing the historic centre, the researchers felt that the top-down approach, separating the traffic issue from the issues affecting heritage, was not effective in managing any of the issues.

The researchers then developed a planning and architectural approach to addressing these issues, covering the following three fields of intervention:

- Mapping and evaluation of heritage value distribution in the inner harbour.
- Traffic diversion and improvements to the pedestrian network.
- Critical qualification of the public space.

The three fields were developed simultaneously and coordinated in order to ensure a meaningful transformation of the historic centre. The viability of the plan resided in the interface of the three fields: to resolve them concurrently, avoiding any heirarchy that would prioritize any of them.

This approach sought to improve traffic flow and pedestrian circulation, thus creating better conditions for appreciating Macau's heritage.

Mapping and evaluation of heritage

Docomomo Macau Research Centre conducted a preliminary mapping of the district and discovered that although the current main tourist route from Senado Square to Saint Paulruins contained the largest concentration of monuments, the planning area, from Rua da Tercena to Avenida Almeida Ribeiro had a much larger number of buildings of architectural value and more heritage clusters of interest, which if converted into tourist zones would more than quadruple the number of heritage buildings of interest in Macau. If public spaces and visibility were organized around these, the pedestrian island network could be expanded towards them and a significant increase of street-front retail would be gained, serving both tourists and locals, and thus solving two of the current issues of the historic centre: lack of walking space and retail space to serve the 30 million visitors and the local population.

Figure 4.5: The existing pedestrian island of the historic centre of Macau shown in bordeaux, and the proposed expansion in turquoise and green.

Traffic redirection

The findings of the study suggest that diversion of the traffic would reduce congestion at historical sites, allowing these to revert to public use. Traffic redirection would also allow a new pedestrian axis to be implemented without disrupting access of vehicles to the surrounding neighbourhoods and commercial activity. In addition, alternative tourist bus drop off areas would facilitate access between the monuments.

Critical qualification of the public space

The research results indicate that enlarging the pedestrian network of the city centre would make walking a more attractive means of accessing the various parts of the city, which would naturally eliminate the level of dependency on cars and return public space to residents while improving their quality of life.

Figure 4.6: Plan showing the intervention area and mockup of the proposal for redesigning the Avenida Almeida Ribeiro.

Conclusion

Through the cooperation and participation of the community, Docomomo Macau Research Centre used a bottom-up planning approach to develop a comprehensive plan. The plan was presented to all of the government committees that deal with the historic centre, and some of the ideas have been adopted to manage the highest tourist density periods, namely the Chinese lunar holidays, Golden Week and the Mid-Autumn Festival.

Docomomo Macau Research Centre continues to work with other partners, using its plan to raise awareness of how the challenges facing the historic centre can be resolved through an alternative planning approach.

Crisis in the management of the Penang Botanic Gardens, George Town, Malaysia

Lin Lee Loh-Lim, Penang Forum

Keywords: Malaysia, geography, tourism, governance, conservation, stakeholder engagement

One of the oldest botanic gardens in Southeast Asia, the Penang Botanic Gardens (PBG) is set amid a lowland Dipterocarp forest of 592 acres. It is jealously guarded and loved by the residents of Penang (Penangites) and has over 2 million visitors annually.

Conservation of the gardens has been threatened by conflicting tourism initiatives, however. In 2007, a Malaysian Ministry of Tourism project to alter the gardens to meet perceived tourist needs resulted in inappropriate changes. Trees were cut down, natural slopes were flattened, formal gardens were destroyed, streams were canalized and bizarre edifices were built. The public outcry was immediate. The ministry, however, was unmoved.

Figure 4.7: The arches erected by the Ministry of Tourism in the historic Penang Botanic Gardens 2010.

In 2010, the erection by the ministry of two massive concrete arches invited further controversy. Renewed public outcry forced the ministry to convene stakeholder meetings to hear the objections. The ministry stood firm, however, so the public chorus of disapproval grew. Then fate took a turn: one arch started to tilt, perhaps due to low quality materials used in its construction. In spite of attestations by engineers proving the arch was tilting, the authorities denied it. The ministry then conducted an online survey and found that 93 per cent of the respondents were against the arches. Not satisfied, the ministry hired the Universiti Sains Malaysia to conduct an on-site user survey, which found that 71 per cent of the PBG users were against the arches. Faced with imminent elections and increased tilting of the wayward arch, the ministry decided to demolish the two monstrosities.

The demolition was another lesson in poor management. It was conducted at night in an attempt to avoid public comment, but media and civil society representatives were present. The arches fell at the first touch of the bulldozer. Following the demolition, civil society pressed for alternatives more sympathetic to the gardens. An open lawn and ponds with water lilies were subsequently installed.

The entire sorry fiasco was the result of failures at many levels, including the failure to understand that the botanic gardens are not primarily for tourism, and the failure of the government to plan and to review in a competent manner, and consult with stakeholders before undertaking significant changes. The Ministry of Tourism is now very wary of new developments in heritage areas. This represents a success for civil society and a lesson in how tenacity can achieve results.

4

Figure 4.8:. Arches replaced by water lily ponds 2018.

Lijiang: A belaguered beauty

Heather A. Peters, Senior Consultant, UNESCO (retired), Ophidian Research Institute

Keywords: China, geography, tourism, authenticity, urban planning, World Heritage Site, commercialization, displacement

Background[1]

The historic town of Lijiang in north-western Yunnan illustrates many of the challenges faced by World Heritage townscapes. Inscribed on UNESCO's World Heritage list in December 1997, Lijiang Old Town represents an extraordinary example of a late 19th to early 20th-century town. It is the cultural centre for the Naxi ethnic minority and was once the seat of Naxi traditional political authority. The town combines the authenticity and integrity of a unique physical heritage site with the traditional intangible cultural heritage of the people who lived there.

The challenges

Almost immediately following its inscription, Lijiang became an important international and domestic tourist destination. Not unexpectedly, this new found tourism served to showcase Lijiang to all of China and to the world. This, in turn, attracted more visitors. However, this tourism put immediate stress on the town's authenticity and integrity, and created a series of problems not previously experienced by the town's authorities.

The managers of the Lijiang World Heritage Site now faced a series of conflicting policy decisions: How could the residents benefit from the tourism development? How could they meet the needs of both the original residents and the visitors? Should they encourage ever-increasing numbers of tourists, or focus on problems linked with overcrowding? Should they support traditional livelihoods and cultural businesses or encourage tourism-driven commercialization catering to visitors? How could they meet the needs of new commercial interests without modifying or even destroying the architectural heritage they had committed to conserve? And, also important, how could the residents of the Old Town retain the spirit and essence of their traditional culture in the midst of the economic development brought about by tourism?

The situation in Lijiang led to a very common, and tragic, problem plaguing many World Heritage townscapes – the gradual displacement of the original residents, both spiritually and physically, from their historic town.

---

1 Except for the reference to UNESCO Advisory Mission Report, the information found in this case study is the result of nearly 28 years of the author's fieldwork and experience in Lijiang. She first visited Lijiang in 1989 as a visiting scholar based at the Yunnan Nationalities University. From 1997 to the present, the author travelled extensively to Lijiang, mostly as part of UNESCO, but including two years with The Nature Conservancy (TNC). The views expressed in this case study are those of the author's, and do not represent those of either UNESCO or the TNC.

The response

Recognising the steady erosion of the town's traditional culture and the impact of this on the original residents, the site managers and other Lijiang authorities devised various strategies to address the challenges. However, many of the proposed initiatives only led to the further commercialization of traditional culture which, in turn, served to underscore the loss of the original. Hence, a short-lived regulation required all shopkeepers, Naxi or Han, to wear traditional Naxi dress, while another policy turned traditional activities, such the evening cleaning of the central square, into performances. This highlighted the loss of authenticity of the Old Town's cultural heritage.

Another failed strategy was one that sought to meet the economic needs of residents. In this case, they decided to permit outsiders to rent property in the Old Town for business purposes. The authorities felt that by collecting rent from their properties, the residents would benefit indirectly from the increased tourism. However, insufficient regulation and enforcement meant that the policy resulted in the further demise of the types of shops that sold daily supplies and provided services to the local residents. The residents therefore continued their out-migration to new apartments in the New Town, leaving the Old Town in the hands of outsiders. This effectively robbed the Old Town of its cultural authenticity.

Solutions

Some attributed Lijiang's problems to the fact that the city was inscribed before a fully-developed management plan had become a mandatory requirement for World Heritage inscription. However, ten years later, when a master plan was finally developed, it still did not present a fully-integrated approach to conservation and development. Rather, it embodied conflicting plans for heritage site management and economic development that only exacerbated the threats seen in Lijiang.

In November 2008, an official UNESCO mission to monitor Lijiang found that the issues had not been resolved. The report recommended that 'in developing the overarching principles for the Conservation Master Plan, a holistic conception of heritage should be adopted and an integrated management strategy used, in which development and conservation are balanced' (Jing, F. et al., 2008, p. 25).

Thus, a first step to addressing the situation would be to review existing heritage management and business plans and integrate them into one holistic plan that reconciles heritage protection and economic development. A plan is needed that not only safeguards what remains of the authenticity and integrity of the traditional built environment, but also strengthens traditional Naxi culture and practices before they completely disappear. A corollary to this first step is to enforce existing regulations regarding the conservation, preservation and restoration of the historic architecture.

A second step is to limit the numbers of tourists visiting Lijiang each day. This needs to be planned in detail by authorities, but this could involve strictly limiting the numbers of hotels and guesthouses, or restricting the numbers of tickets sold for each museum and activity in Lijiang. This would immediately upgrade the quality of the visitors' experiences, and reduce the impact on Lijiang's resources, including both the physical wear and tear on the architecture, and the pressure on the town's water supply – a more recent and growing problem.

The damage caused by years of out-migration of local residents cannot be fully reversed. However, a more enlightened tourism policy, which encourages the participation of local Naxi and supports and strengthens traditional cultural industries, could generate a revival of Naxi ownership of their heritage town. The question remains, is it too little, too late?

(Right) **Figure 4.9:** Lijiang Canal
(Source: David Feingold)

(Below) **Figure 4.10:** Lijiang Pizza Hut
(Source: David Feingold)

References

Jing, F., Logan, W. and Kaldun, B. (2008) *Advisory Mission to the Old Town of Lijiang World Heritage Property, China.* Report prepared for the mission undertaken by the UNESCO Beijing office, November.

Impacts of tourism on Old Phuket Town, Thailand

Yongtanit Pimonsathean, Associate Professor, Urban Design and Development International Program (UDDI), Faculty of Architecture and Planning, Thammasat University

Keywords: Thailand, geography, tourism, conservation, tangible heritage, intangible heritage, stakeholder engagement, displacement

Old Phuket Town is a conglomeration of mixed Asian-European architecture that emerged as a consequence of the international tin trade and mining industry, which rose to prominence in the Malay Peninsula between the mid-19th and mid-20th centuries.

Conservation initiatives in Phuket, instigated in the 1980s by a local heritage group, were among Thailand's earliest homegrown efforts to protect local culture. In 1994, the group succeeded in declaring as a conservation area a commercial main street and early residential quarter, covering an area of 33.6 hectares. Subsequently, in 2017, the conservation area was extended to 276 hectares.

The local conservation efforts have aimed to protect both tangible heritage (including shop houses and mansions) and intangible heritage (such as local language, clothing, food and socio-religious practices). Success has been achieved through a cooperative platform and an active network comprising the municipality, community-based organizations, a foundation, a private school alumni association, a cultural council and local cultural associations.

Tourism was not the initial impetus for conservation in Phuket. Instead, initial efforts to conserve the heritage of Phuket stemmed from a desire to maintain the traditional way of life and the beauty of the townscape. Since the turn of the 21st century, however, hypermarkets and mega retail stores in the suburbs began to threaten local businesses in the conservation area, and residents began to see tourism as a means of safeguarding local businesses. With the growth of heritage tourism in Southeast Asia, many shop houses in Phuket were converted into businesses targeting tourists, including hostels, souvenir shops, restaurants and bars, thus generating income for residents. Another means of generating income for local businesses was the community's decision to open one of the streets of the old town as a weekend 'walking street' and market.

Tourism in Old Phuket Town has had both positive and negative aspects. On the positive side, it provides new economic opportunities for local residents. On the other hand, the tourism boom has led to an increase in land values and rents that has accelerated the transfer of property ownership and tenancy, resulting in the displacement of original residents. Fortunately, so far in Phuket the original residents still own the majority of the buildings.

4

Another negative impact of tourism is large-scale developments that are inappropriate for the context. One such case was the development of a large hotel in 2015/16. This case has, however, raised public awareness of the need for more comprehensive development control measures to help preserve heritage buildings and the historic townscape.

A further issue related to tourism is local crime and noise. In the late 1990s and early 2000s, nightlife businesses such as pubs and bars were launched to meet tourist demands, but this raised crime rates and noise levels. A social pressure campaign by residents subsequently resolved this issue, however.

Another tourism-related issue affecting the old town has been the spread of franchise businesses, such as convenience stores. While providing goods for tourists, such businesses are considered threats to both the local culture and the economy. Local shops cannot compete with the prices for goods and services from franchise convenience stores, so go out of business, leading to a loss of livelihoods for residents. Furthermore, the profits of franchise businesses do not stay in the community, with the result that local investments decline.

Balancing conservation and tourism in Old Phuket Town is a dynamic process and it is a challenge to sustain local physical and intangible cultural assets in the current circumstances. However, the will of the local communities and their active network are a strong force in the combat against the threats.

Figure 4.11: The 19th century buildings in Old Phuket Town.

Cultural tourism in Amritsar – celebrating cultural diversity through conservation

Gurmeet S Rai, Conservation Architect and Heritage Management Specialist, CRCI (India) Pvt Ltd

Keywords: India, geography, tourism, conservation, engagement, cultural heritage

Introduction

The city of Amritsar, named after the Amrit Sarovar (pool of nectar), the holy tank within which the shrine of Harimandir Sahib is situated, is one of the foremost places of pilgrimage in India. Revered by not only the Sikhs, but also Hindus and other faiths, this historic city has played a prominent role in the history of northern India, including in the freedom struggle, and is a much-visited cultural tourism destination.

The city has been a significant trading zone and commercial centre since the 1500s. Its location on the Grand Trunk Road, which joins the Silk Route at Kabul, has geo-political significance, which was recognized by the Sikh Gurus, particularly the fourth – Guru Ramdas – who excavated the sacred sarovar in 1573. Guru Ramdas was also instrumental in developing the local economy of the area; he invited members of 52 crafts and trading castes and established a working community of skilled artisans and craftsmen in the vicinity of the sarovar.

The administrative setup of the city is what determined its success in trade and in the growth of various crafts. The city's sardār (chiefs) each constructed their own *buṅgā* (houses) around the principal sarovar and setup their respective *kaṭrā* (wards), encouraging traders and craftsmen to reside in them. The relative stability in the region led to greater numbers of worshipers visiting the holy city, and this helped increase the residential population, including trades people, in the area, resulting in Amritsar becoming one of Punjab's primary trading centres by the end of the of the 18th century. Thus, a link between faith and commerce flourished, which ensured the survival of the settlement, despite several attacks on the Golden Temple complex during the mid 1700s.

In terms of its architecture, the city flourished most under Maharaja Ranjit Singh (1780-1839) – one of the most influential and revered Sikh leaders. He was responsible for the fortification of the city, with the construction of a double wall and a moat around the city, with twelve gates and corresponding bridges, and the heavily-armed Gobindgaṛh Fort. Another remarkable building constructed under his rule was his summer palace, Ram Bagh. But he is remembered most for his funding of the gold plating of the dome and exterior of the Darbar Sahib, along with some parts of the interior.

Cultural heritage conservation to enhance tourism

In 2015, the Government of Punjab, through its Department of Tourism, launched an initiative to enhance the city's tourism potential through conservation of its cultural heritage. Two significant historic sites were identified for conservation: Gobindgarh Fort and Ram Bagh Garden. While Ram Bagh was already a protected monument under the responsibility of the Archaeological Survey of India, Gobindgarh Fort was being used and managed by the Indian army. Ownership was transferred to the Department of Tourism. Management plans were prepared for both sites, with conservation and revitalisation being the primary focus.

At the same time, political parties made a push to improve the principal access to the Golden Temple. This project entailed making the final 300 metres of this access road a pedestrian zone, along with rendering the building facades and installing decorative works, pavers, street furniture and art work. While this intervention has helped reduce traffic, it can be best described as a 'façade improvement', rather than true conservation, as it was done without an understanding of the local architecture and cultural traditions, which was largely due to a lack of community consultation.

This reflects the reality in India: cultural heritage management and cultural heritage tourism operate in two distinct silos. Engagement of communities with their heritage is mostly found to be within the realm of their personal inheritance, and extends, at the most, to engagement with religious sites of their own religious beliefs and practices. Little is seen by way of engaging with the 'other', whether in public spaces or shared cultural spaces.

Sites of conservation in the city – demonstration of equitable processes in urban conservation

In the recently-launched urban conservation HRIDAY programme, implemented by the Ministry of Housing and Urban Affairs, a deliberate effort has been made to make cultural narratives of diverse groups of people accessible, and hence recover shared cultural memory for a more inclusive experience of the spirit of the place, for tourists and the community alike.

Amritsar was identified as one of the 12 historic cities for infrastructure improvement under the HRIDAY programme. The programme aims to upgrade urban infrastructure to protect and enhance the cultural experience of the place. Heritage zones were identified in the city along with specific conservation and infrastructure actions. This process led to the realisation that infrastructure for tourism enhancement in the walled city of Amritsar needed to be nestled within a comprehensive mobility plan, with an integrated non-motorised transport system.

The restoration of Ram Bagh Gate was one of the HRIDAY projects. The historic building was unprotected so only survived demolition as it was being used as a police station. The station was relocated so as to recover the historic building for the public good. The gate lies at an important junction of roads connecting

Ram Bagh Garden with the Golden Temple, and was used by Maharaja Ranjit Singh when he visited the temple. A segment of the rampart connected to Ram Bagh Gate houses a printing press and a primary school built during the colonial period.

In recent years the gate, the printing press and the primary school have been restored, along with a few other industrial heritage sites, namely a colonial period pump house, power house and office of a deputy commissioner. The local government, with the support of the Government of India, is in the process of active adaptive re-use of these buildings and sites. In addition, public arts projects are being developed to provide a platform for active community engagement and participation of local youth.

How heritage trails affect historic cities, Lahore, Pakistan

Ayesha Pamela Rogers, Director, Rogers, Kolachi, Khan & Associates

Keywords: Pakistan, geography, tourism, conservation, cultural heritage, heritage trail

Tourism in Pakistan is on the threshold of a resurgence following a long period of disruption due to terrorism and insecurity, and a resulting reluctance to travel, along with a lack of visitor infrastructure. As part of an informal tourism policy, cultural tourism in the country's many historic towns and cities is being developed, and national tourists are showing increased interest in visiting and experiencing traditional urban centres. A visitation tool that is being developed is the heritage trail, although, as this case study will discuss, it is interpreted in the Pakistan context.

The accepted definition of a heritage trail is a pathway that links the cultural heritage of the area to form a "themed, interpreted journey for visitor education and enjoyment" (Silbergh et al., 1994, p. 123). According to MacCleod (2012), a heritage trail is by nature flexible in its themes, low cost and requiring little infra-structural investment. A heritage trail is a direct application of the local bottom-up approach to heritage tourism, involving interaction between the three players in heritage tourism: the place, locals and visitors (Middleton and Hawkins, 1998).

Heritage trails are used widely in tourism in historic Asian cities, including in old Delhi, Singapore and Hong Kong. Trails vary in the extent of conservation and redevelopment along their route; the amount and quality of interpretive materials for visitor understanding of the place; the degree of local community control and input; the overall sustainability of the trail; and the type of tourist experience.

In Pakistan, the first heritage trail introduced as a tourism tool was the Shahi Guzargah (the Royal Trail) in Lahore Walled City. This trail begins at historic Delhi Gate and leads to Akbari Gate. It passes through bazaars and urban open spaces, linking important heritage places such as Shahi Hammam and Wazir

Khan Mosque, along with traditional mansions. The Guzargah is being further developed, in stages, by the Walled City of Lahore Authority (WCLA) and the Aga Khan Trust for Culture/Aga Khan Cultural Service Pakistan (AKTC/AKCSP).

Recently the trail approach was adopted by the historic city of Peshawar, where a heritage trail is being constructed to link Ghanta Gharthrough Baazar-e-Kalaan and Sethian Mohallah, a neighbourhood with seven palatial wooden haveli. The trail culminates at the archaeological complex of Gor Gathri. The project is being carried out under the Khyber Pakhtunkhwa Directorate of Archaeology and Museums, again in cooperation with the AKTC/AKCSP. It is expected that other historic cities, such as Multan, Gujrat, Rawalpindi and Karachi will soon also develop heritage trails.

Conservation in both the Lahore and Peshawar trails, is designed to restore the streetscape in a way that provides a so-called 'window to the past'. The interventions have included improvements to services and utilities, in particular improving drains, widening and resurfacing roads, and removing encroachments and alterations to facades of historic buildings (nearly 850 along the Shahi Guzargah alone).

The authorities also gave 'a cultural and historical touch' to structures along the trail, with the arbitrary addition of carved wooden balconies and windows on buildings. Such changes are part of a commodification process, which does not reflect the factual record of any past period. Instead, it is what Daher (2005) calls 'urban cosmetics', which involves modifying historic areas to meet tourist demand for a particular aesthetic, and prioritising commercial values over authenticity and conservation values. Much of the development along Peshawar's trail is a designer's idea of a historic precinct, creating a past that never existed (Urry and Larsen, 2011). This makes historic areas more like museums than places where people live and work. In Peshawar, the desire to retain a cosmetic streetscape has led to the warnings and even arrests of merchants who have violated the new image by hanging their wares on the ornate iron lampposts that were installed to decorate the pavements.

The theme guiding tourism initiatives along Lahore's Shahi Guzargah is 'shop, eat and tour inside the Walled City', but the tours are not accessible to many national visitors, as they are expensive by local standards. Furthermore, although described as a 'heritage trail', there is no signage along the route, no information about the places of interest and no easily-available maps for self-guiding tourists. Thus, while it is called a heritage trail, it meets none of the basic requirements of one. Furthermore, the interpretation of the Walled City for visitors is as an exotic Mughal backdrop for commercial tourism activities. This fails to accurately represent the complex culture and historical layering of the place.

Lahore's market merchants are united in their appreciation of the new road surface, drains and cleanliness that have resulted from the heritage trail project, but they are much less appreciative of the closures for protocol events, gentrification and inappropriate tourist behaviour in religious places, as well of as what they see as WCLA interference. Similarly, residents have mixed feelings about the interventions in adjacent residential areas, which have resulted in increased property values and led to long-time residents selling to outsiders and then moving out of the Walled City. Overall, the most common lament is that the changes have disrupted the traditional social ties that previously bound communities together (Cermeño and Mielke, 2016). Indeed, this model of heritage trail as a strip of 'restoration' and redevelopment for tourism has cut right across the social and geographical fabric of the old city, severing the complex networks and resulting in a historic city cut in two.

This kind of 'place change' (McKercher, Wang and Park, 2015) has dramatic impacts on both residents and the local heritage. While some believe this can integrate 'the goals of urban heritage conservation and those of social and economic development' (Bandarin and van Oers, 2012, p. 212) others believe this risks losing the authenticity of the place, putting heritage exploitation above conservation. It is necessary to assess the impacts of heritage trail development on the Walled City because, as stated in the Hoi An Protocols, "if the lifestyles and traditional characteristics are destroyed, the conservation of the buildings will be nothing but a theatre prop, devoid of the flavour and value system that produced the special attributes of historic cities" (Engelhardt and Rogers, 2009).

Figure 4.12: A view of the façade treatment along the Lahore Walled City heritage trail; the application of new carved wooden features, old style lamps and decorative draperies to give an historical and cultural touch to modern structures.

References

Bandarin, F. and van Oers, R. (2012) *The Historic Urban Landscape: Managing Heritage in an Urban Century*. London: Wiley.

Cermeño, H. and Mielke, K. (2016) Cityscapes of Lahore: Reimagining the urban, *THAAP Journal*, 110-139.

Daher, R. F. (2005) Urban regeneration/heritage tourism endeavours: The Case of Salt, Jordan 'Local Actors, International Donors, and the State', *International Journal of Heritage Studies*, 11 (4): 289-308.

Engelhardt, R. A. and Rogers, P. R. (2009) *Hoi An Protocols for Best Conservation Practice in Asia: Professional Guidelines for Assuring and Preserving the Authenticity of Heritage Sites in the Context of the Cultures of Asia*. Bangkok: UNESCO.

MacLeod, N. (2012) Cultural routes, trails and the experience of place, in M. Smith and G. Richards (eds.), *The Routledge Handbook of Cultural Tourism*. London: Routledge.

McKercher, B. Wang, D. and Park, E. (2015) Social impacts as a function of place change. *Annals of Tourism Research*. 50, 52-66.

Middleton, V. T. C. and Hawkins, R. (1998) *Sustainable Tourism: A Market Perspective*. Oxford: Butterworth-Heinemann.

Silbergh, D., Fladmark, M., Henry, G. and Young, M. (1994) A strategy for theme trails, in J. M. Fladmark (ed.), *Cultural Tourism*, London: Donhead

Urry, J. and Larsen, J. (2011) *The Tourist Gaze 3.0.*, London: Sage Publications.

Tourism risk preparedness, Kaesong, Democratic People's Republic of Korea

Sharif Shams Imon, Assistant Professor, Institute for Tourism Studies, Macao

Keywords: North Korea, geography, tourism, World Heritage Site, governane, tourism development

Kaesong, a city located a few kilometres to the north of the line that divides the Korean peninsula, has a history of more than 1000 years. It was the capital of the Koryo (also spelled Goryeo) Dynasty (AD 918-1392) and it represents an amalgamation of geomantic concepts, which are visible in the planning of the ancient city and in its early architecture.

In 2013, 12 components associated with the Koryo Dynasty were inscribed on the UNESCO's World Heritage list. At the same time, the World Heritage Committee recommended the creation of tourism and interpretation plans for these components. For a site with highly controlled access and very low number of international tourists – about 18,000 people visited the entire country in 2013 – this recommendation may seem unnecessary, but, for an unprepared site, an abrupt increase in tourist numbers could lead to multiple problems.

Figure 4.13: Arrival of a Chinese tour group at Seonggyungwan, Kaesong.

As of 2018, Kaesong's level of tourism development is low. It sits somewhere between the 'involvement' and 'development' stages of Butler's tourist area cycle of evolution (1980): specific facilities for tourists exist, along with organised travel arrangements, and the city has a well-defined tourist market. But tourism is set to develop quickly in the near future. The recent thawing of the relationship between the two Koreas and the prospect of peace in the peninsula is likely to lead to a relaxation of travel restrictions and a rapid increase in tourism in the country, especially in Kaesong, a World Heritage site only a short distance from the border with the Republic of Korea.

Cessation of conflict, enhanced access in the form of a better transport connection such as a new rail link or an airport, and enhanced visibility because of World Heritage listing, are triggers that often lead to increases in tourist numbers. While such triggers have a predictable effect, so far local heritage site managers in Kaesong have been caught unawares. A recent change in government's tourism policy led to a rapid increase in Chinese tourist numbers, but the heritage sites in Kaesong were not prepared for this. Parking places at more popular heritage sites in the city are already reaching their capacity, and the presence of large tour groups is beginning to make the sites noisy and crowded. Thus, there is an urgent need for better tourism risk preparedness in Kaesong.

Unfortunately, there is a divide between heritage site management and tourism development in Kaesong, and no coordination between them. Site management is a city-level responsibility, handled by the Kaesong Cultural Property Management Office, while tourism is controlled at the national level by the Bureau of Tourism and the Foreign Affairs Department. A long delay in developing a tourism management plan and the weak capacity of site managers to address tourism pressures has made the situation even more challenging. If these issues are not addressed soon, Kaesong may become one of the many heritage sites around the world that are struggling to maintain their integrity in the face of overwhelming tourism pressure.

References

Butler, R. W. (1980) 'The Concept of a Tourist Area Cycle of Evolution: Implications for Management of Resources', *Canadian Geographer / Le Géographe canadien*, 24 (1), 5-12.

Heritage conservation and tourism development in Luang Prabang, Lao PDR

Wantanee Suntikul, Assistant Professor, School of Hotel and Tourism Management, The Hong Kong Polytechnic University

Keywords: Lao PDR, geography, tourism, engagement, World Heritage Site, urban development, heritage regulation

In 1995, UNESCO listed the historic town centre of Luang Prabang, Lao PDR, as a World Heritage Site. This has led to a rise in tourism, with the number of tourism-related businesses (tour agents, hotels, guesthouses and restaurants) growing from 58 to 820 between 1997 and 2016, and the number of tourists increasing from 237,683 in 2009 to 463,319 in 2016 (Luang Prabang Provincial Tourism Office, 2006; Ministry of Information, Culture and Tourism, 2016).

Many tourism businesses are housed within 'heritage' structures, which are supposedly protected by regulations designed to preserve the unique historical architectural character of the place. Demolition of heritage buildings and non-conforming new construction indicates that these regulations are not being adhered to, however.

A 2002 UNESCO report found weaknesses and lack of coordination in the administration of Luang Prabang's World Heritage assets, and noted that illegal construction of buildings demonstrated "non-respect for the building permit system" (UNESCO, 2002, p. 23). A periodic reporting exercise in 2003 identified tourism as a major factor in the acceleration of urban development in Luang Prabang (UNESCO, 2003) and observed that although authenticity and integrity remain, they "are under serious threat" (UNESCO, 2003, p. 25).

Recognizing the threats, in 2005 the Government of the Lao People's Democratic Republic issued a new national heritage law, defining and classifying both tangible and intangible heritage, establishing rights and duties for their protection, and setting up a National Heritage Fund. These measures allowed for restrictions on alterations, additions and other physical changes on heritage-listed buildings, in terms of architectural style materials and scale. However, unapproved changes continued to be made, in defiance of the new regulations. Illegal construction and change of uses of land (from traditional to tourism uses) were identified as two primary threats (Boccardi and Logan, 2007). Given this situation, in 2007 UNESCO considered placing Luang Prabang on the World Heritage in Danger list.

Living costs have skyrocketed as a result of the speculation brought by tourism-related development, leading to many residents leaving the town centre. Furthermore, renting one's property to a tourism business has offered locals an added economic incentive to move out of the historic core (Suntikul and Jachna, 2013). The loss of local people has led to a decrease in participation in important cultural activities, such as the binthabat, the daily practice of giving offerings of food to monks, who form a long procession through the city streets with their alms bowls every morning. This practice has increasingly become an attraction for tourists, even as local people's participation declines.

There is an ambivalent relationship between tourist enterprises and heritage preservation, involving a trade-off between the advantages that the protected heritage environment brings for tourism businesses and the constraints of preservation rules on these businesses. On the one hand, tourism-related businesses benefit from the atmosphere and aesthetic provided by heritage buildings, and the profits earned from tourism provide revenue for converting and maintaining heritage buildings. On the other hand, the costs of undertaking repairs to heritage buildings using approved materials are high and prohibitions restrict business owners in extending their structures (to expand their businesses). Furthermore, business owners perceive a lack of clarity in preservation regulations and lack of efficiency and professionalism in the administration of these regulations (Suntikul and Jachna, 2013).

Luang Prabang exemplifies a situation found in many heritage tourism destinations. In such cases, it is crucial that local people and the activities that sustain local livelihoods not be seen as threats to heritage properties. Rather, residents should be engaged in dialogue, seeking synergies between preservation of the inheritance of the past and nurturing its future-oriented development. The way forward must involve collaboration between stakeholders, including the government, heritage bodies, commercial enterprises and residents. Such an approach can facilitate conservation of the town's historic character while at the same time enabling the town to meet the social and economic needs of local people.

References

Boccardi, G. and Logan, W. (2007) *Reactive monitoring mission to the town of Luang Prabang World Heritage property*, Lao People's Democratic Republic, 22-28 Nov.

Luang Prabang Provincial Tourism Office (2006) *Statistical report on tourism in Luang Prabang.* Luang Prabang: Luang Prabang Provincial Tourism Office

Ministry of Information, Culture and Tourism (2016) *Statistical Report on Tourism in Laos*, Vientiane: Ministry of Information, Culture and Tourism. http://www.tourismlaos.org/files/files/2016%20Statistic%20Report.pdf

Suntikul, W. and Jachna, T. (2013) Contestation and negotiation of heritage conservation in Luang Prabang, Laos. *Tourism Management.* **38**, 57-68.

UNESCO (2002) *Report of the Rapporteur. Convention concerning the protection of the world cultural and natural heritage*, 26th session, 8-13 April 2002. https://whc.unesco.org/archive/2002/whc-02-conf201-15e.pdf

UNESCO. (2003) *Periodic reporting exercise on the application of the World Heritage convention. Section II. State of conservation of specific World Heritage properties.* State Party: Lao People's Democratic Republic. Property name: The Town of Luang Prabang. Paris: UNESCO.

Chiang Mai: Slow city – no thanks; creative – yes

Martin Vensky Stalling, Senior Adviser, CMU Science & Technology Park, Secretariat of Creative Chiang Mai

Keywords: Thailand, geography, tourism, governance, sustainability, community engagement

How can cities that depend on tourism ensure livability and sustainability while also meeting the need for local jobs? Thailand's second-largest city, Chiang Mai, shares this common challenge.

Chiang Mai's most defining feature is perhaps its diversity. Culturally, it is far from homogeneous. As well as various ethnic groups, it has multiple religious communities, including a significant Muslim population, and it has a large number of foreigners who have made the city their home. Chiang Mai not only has amazing food, temples, culture and arts, it also has eight universities, a science and technology park, maker spaces, co-working spaces and digital nomads. The charm of the city, its unique history, culture and natural surroundings have made Chiang Mai not only an excellent place to live but also one of the most popular cities in the world for tourists.

Growth in tourism and the poorly-managed development that has resulted from tourism, have adversely affected the city and its people, however. Issues include the proliferation of businesses that focus solely on the tourist market, including shops and vendors that are not in harmony with the townscape (e.g. shops decorated in shrill white, selling latex products) and the many (often unlicensed) hotels and hostels in residential areas, which reduce the quality of life for local residents. The influx of Chinese tourists has been particularly challenging. Businesses owned by Chinese offer services in ways that are not in keeping with Chiang Mai culture. Furthermore, some of the business models that have emerged around Chinese tourists have excluded locals.

Tourism remains a major source of income and employment in Chiang Mai, however. Therefore, although government agencies are seeking to reduce the impacts of tourism and make it more sustainable, they are under pressure to refrain from doing anything that might adversely affect the tourism industry.

But the conventional approach of offering visitors traditional home stays, handicraft stalls, local food vendors and a museum has reached saturation point. The current trajectory of tourism can only lead to the deterioration of the elements of Chiang Mai that make it so alluring. One of the major trends in the travel industry today is that many tourists are seeking quality experiences. Visitors want a clean, safe and accessible city, with walkable streets. Visitors particularly appreciate local shops and interesting food venues, not artificial local markets that sell the same things found everywhere else in the world.

To preserve the city's scale and the elements that make it attractive to tourists, Chiang Mai must offer visitors better and more sustainable activities, products and experiences. A good model for the future development of tourism in Chiang Mai is to bring in new ideas, organize well and engage the local community.

Chiang Mai has a large creative community. The flourishing contemporary art and creative community is often neglected by policy-makers and government agencies, but embracing this and other facets of Chiang Mai's diversity would make Chiang Mai a thriving, livable city that is attractive for locals and visitors alike. While the government spends money on big events for tourists, that compounds the issues associated with tourism, the local creative community has developed popular markets, events and spaces. Some of them seek to attract both Thai and foreign tourists, while others, such as Thapae East, a hip venue close to the city centre, are now firmly part of the city's youth culture and creative texture.

Figure 4.14: One of Chiang Mai's many craft markets.

Many exciting initiatives have sprung up in recent years. Inspired by projects like 'handmade chiangmai' and training offered by the Thailand Creative Design Centre (TCDC), entrepreneurs are offering workshops and classes in cooking, pottery, weaving and other crafts. Meena Rice Based Cuisine, Blackitch Artisan

Kitchen, May Kaidee, Rustic and Blue and Cuisine de Garden are some innovative examples. Chiang Mai also boasts a creative coffee scene that seeks its equal.

New initiatives in community-based tourism include Local Alike, which uses chic online tools to allow visitors to find meaningful, socially-responsible experiences run by locals, ensuring the profits stay in the community. Another inventive idea to promote responsible tourism is Chiang Mai's new heritage trail, developed with the Hong Kong firm 'iDiscover', which enables community members to harness technology to identify local hotspots that are of interest to visitors and locals alike.

MAIIAM, Chiang Mai's award winning contemporary art museum, and the Chiang Mai Art (Gallery) Map by Chiang Mai Art Conversation have put the city's flourishing contemporary art scene on the map; creating new destinations for visitors. Meanwhile, the annual Nimman Art and Design Promenade, a week-long art market, has inspired events, activities, designers and craft makers. Similarly, the annual Chiang Mai Design Week is bringing new activities and diversity into the city centre.

Figure 4.15: TEDxChiangMai after party at Thapae East Creative Venue.

Makerspace Thailand, established by Nati Sang, a Thai entrepreneur, and Punspace, co-working spaces established by two Thai IT experts, have quietly become must-visit destinations for digital nomads, makers and people interested in crafts. The activities and events at such venues include TEDx ChiangMai and Design Week, which have given Chiang Mai a new image, moving it beyond its positioning as a city of traditional culture and temples.

A pioneering local initiative is Oxotel. The owners converted an abandoned building into a stylish modern hostel, which has won several design awards. With its fusion architecture, cool interior design and arty café, Oxtel has become a destination in itself. Oxotel's value is enhanced by its location within a community of traditional silver craft makers, allowing visitors to blend the old and new, tradition and modernity. Another local initiative is 'Green Beauty Scented', which promotes sustainable urban development, focusing on preserving and improving Chiang Mai's precious green spaces.

Local communities in Chiang Mai, are doing what those in Japan and elsewhere have done, they are building on 'what is on hand' (Kerr, 2018) to create new livelihoods and income sources, bringing together their cultural knowledge and local environmental and heritage resources to create attractive products and services. Thus, drawing on their creativity, the people of Chiang Mai are using their rich culture, heritage, local wisdom and environment to drive a thriving economy, and are having a transformational impact. Governmental support, in the form of funding and training, would enable more local people to benefit from creative industries and make tourism sustainable, for the long-term benefit of both residents and visitors.

References

Kerr, A. (2018) Rural revival using what's on hand, TEDxChiangMai, 10 February.

4

Conservation in Broken Hill, Australia

Elizabeth Vines OAM, FRAIA, M.ICOMOS, Architect, Partner, McDougall & Vines, Conservation and Heritage Consultants; Adjunct Professor, Deakin University, Melbourne

Keywords: Australia, geography, tourism, conservation, built heritage, cultural heritage

Broken Hill, a town in the Australian desert with a population of 19,000, is significant for its unique mix of architecture and mining infrastructure, set in a vast arid landscape. The town was founded the late 1880s and showcases architecture of a variety of stylistic sources, including works by significant architects from Melbourne, Adelaide and Sydney. The remaining humble miners' cottages or *tinnies*, constructed in corrugated iron, are testimony to the harsh living conditions of the early miners. In January 2015, Broken Hill became the first town in the country to be listed on the Australian Heritage Register. The national listing recognises the town as being significant in the development of Australia and acknowledges over 130 years of continuous mining operations and technical developments, as well as the town's pioneering role in the development of occupational health and safety standards, and its early practice of regenerating the environment in and around mining operations.

Over the past 30 years, Broken Hill has developed a comprehensive heritage management programme, with heritage-based planning policies and grants programmes to facilitate the retention of its built and social heritage. A heritage advisor, funded by local and state governments, provides home owners with free technical advice, and local committees ensure that the community is well represented in managing and promoting the built environment of the city. Locals and visitors are kept informed about the town's heritage and the importance of good quality conservation via publications, activities and events, including a comprehensive history, conservation guidelines, self-guided driving and walking tours, and an annual heritage week. Because of this, Broken Hill is seen as a model for heritage conservation in Australia.

The town's built heritage faces threats, however. Due to its isolation, property values are comparatively low, and conservation, repair and adaptive re-use works are expensive. Small projects are eligible for modest heritage grants, but larger-scale conservation projects require substantial funding, which is not easy to find. The retention of now redundant mining structures is also problematic, as these are located on active mining sites. They are of interest to tourists, are an essential part of the town's story and important visual landmark elements contributing to the city's character and historical development, but visitor access is problematic, with liability and safety issues severely limiting tourism opportunities. Ambitious tourism initiatives, which once provided guided access to these sites by former miners, collapsed due to insurance and liability issues. Retention of these large structures is seen as a major challenge for the operating mining companies, who see these structures as liabilities in view of the cost of ensuring their safety.

Figure 4.16: The Living Desert Flora and Fauna Sanctuary, Broken Hill.

Promoted as the 'accessible outback', Broken Hill has a strong community spirit, but its fortunes vary with the prices of silver, lead and zinc. The economy is supported by tourism initiatives showcasing not only its mining history, but the region's rich indigenous heritage and local artist community, which are essential elements in its cultural significance. Major artistic attractions include the Desert Equinox and the Living Desert Reserve. The latter features sandstone sculptures displayed on the desert skyline. Such initiatives draw on the town's creative resources and combine these with its cultural, built and natural heritage to ensure the tourism industry is sustainable and benefits the community in the long term.

Livelihoods, tourism and heritage conservation in post-earthquake Kathmandu Valley, Nepal

Kai Weise, ICOMOS Nepal

Keywords: Nepal, geography, tourism, conservation, governance, heritage impact

Kathmandu Valley is a World Heritage site comprising seven groups of monuments: three squares (Kathmandu, Patan and Bhaktapur), two Buddhist *stupa* complexes (Boudha and Swayambu) and two Hindu temples (Pashupati and Changu Narayan). The site is largely urban and represents a vibrant living culture that stretches back into the misty realms of legend.

Tourism in Kathmandu Valley is a source of livelihoods for many in the local community, with numerous residents operating curio stalls and shops in and around the site's public spaces. Such businesses have had a negative impact on the historic setting, however, with priest's houses in Swayambhu being converted into shops, and historic squares becoming covered with stalls selling souvenirs. These issues are becoming more serious as visitor numbers increase.

The links between tourism, livelihoods and heritage conservation were highlighted following the 2015 Gorkha Earthquake, which damaged large parts of the monuments. The disaster led to a drop in tourism, and both the site managers and local communities lamented their diminished income. The local site managers decided to open the sites to tourists so they could collect entrance fees. Initially, visitors were allowed to enter the sites at their own risk, and no signage or safety measures were put in place. However, the dilemma was of course that if the tourists were charged, safety had to be ensured. This was the topic of much debate between UNESCO, the central authorities and the local site managers. For safety reasons it was necessary for the monuments to be stabilized before allowing visitors to enter but, following pressure from those whose livelihoods depended on tourism, politicians pushed for immediate opening. Finally, with minimum signage and some barricades around dangerous areas, the sites were opened officially to tourists within two months of the earthquake.

The authorities pushed for rapid reconstruction, setting impossible deadlines, with little understanding of the circumstances. Under pressure to show progress, particularly in view of the highly acclaimed Post Disaster Needs Assessment process, the government tendered out rehabilitation projects to random contractors who had no inkling of heritage conservation, and no knowledge of traditional techniques, materials and procedures. Faced with instances of damaged monuments being torn down and then reconstructed with concrete columns and beams, activists stepped in and stopped such projects, but the damage was done.

For monuments to be restored appropriately, the traditional skills and knowledge of artisans must be maintained, which in turn requires that artisans' work is economically viable and is also respected and valued. When knowledge is not valued, it is lost. For example, knowledge of how to create timber joints, using timber elements, is quickly vanishing because metal elements are perceived as being better. Knowledge needs to be documented and passed on to the new generation of artisans. But for the younger generation to carry on this tradition, they must have a sense of security in the future of their profession and acknowledgement of the value of what they do. This requires a change in attitudes towards vernacular architecture and materials, as well as in the government's system of implementing restoration projects.

In the post-earthquake rehabilitation of monuments and sites, along with ensuring the continuity of skills and knowledge, it is essential to also ensure the continuity of other forms of intangible cultural heritage. This means, for example, ensuring that rituals and festivals continue to be performed. Therefore, even though the circumstances were difficult, with rubble having to be cleared, the chariot festivals of Machhendranath, Bisketjatra and Indrajatra were held following the earthquake. Likewise, the annual tantric rituals of Shantipur in Swayambhu were carried out, which required the removal of collapsed walls and murals.

Recognising the need to preserve both tangible and intangible heritage while also fostering tourism and local livelihoods, an initiative was launched to present the post-earthquake rehabilitation process itself to visitors. Tourists are now being given the opportunity to tour the reconstruction site in Hanumandhokha

Palace Complex, for example. This has allowed visitors to appreciate the traditional knowledge and skills involved in the rehabilitation of heritage structures. Another example is an exhibition at the Hanuman Dhoka Palace Museum in Kathmandu that explains the rehabilitation activities. Artisans working on wood carvings have become quite an attraction, giving them a greater sense of pride in their workmanship and their cultural and social traditions.

Figure 4.17: Tourist taking photos of traditional artisans working on wood carvings for the Hanuman Dhoka Palace restoration.

Figure 4.18: ICOMOS ICORP (International Scientific Committee for Risk Preparedness) on the Road Project interviewing a traditional wood carver at Hanuman Dhoka Palace.

Towards sustainable cultural tourism in Chettinad, India

Minja Yang, President and Professor Raymond Lemaire International Centre for Conservation Katholieke Universiteit Leuven (RLICC/ KU Leuven)

Keywords: India, geography, tourism, tangible heritage, intangible heritage, community participation, urban planning, cultural mapping

In 2006, the UNESCO New Delhi Office launched the Indian Heritage Passport Programme, with two main aims: (i) to promote sustainable cultural tourism, so as to support local job creation, thereby preventing out-migration in search of employment and promoting poverty reduction along cultural routes, and (ii) to enhance the safeguarding of cultural heritage of non-monumental character, which are not under legal protection, so are threatened by decay and demolition. Conscious of the danger that rural tourism can engender in terms of aggravating social and economic inequities, this UNESCO programme had an interdisciplinary strategy to promote culture-based development through involving the local inhabitants in the knowledge economy.

The programme began with mapping the destination's natural, tangible and intangible cultural heritage. This cultural mapping and urban analyses were initiated through a workshop organised with Anna University of Chennai and the École de Chaillot, a school of monument conservation in Paris, and were continued periodically over the following years with other national and international partners. Student interns from France, Italy, Belgium and England joined those from universities in India, to enrich the documentation on not only the tangible and intangible heritage but also the ingenious rain water harvesting and drainage systems. In addition, the UNESCO programme partnered with the National Institute of Open Schooling (NIOS) of India to promote literacy and skills training for the community along the cultural route. This required developing a training module on tourism for neo-literates within the framework of the UNESCO LIFE (Literacy Initiative for Empowerment) programme.

To create synergies with the government's Digital India programme, UNESCO also established, where possible, community multimedia centres to provide the community with the facilities and training required to access the internet, and hence the world of information. At some sites, UNESCO also provided training in how to create websites to advertise the attractions of the cultural route and to facilitate e-reservations. Moreover, UNESCO included, as subjects in public awareness-raising workshops for the local inhabitants, traditional Tamil building and hydro-engineering technologies, and the region's importance in the ecosystem of the Gulf of Mannar, which hosts a UNESCO Biosphere Reserve. The goal of this was to increase the local population's interest in the landscape and in the ecological practices inherited from their ancestors. Passing on knowledge of traditional technology, as part of intangible heritage, is a facet of the outstanding universal value of the area, and it serves as a foundation of value-based knowledge tourism.

One of the project sites was Chettinad (Chetti: community of traders, Nadu: country). Located northeast of Madurai, on a semi-arid plain of 1550 square kilometres in the heart of Tamil Nadu in South India, the Chettinad region is inhabited primarily by some 110,000 Chettiars – once traders and financiers who in the late 19th and early 20th century made their fortunes by extending their businesses across Southeast Asia. The well-defined geo-cultural territory of Chettinad includes two towns and 73 villages.

Since the time the community settled in the area, the Chettiars have upheld a vision of urban planning and development that makes this area outstanding in terms of its built heritage. Their traditional villages, constructed as ideal towns in accordance with the sophisticated rules of the ancient Tamil science of urban planning, are characterised by clan temples, sacred groves and remarkable traditional water management systems constructed with local laterite stone. The urban ensemble is composed of orthogonal streets and rectangular plots, with a succession of houses with inner courtyards framed by wide sloping roofs to collect rainwater and to cool the air.

In the late 19th and early 20th centuries the Chettiars juxtaposed on their ancestral villages new ideas in planning and architecture, acquired through their international exposure. The Chettiars introduced *ooranis* (ponds) in the villages and *erys* (reservoirs) in the surrounding countryside. To construct and decorate their palatial mansions, and display their wealth, the Chettiars imported materials and expertise from all over the world, including teak from Burma, marble from Italy, cast iron and steel from Britain, tiles from Japan and chandeliers from Belgium. Requiring the best, the Chettiars also called upon skilled craftspeople from various regions of India, such as for wood carving, frescoes and egg-plastering. Local expressions of the Art Deco style, which were largely constructed during the 1930s and 1940s, reflect the international architectural and decorative vogue of the era and represent another layer of the remarkable built heritage of Chettinad. In the 1940s, economic changes led to the abandonment of many of the buildings, and many structures have since been razed. Those that remain are mostly in a dilapidated condition.

In the 2000s, on the initiative of two French architects, both long-time residents of South India, a steering committee of resident and non-resident Chettiars was established through a non-governmental organisation, Arche-S, to encourage the participation of the local inhabitants and to guide the development of tourism in Chettinad. At the same time, to expand appreciation of the site and gain protection of its composites, the process of gaining World Heritage status was initiated. The first cluster proposed for the World Heritage tentative list comprised nine villages and one town, chosen for their proximity to Kanadukathan, the village where the Raja's Palace is located and the starting point of a knowledge-based cultural tourism trail.

While activities initiated under the UNESCO cultural routes programme are ongoing, their long-term success and sustainability depend on the participation of local inhabitants and on local government support. Without some form of legal protection, which even after ten years is yet to be granted, and with the continued concentration of investment in the major cities of India, the future of small towns and villages, despite their exceptional heritage value, is less than promising.

To promote spatial and social equity in a country like India, where the majority of the population remains rural, despite the rapid pace of urbanisation, it is essential to maintain the rural-urban linkages of the sort demonstrated by Chettinad. The employment and development potential of the 73 villages and the two towns of Chettinad as a 'slow tourism' cultural route should be combined with creating closer business connections between Chettinad and Chennai and Madurai, which have become important digital hubs in the region. This should be considered with more strategic vision by the state government and the business sector if the current trend of migration to increasingly polluted, over-crowded mega cities is to be discontinued.

5 Managing Urban Heritage Areas in the Context of Sustainable Tourism: Planning and Management

In this chapter, the case examples relate to planning and management, which encompasses urban planning, governance, implementation, holistic approaches, integration, carrying capacity and empowerment and participation.

A protection and management plan for the historic centre of Macao

Carla Figueiredo, Architect and Senior Adviser, Cultural Heritage Department of the Cultural Affairs Bureau of Macao S.A.R. Government

Keywords: China, geography, urban planning, conservation, World Heritage Site, heritage management

Macao's heritage has been managed since 1953 based on legal frameworks that were put into effect at that time. Changes in the law in 1976 have since led to more systematic management. This has enabled the most representative examples of the rich cultural and architectural legacy of the city, with its history of more than 450 years, to endure.

Nonetheless, the historic core needs particular care. For this, a protection and management plan is required. This very important institutional development will specify the most appropriate city management instruments for protecting the principal attributes associated with the cultural value and visual interface of the group of buildings and surrounding urban setting inscribed in the UNESCO World Heritage list in 2005.

As well as fulfilling the aspirations put forward in Heritage Protection Law 11/2013, in effect since March 2014, the protection and management plan for the historic centre of Macao will also provide a sustainable basis for ensuring compliance with the recommendations of the World Heritage Committee. Moreover, it will provide a solid foundation for the long-term vision communicated by the Government of Macao S.A.R. in its efforts to preserve the city's invaluable cultural resources.

The protection and management plan is based on a public-consultation process, which has included numerous clarification sessions and a broad debate in the media, with input from people from all walks of life. Interventions by the public demonstrate a good level of research into the subject, the gathering of technical knowledge and a will to share constructive ideas.

The positive dialogue that has ensued from the consultation process was motivated by the rich content of the plan, which identifies the most notable visual corridors and streetscapes of the historic centre and construction restrictions for each district and architectural unit. It also demands a strong scientific basis for conservation works, greater accountability, and a sense of purpose for the day-to-day action-plans, maintenance tasks and conditions of usage. These are strongly supported by risk-assessment monitoring that recognizes the principal latent pressures, including the ongoing development of the city, an increase in tourist numbers, and the need for an efficient disaster response system.

The plan presents an integrated approach for the protection and management of the character and livelihoods of the historic centre, including the intangible heritage expressions of the city, while also providing for the continuous updating of infrastructure to support quality cultural tourism experiences, a balanced transportation and circulation network, coherent urban furniture installations and public facilities, the maintenance of green spaces, and continued investment in education, research and the promotion of cultural values, along with efficient interpretation support to enhance the story-telling capacity of Macao's heritage legacy.

In tune with the plan's specifications, 11 important visual corridors, 19 picturesque streets and 24 significant urban fabric structures have been identified. Detailed descriptions of the respective attributes and protection mechanisms have been prepared for these, thereby ensuring adequate safeguarding of the most important features associated with the historic centre.

The plan's attention to detail is reflected in the sub-division of the visual corridors into three types of visual linkages, namely: between the monuments and the seaside, between the monuments and relevant public spaces and between the monuments themselves, as well as the various viewpoints and their inherent articulation. This indicates a clear understanding that the historic centre is a living organism that requires a complex network of evaluation channels to assess its condition at any given time.

Centred on the core spatial units targeted for protection, the plan focuses attention on the actions and interventions that could impact the preservation of these units, including the quality of the conservation works, further specified as a list of basic principles for such works, and the need for construction restrictions specific to each block and street and their surrounding environments.

The plan also provides for the design of efficient usage and maintenance action plans, with the identification of practical factors such as capacity limits, circulation of visitors and human resources for management and monitoring tasks. Furthermore, the plan recognizes that the functions and uses of heritage sites need to be consistent with the spirit of each structure and each place. Recognizing the key threats to heritage properties in Macao, including fire, typhoons and termites, the plan also includes risk-assessment measures and takes a preventive stance, while also recognizing the importance of regular monitoring.

The upcoming implementation of the protection and management plan for the historic centre will hopefully inspire the spirit of a future master plan for the entire city, with the necessary coordination of principles and actions.

Heritage management in the historic city of Jaipur, Rajasthan

Dr. Shikha Jain, Director, DRONAH (Development and Research Organisation for Nature, Arts and Heritage), India

Keywords: India, geography, urban planning, historic urban landscape, governance, conservation, stakeholder engagement

Jaipur, a historic walled city in India, is an exemplar of urban planning. The city was designed with extraordinary foresight and is probably the only 18th-century walled city in India that has coped with present day urban pressures.

The city is unique in its architectural heritage, reflecting Jaipur's history as both a centre of trade and commerce and a creative hub for the arts and crafts. It is also a city with a distinct artistic identity.

The Archaeological Survey of India, the Government of India and the Rajasthan State Archaeology Department protect the major monuments and sites in and around Jaipur. Additionally, a special body, the Amber Development and Management Authority (ADMA), was created by the Government of Rajasthan in 2005 for the upkeep and maintenance of state archaeological protected monuments. It is a very good example of a government-created agency with a revenue generation model for the upkeep of historic sites. A number of non-governmental bodies are also actively involved in heritage conservation, raising awareness of the value of conservation and bringing the stakeholders and partners to a common platform.

The city exhibits interesting cases of urban conservation initiatives by the public and private sectors that have thrived, generating income for local craftspeople. These efforts have managed to retain the local character and urban vocabulary in terms of materials, craftsmanship and cultural traditions.

The city is actively involved in the UNESCO Creative Cities programme. In addition, Jaipur was selected as one of 100 'smart cities' under the Smart City Mission of the Ministry of Urban Development (MoUD), launched in 2015. It was one of the few cities where citizens collectively decided and voted for heritage planning for a nominated area of the walled city. In 2015, India nominated the Walled City of Jaipur as a World Heritage site.

The Jaipur Heritage Management Plan, prepared in 2007, is one of the first initiatives of its kind in India — a city level plan for heritage management. It later became part of the Jaipur Master Plan 2025. The Municipalities Act of 2009 (amendment) and Jaipur Building Bylaws of 1970 guide the control of the urban character of Jaipur, and have helped in retaining the original architectural form of the market areas. Jaipur City has also developed specific architectural control guidelines for its various markets, recognizing the distinct features of each of them, though these are yet to be formally adopted by the municipal corporation.

The city's plan envisions 'innovative and inclusive solutions' that involve the use of technology, information and data to make infrastructure and services better, so as to enhance the quality of life of the residents. This plan focuses on carrying out urban conservation and adaptive re-use projects in the historic walled city area, incorporating all previous area-specific management plans and vision plans for the city's heritage.

Interventions have been undertaken to preserve the historic urban character and improve services. These include urban façade conservation and improvement, façade illumination, traffic control and the provision of adequate physical infrastructure and services.

Implementation of urban heritage-related projects is challenging in Indian cities as heritage sites are often located in congested areas facing developmental pressures such as heavy traffic, high real estate values and multiple ownership issues. As Jaipur demonstrates, the successful and effective implementation of any plan in a historic area requires the support of all relevant interest groups. In such situations, with living heritage and where stakeholders have centuries of association with a site, it is essential that conservation professionals look beyond conventional guidelines and engage in dialogue with the residents in order to ensure their interventions are appropriate.

The battle to conserve the Mumbai Mills

Tasneem Zakaria Mehta, Former Vice Chairman INTACH And Mumbai Convenor

Keywords: India, geography, governance, urban planning, heritage impact, stakeholder engagement, adaptive re-use

Located in the heart of Mumbai, midway between the heritage-rich southern fringe and the new developments in the north, the mill lands, which cover approximately 600 acres, offer the city a unique opportunity to regenerate a historic industrial area through enlightened urban planning.

The 58 mills on this land were built in the latter part of the 19th century, in an area that came to be known as Girangaon ('village of mills'), to cater to the rising demand for cotton fabric in Britain after the American civil war halted the supply. Mumbai's prosperity and development were a direct result of the affluence generated by this trade.

The heritage structures on this land are similar to those in Manchester and Birmingham. Built from local grey basalt stone, with an extensive use of teak for decorative elements and trusses for the north lights, the imposing three- and four-storey buildings feature impressive chimneys and unique roof-scapes.

The mill lands formed the heart of working class Mumbai in the late 19th and early 20th centuries, and featured a tight knit socio-economic unit, with workers residing close to the mills in one-room tenements known as chawls. The area spawned its own variant of theatre, music and literature to cater to this new working class. By the turn of the 21st century, however, many of the mills had become defunct and those that continued did not modernise, resulting in their steady decline. By the 1980s the mills had become economically unviable. Mill workers were laid off, leading to strikes, and the area erupted in violence.

Figure 5.1: Mills of Bombay.

In an effort to address this difficult situation, the government invited the eminent architect Charles Correa to head a committee to create an urban master plan for the area that would address the needs of the various stakeholders. Correa's plan delineated areas for public access to address the concerns of the mill workers, the mill owners and the government; suggested adaptive re-use for many of the heritage structures; proposed new zoning and public facilities around transport hubs; and included arrangements for public housing, to address the huge deficit in urban housing that bedevils Mumbai. However, the plan was never implemented and the mill owners, in collusion with officials, sold off much of the land on a piecemeal basis. Instead of coherent design and regulation guidelines that would have ensured the creation of services and amenities that would benefit the city, developers built a dense cluster of office and residential buildings and malls, which have produced an urban nightmare.

In 2005, when it became apparent that much of the city's rich industrial heritage would be lost if urgent action was not taken, the Mumbai chapter of the Indian National Trust for Art and Cultural Heritage (INTACH), along with Tasneem Mehta and Darryl DeMonte, submitted a public interest litigation against the Government of Maharashtra, the Mumbai Municipal Corporation, the Mumbai Heritage Conservation Committee, the Mumbai Metropolitan Regional Development Authority, the Maharashtra Housing and Area Development Authority, the National Textile Corporation, the Maharashtra State Textile

Corporation and 23 mill owners, to petition the court to save the magnificent heritage mills of Mumbai's ailing textile industry.

In an effort to gather information that would convince the government to respond, INTACH held a major conference in collaboration with INTBAU, an arm of the Prince of Wales Trust in England. Moreover, Tasneem Mehta, the convenor of INTACH Mumbai, visited several of the mill sites in England that the Prince's Trusts had helped convert for institutional and commercial purposes. Based on the knowledge gained through these visits, she made presentations to senior government officials and worked with the Bombay Environmental Action Group to push for a master plan that would protect the heritage structures through adaptive re-use. INTACH also held meetings with several senior officials, builders and other stakeholders, who also participated in the week-long workshop and conference.

It was hoped that sensitive regulations and adaptive re-use of the grand old heritage structures, the water bodies and the large sheds, with their beautiful skylights, would provide a much-needed green and open recreational area, as well as space for new facilities for the city. However, greed and a lack of political will instead resulted in the subversion of the original regulations and the loss of these structures and land to private speculators.

Figure 5.2: Textile mills.

The government clearly had no intention of implementing any plan. The sole motive of the land sales was profit. Public interest was given lip service but never heeded. In fact, the regulations allowing development in the area were so lax that a major fire broke out in the Kamala Mills area in 2017, and 19 lives were lost. Meanwhile, the workers who were promised reemployment and re-skilling never received any benefits.

The Bombay Environmental Action Group took out public interest litigation against the government for subverting DCR 58, which was concerned with the proper distribution of land, and against the piecemeal sale of the mills. They won in the high court, but lost in the supreme court. The INTACH Mumbai chapter supplemented this litigation with one that directly aimed to protect the mill heritage and, as a consequence, four large mills have been saved. Stakeholders have proposed creating a textile museum and other public facilities on these sites.

As of 2018, the final judgement has not been made, however, as successive governments have stalled the process and the courts have deferred the verdict. The government has frequently amended the development control regulations to enable the dismemberment of this significant parcel of land that could change the face of Mumbai. INTACH continues to pursue protection of the sites to ensure that the land is used for public purposes.

Ahmedabad's urban renewal: a model for heritage conservation in India's cities

Debashish Nayak, Founding Director, Centre for Heritage Management, Ahmedabad University

5

Keywords: India, geography, conservation, heritage impact, urban renewal, built environment

As society evolves in response to change, so does its expression of heritage. Most Indian cities have core areas of strong architectural and urban character that have traditionally been places of life, vitality, wealth, power, enlightenment and culture. These areas embody community history, emphasising tradition, heritage and culture through architecture and urban form. These attributes do not accrue in a day or a decade, they represent centuries of growth, during which new elements are constantly juxtaposed with older ones.

Familiarity leads to indifference, however, so citizens become insensitive to their environments. Furthermore, today, historic structures in cities tend to be perceived as being incongruous with modern needs. They are seen as inefficient, unproductive and even inconvenient, and many residents seek to replace heritage buildings with contemporary structures. But modern structures often lack any connection to the local culture, history and identity of the city, and the removal of historic structures erase important historical markers.

It is therefore necessary to inculcate awareness in citizens of the social and cultural importance of the built environment, and to help them develop a harmonious relationship with it, so as to avoid losing memories of glory and pride. Urban renewal is a way of achieving this. It rebuilds not just the city but people's relationships with it. Old buildings and civic spaces are reinvented so that they are perceived as assets rather than liabilities.

In the 1980s, the Ford Foundation initiated systematic studies of three historic Indian towns in collaboration with their local municipal bodies. As part of this, it sent civic officials from Ahmedabad, Jaipur and Hyderabad to the International Centre for the Study of the Preservation and Restoration of Cultural Property (ICCROM) in Rome for a 16-week programme in urban conservation. The knowledge gained from the ICCROM programme was invaluable in conserving the Walled City of Ahmedabad, which became India's first World Heritage city.

Over the years, the Ahmedabad Municipal Corporation (AMC) has launched various heritage conservation and development initiatives in the Walled City, and the success of these initiatives is such that the AMC can offer insights to assist other cities in conserving their heritage.

In 1996, the AMC invited CRUTA Foundation of Calcutta to launch a process within its managerial setup to address heritage issues in the city. From this emerged, under AMC's auspices, India's first municipal heritage cell and, in 1997, its first heritage walk. The programmes that ensued included celebrations of heritage days and weeks; documenting and restoring buildings (with India's first bank loans from HUDCO, and later subsidised by the French government along with free technical support); creation of community spaces inspired by local history; and the training of volunteer guides. In addition, the AMC initiated and amended heritage regulations, with modifications in such areas as property tax, land use and disaster risk management. The AMC has also encouraged the media to engage with the community and to write articles that enable community members to gain an appreciation of their history and heritage. In addition, the AMC has established links with national and international agencies and organisations, which have increased appreciation of Ahmedabad's heritage.

Figures 5.3 and 5.4: Volunteer guides conducting the Ahmedabad Municipal Corporation initiated 'Heritage walk of Ahmedabad'.

The Ahmedabad model is a guiding example and around 50 Indian cities have sent their municipal officers to Ahmedabad for training. Experience has also been shared with major towns and cities in the state of Ahmedabad through the Gujarat City Managers' Association.

'The Central Axis of Beijing' should not be a World Heritage site

Que Weimin, Urban and Environmental Sciences College, Peking University, Beijing

Keywords: China, geography, World Heritage Site, urban planning, cultural heritage

The UNESCO World Heritage Committee does not specifically seek the 'spirit of World Heritage' when identifying World Heritage Sites, but this concept underlies the World Heritage movement (UNESCO World Heritage Committee, 1994). The nomination of the Central Axis of Beijing as World Heritage is contrary to the ideals represented by this 'spirit'.

On 29 January 2013, the National Commission of the People's Republic of China for UNESCO submitted the Central Axis of Beijing to the World Heritage Committee for inclusion on the World Heritage list (UNESCO World Heritage Committee, 2013). While the submission meets four of the ten selection criteria (UNESCO World Heritage Committee, 1977), the submission is unsuitable for inclusion as a World Heritage site.

The three justifications for including the Central Axis of Beijing as World Heritage are that the central axis illustrates "urban planning in the Yuan, Ming and Qing dynasties, as well as the People's Republic of China" (UNESCO World Heritage Committee, 2013); that this central axis is the south-north central axis of the Ming-Qing Dynasties; and that this axis represented 'the world centre' in ancient texts. But all three justifications are irreconcilable with historical facts.

The central axis method is not recorded in any Chinese classic texts, or in any of the 43 studies of Zhou Li published during the period between the Hang (206 BC – AD 220) and Qing (1644-1911) dynasties. Furthermore, the contents of the south-north central axis and the Central Axis of Beijing are quite different. Moreover, the viewpoint of the central axis being 'the world centre' is a doubtful interpretation of an early text (Li, 1473). Several other ancient capitals were also recorded as 'the world centre' in Chinese classics (Li, 1795); as observed during the Qing Dynasty (Wu, 1795).

Although the city wall, the street system of Dadu (1272-1638) and the former Beijing Walled City of the Yuan Dynasty, were planned according to the norms recorded in Zhou Li, the design of the walls did not observe the norms and the street plan did not comply with the criteria.

The Central Axis of Beijing is not located at the centre, between the west and east boundaries of the old Beijing walled city; it crosses the meridian at an angle

(Zhang, 1998; Kui, 2005), and the width of the planned red line for construction varies depending on the section. Furthermore, it is not a straight line (Chen, 2003).

The submission of the Central Axis of Beijing is such that, the historical period does not match its description. It is described as follows:

> As an outstanding example of feudal China's capital, the old city of Beijing enjoys a prominent position in the world history of urban planning and development. … The Central Axis ingeniously organizes the imperial palaces, the imperial city, temples and altars, markets, streets from feudal times and the Tian'anmen square complex built after the founding of the People's Republic of China in 1949.

But 'the People's Republic of China' is obviously not 'feudal China'. Moreover, the negative impacts of recent development are not mentioned.

Its substantial heritage content, the tangible historic architecture along the north-south central belt in old Beijing City and the intangible central axis of Forbidden City, both to the north and south, confuse the nature of cultural heritage between the tangible and the intangible, and illustrate an inconsistency between the site's name and its content. The heritage value of the central axis in the Forbidden City is denied by the nomination of the Central Axis of Beijing. Furthermore, the submission represents a re-nomination of two World Heritage sites, the Forbidden City (UNESCO World Heritage Committee, 1987) and the Temple of Heaven (UNESCO World Heritage Committee, 1998), as these are annexed within The Central Axis of Beijing.

In brief, the nomination of the Central Axis of Beijing is contrary to the strategic objectives: credibility, balance, authenticity and integrity, and to the spirit of World Heritage. To safeguard China's international image as a country with coherent World Heritage, it is recommended that the Central Axis of Beijing be removed from the UNESCO World Heritage Tentative List.

References

Chen, Yongde (2003) Discussion on alignment of Beijing Central Axis, *Beijing City Planning and Construction Review*, **4**, 109-110.

Kui, Zhongyu (2005) Analysis of the Deviation of the Beijing Central Axis from the Meridian, *Geo-Information Science*, **7** (1), 25-27.

Li, Jingde (1473) *Zhu Ziyu Category*, Vol. 2, Chinese Basic Ancient Books Library - Chen Wei block printed edition, p. 19.

Li, Tao (1795) *A Comprehensive Review of the Six Dynasties*, Vol. 10, Chinese Basic Ancient Books Library. The four sections of books of pavilion of literary profundity in the Qing Dynasty, p, 65.

UNESCO World Heritage Committee (1977) Operational Guidelines for the Implementation of the World Heritage Convention. http://whc.unesco.org/en/guidelines/

UNESCO World Heritage Committee (1987) Imperial Palaces of the Ming and Qing Dynasties in Beijing and Shenyang, http://whc.unesco.org/en/list/439/

UNESCO World Heritage Committee (1994) Global Strategy for a Representative, Balanced and Credible World Heritage List, http://whc.unesco.org/en/globalstrategy/

UNESCO World Heritage Committee (1998) Temple of Heaven: an Imperial Sacrificial Altar in Beijing. http://whc.unesco.org/en/list/881/

UNESCO World Heritage Committee (2013) The Central Axis of Beijing (including Beihai). http://whc.unesco.org/en/tentativelists/5802/

Wu, Changyuan (1795) *Chen Yuan Shi Lue (An Outline of Past Beijing)*, Chinese Basic Ancient Books Library -The Carved Book of the North Pond, pp.3-4.

Zhang, Jinyuan (1998) Geographical coordinates, Beijing Central Axis and Beijing City Coordinate System, *Municipal Technology*, (1), 62-63.

Further reading

Liu, Junwen (2005) *Edi*, Chinese Basic Ancient Books Library, Beijing erudition, Digital Technology Research Center, Peking University Edition.

UNESCO World Heritage Committee (2002) Budapest Declaration on World Heritage

UNESCO World Heritage Committee (2012) Celebrating 40 years of World Heritage 1972-2012. http://whc.unesco.org/en/40years

UNESCO (2015) Policy document for the integration of a sustainable development perspective into the processes of the World Heritage Convention. http://whc.unesco.org/en/sustainabledevelopment

United Nations General Assembly (2015) Transforming Our World: the 2030 Agenda for Sustainable Development, A/RES/70/1 http://www.un.org/sustainabledevelopment/development-agenda

5

Conserving the Vernacular in Singapore

Ian Tan, PhD candidate, Department of Architecture, University of Hong Kong

Keywords: Singapore, geography, urban planning, stakeholder engagement, heritage protection, cultural heritage, displacement

Investment in heritage

While Singapore is small in size, with a territory of 720 square kilometres, the city state has invested considerable resources in protecting its heritage. As of 2018, Singapore has conserved about 7000 buildings, mostly in the city's historic districts, gazetted 72 historically significant buildings as national monuments and inscribed its Botanic Gardens as a World Heritage site.

The removal of kampong

While much has been conserved, the rapid pace of urbanization and a steep increase in the population led to Singapore's vernacular villages, known as *kampong*, being cleared for the construction of high rise housing.

In the 1957 census, a quarter of Singapore's population lived in kampong. Such villages were located along rivers, the seafront, trunk roads and the railways, so people lived close to where they worked (e.g. in fishing and farming). Until the 1980s, kampong were even found in sub-urban areas. The kampong formed the cores of large communities. But between the 1960s and 1980s, the populations of these communities were resettled to make way for 'new towns', high-rise, densely-populated housing estates that stand in strong contrast to the kampong house, essentially a single storey timber post and lintel construction raised on stilts.

As of 2018, only two kampong areas remain in Singapore. Kampong Buangkok, the last remaining kampong on mainland Singapore, and the kampong of Pulau Ubin, an island off the north-eastern coast. The former consists of 26 houses while the latter has more than 70 houses.

Conserving Pulau Ubin's heritage for Singapore's future

Pulau Ubin, which has an area of 10 square kilometres, was once a cluster of five islets separated by tidal rivers. It was united by bunds to form a single island. Pulau Ubin is overseen by the National Parks Board, which takes care of both the natural habitat and the island's stock of vernacular kampong houses.

In the past, Pulau Ubin supplied materials that were crucial to Singapore's economy. The island had granite quarries, rubber plantations and prawn breeding farms. These industries declined in the 1970s as Singapore moved into new activities. Today, most island residents are retirees or work in the service industry, including as ferry workers, restaurant staff and bicycle rental operators.

Pulau Ubin is home to Chek Jawa Wetlands, one of Singapore's richest natural areas. At low tide, visitors can observe the interaction between the flora and fauna in various ecosystems, including sandy beach, rocky beach, seagrass lagoon, coral rubble, mangrove and coastal forest.

Community involvement

Pulau Ubin was once threatened by development. In 2000, the government planned to reclaim the tidal land at Chek Jawa. This was met with negative feedback and much media attention, however. This attention raised public interest in the island, and thousands of visitors flocked to visit the wetland treasure. Consequently, the government cancelled its plans and instead announced new amenities to protect and showcase the wetland. These amenities were completed in 2007 and include a visitor centre, a 20-metre tall viewing tower and a tidal boardwalk.

Aware of keen interest among Singaporeans to participate in preparing future plans for Pulau Ubin, in 2014 the government initiated the Friends of Ubin Network (FUN). It brought together members of various heritage and nature groups, volunteers and public agencies to discuss how to enhance and protect the island's heritage, natural environment and biodiversity.

Plans for the future

The government, civic groups and universities embarked on outreach, research and documentation projects on Pulau Ubin to gain an in-depth understanding of the island. Aside from a project to generate public awareness of the island's built, cultural and natural heritage, three main initiatives are underway for protecting Pulau Ubin's heritage. They are:

- **The Pulau Ubin cultural mapping project**: The National Heritage Board commissioned a year-long study on the social and cultural life on the island. Interesting aspects included mapping stakeholder profiles, such as the local visitors, business owners, former and current residents as well as documenting social events and religious activities throughout the year.

- **Pesta Ubin**: A bottom-up initiative initiated by a group of Ubin enthusiasts, with the support of the FUN network. Pesta Ubin is an annual month-long festival. Activities highlight the island's attractions, including the kampong, natural habitats, adventure sports and sea sports.

- **Student projects**: The Department of Architecture at the National University of Singapore (NUS) has conducted various student documentation and design projects in recent years, including the Naturing Ubin Masterplan project, launched in June 2015, and the Pulau Ubin Lives Symposium, held in April 2018.

FUN and the various public projects in Pulau Ubin demonstrate how stakeholder engagement can lead to deeper public appreciation for natural and cultural heritage, and can empower the public to play a part in conserving heritage for future generations to enjoy.

Meeting future challenges in land planning

As the island's population declines due to an aging population and the flow of youth to the mainland, the island's intangible cultural heritage, including traditional skills and practices, religious rites and rituals and the villagers' way of life, are at risk of disappearing. Fostering a strong cultural identity and pride in tangible and intangible cultural heritage is the first step in ensuring Pulau Ubin remains endearing and is sustainable as a destination for Singaporeans and overseas visitors. Moving forward, this requires stronger public-private partnership, so as to meet future challenges, along with further outreach efforts, to instil pride in the island's heritage and ensure its continuation.

Bibliography

De Koninck, R. Drolet, J. and Girard, M. (2008) *Singapore: An atlas of perpetual territorial transformation*, Singapore: NUS Press

Friends of Ubin Network (2014) Pulau Ubin. http://ubin.mnd.gov.sg/MS/PulauUbin

Friends of Pulau Ubin (2018) What is Pesta Ubin? https://pestaubin2018.blogspot.hk/p/about.htm

National Heritage Board (2017) Pulau Ubin Cultural Mapping Project, https://roots.sg/learn/resources/virtual-tours/pulau-ubin

National Parks Board (2012) Pulau Ubin and Chek Jawa. https://www.nparks.gov.sg/gardens-parks-and-nature/parks-and-nature-reserves/pulau-ubin-and-chek-jawa

Tang, K. F. (1993) *Kampong days: Village life and times in Singapore revisited*, Singapore: National Archives of Singapore.

Chao Phraya Riverside, Bangkok: A contested cultural landscape

Montira Unakul, UNESCO, Bangkok, Thailand

Keywords: Thailand, geography, historic urban landscape, urban planning, preservation, urbanization, development

At the heart of Bangkok, the Chao Phraya River has been the lifeblood of the city since Bangkok was founded in the late 18th century. The present day riverscape is the result of centuries of human manipulation. Even the original natural water course was altered; a series of canals gave rise to Chao Phraya's present-day form. Beyond facilitating transportation, connection and water flow, the re-shaping of the river created Rattanakosin Island, a mandala of royal power for the current dynasty, modelled on the former capital of Ayutthaya.

Over the course of two centuries, the riverfront has accumulated layers of building development, from historic waterside communities to high-rise residential and commercial projects. This has resulted in tensions among the various interest groups. Discord over the riverside cultural landscape has been played out through conflicting narratives of identity at the local and national levels, as well as through various trajectories for urban planning.

Proponents of historic preservation have championed the heritage listing of the Chao Phraya River cultural landscape as a World Heritage site, a national heritage site, and even, in the case of enclaves such as KudeeJeen, a community heritage site. Heritage designation would provide a means of safeguarding key historic monuments, buildings and structures, such as the iconic Wat Arun and Wat Pho, as well as ancient communities, waterways and other underlying infrastructure. To this end, the Bangkok Metropolitan Administration has commissioned a number of projects, including the Masterplan to Revive Chao Phraya

River in Bangkok (2009-2010) and a 2015 feasibility study towards national heritage recognition.

The proliferation of plans has done little to keep the cultural landscape intact, however. As a cultural landscape, the historic character and context of the Chao Phraya River is under increasing pressure from inappropriate modern infrastructure and development. The relationship between built settlements and the riverside has changed rapidly, and the historic nature of riverside living and riverside access may soon be lost.

Earlier proposals for waterside planning, such as the mid-1990s MIT Bangkok Plan, were criticized as introducing European ways of buffering the waterfront, very different from the vernacular forms of architecture and urbanization, which ensure seamless proximity to the water's edge. The military government's recent proposal to re-sculpt the river with a new 20-metre wide promenade designed to serve recreational pedestrians and bikers has raised major concerns among local residents, professionals and civil society about negative environmental, cultural and social impacts. Meanwhile, private sector developments, such as the much-publicized ICONSIAM, which will introduce the country's tallest building amidst a sprawling mixed-use development within a stone's throw of the old city, are carried out in conformity with the letter of the urban planning laws, but will create irreversible changes to the river's character.

The historic landscape, settlements, monuments and communities have national and possibly world class value. A light-handed and sensitive approach is needed to maintain the riverside's character. Major new developments and infrastructure would disrupt the urban fabric and bar existing communities from the waterfront.

At the local scale, experts have proposed various approaches to riverside development, including reviving vernacular architecture and urban planning models, which allow residents to live in proximity to the water and its seasonal cycle. At the macro-scale of the entire river system and basin, the massive 2011 floods reminded policy-makers and citizens alike of the urgent need for holistic environmental and land use management, so as to regulate the river more effectively, from its upstream watershed to its outlet in the Gulf of Thailand.

Successful planning for the Chao Phraya River landscape requires a balance between (i) protecting the cultural and historic assets and character of the river, (ii) respecting the rights and ways of life of communities along the river, (iii) preserving the ecological functions and context of the river, and (iv) improving the function of the river in terms of flood management. Moving beyond a superficial approach that sees the riverside simply as a dramatic backdrop for evening dinner cruises and elaborate state ceremonies requires a multi-faceted and participatory assessment of the multiple values associated with the river landscape as a natural and cultural system. An inclusive approach such as this would inform a visioning exercise that befits the status of the river as a publicly-owned good to be used for public purposes for the benefit of the nation and beyond.

Ger area cultural heritage, tourism and community enhancement, Ulaanbaatar, Mongolia

Urtnasan Norov, Doctor, Professor, Philosopher; member of Advisory Committee of ICOMOS and President of National Committee for ICOMOS

Keywords: Mongolia, geography, urban planning, development, cultural heritage, stakeholder engagement

Cultural heritage (tangible and intangible) has vital value as it serves as a repository of identity, memory and sense of place. It also contributes to making cities distinctive. Therefore, consideration of cultural heritage factors and heritage places in city planning and development is very important.

The capital of Mongolia, Ulaanbaatar, is a modern city with a history of only about 70 years. It has two distinct parts: a formal urban core area and a surrounding '*ger* district' area. While people in the urban core live mainly in apartment buildings, in the ger districts people dwell in traditional Mongolian ger (round dwellings with felt covers) or in small wooden houses, in fenced-off enclosures. The ger districts have little infrastructure and few services and facilities, with most residents lacking access to clean water and sanitation systems.

Around 800,000 people live in the ger districts, making up roughly 60% of the city's total population. As with other city areas, the ger districts are defined not only by their physical structures but also by the living intangible culture and spiritual life of the residents.

The city authorities have elaborated several development plans in recent decades, but these have, unfortunately, ignored cultural heritage factors. Recently, however, the authorities have recognized the need to change the planning paradigm and integrate heritage values and sustainability concepts into planning processes, involving various stakeholders.

In this regard, the Ulaanbaatar City Government recently submitted an application to the Cities Development Initiative for Asia (CDIA) for a pre-feasibility study (PFS) titled, 'Ulaanbaatar ger area cultural heritage, tourism and community enhancement'. The overall objective of the PFS is to identify both tangible assets and intangible cultural heritage in the ger districts, and integrate them into planning, so as to provide greater economic opportunities and better living conditions for inhabitants.

To achieve this, the project has identified six packages for development and investment in the ger districts. Each package identifies and promotes cultural heritage values at a different level: historic, architectural and artistic, spiritual and religious, scientific, research and education, and employment and livelihoods. Three of the packages include improvements to historic monasteries and the urban fabric that surrounds them. Four packages feature major infrastructure improvements to ger districts. All investment packages are well aligned with government and community objectives and with efforts to increase tourism and improve cultural heritage conservation and management in Ulaanbaatar City. They have been identified as such in the Master Plan for Ulaanbaatar, 2017-2020.

Figure 5.5: General view of Capital city of Ulaanbaatar.

Figure 5.6: Mongolian Ger. Traditional round conical felt dwelling of nomadic people.

Reflections on the case examples

The various case examples presented here demonstrate that historic areas in Asia are facing numerous challenging issues, including:

- Pressures from development stakeholders interested in increasing the density and scale of use of their sites.
- Bureaucracies are not empowered and equipped to deal with these pressures.
- Increasingly large visitor numbers are disrupting social and community networks and values.
- Over-commercialization, especially by outside interests.
- Insensitive infrastructure development.
- Lack of affordable housing, which limits the number of local people that might stay in a historic area.
- Resident populations are declining.
- Populations are aging.
- Land tenure is contested.
- Loss of heritage, tangible and intangible, in its many forms.

In response to these challenges, there is a call for the incorporation of longer-term integrated conservation strategies into urban development planning frameworks, with the overall objective of achieving a balance between preservation and development.

A recurring theme among the cases examples is the call for holistic planning to reconcile heritage conservation and urban development, through the engagement of all stakeholders (including administrators, communities, business and professional people, and heritage advocates), many of whom are not regularly or systematically brought into urban planning and management processes.

Among the case examples are repeated reminders that historic urban areas were founded prior to the contemporary context and have evolved over time in response to the changing social and economic needs of communities, and these areas continue to exist in a context of continued development and urban renewal. While changes have been made in these areas, much has also remained the same, with the forms and scale of historic urban areas enabling the resident populations' intangible heritage to endure. Given the importance of this heritage, the needs of the customary residents of historic districts need to be prioritised and must be accommodated in plans that seek to meet the demands of modern society, including urban densification and infrastructure upgrades.

The need for enforcing existing (and therefore presumably agreed-upon) urban and heritage regulations is seen by many as an important first step. The case examples express frustration that municipal officials in one jurisdiction after another simply ignore existing laws, or do not use the management tools available to them to enforce regulations. Many of the case examples identify this lack of competent, responsive governance at the municipal level as the major threat to the protection and conservation of the historic urban environment, above the other two very real and acknowledged threats: overtourism and speculative property development. The case examples emphasise that there is a need for Asian cities to adopt additional development control tools, including: the designation of historic precincts, zoning by-laws, regulations pertaining to historic buildings, and heritage impact assessment. Such tools are recognised as essential components in the urban conservation processes in other parts of the world, where modern urban strategic planning has been successful in incorporating heritage districts into holistic urban development models.

Tourism, including in historic areas and areas with rich heritage resources, is clearly seen in many of the case examples as an opportunity to sustain local livelihoods and is not necessarily viewed as a threat to either the tangible or intangible heritage asset base of the community. Many case examples see the power of tourism to create jobs and economic development, particularly in rural areas that are losing populations. Overtourism is seen as an issue, however, with several case examples calling for limiting the number of tourists, especially in high seasons and at particular times of the day, while others call for careful management of retail uses in historic areas. Other case examples call for responsibly managed tourism that promotes traditional and endangered local trades and crafts, thereby tying heritage conservation and tourism into larger poverty alleviation initiatives.

5

A very specific and omnipresent threat to heritage districts referred to the case examples is the expansion and development of modern transportation infrastructure to provide increased visitor access. In particular, several case examples comment on the impact of inserting modern transportation infrastructure into historic districts.

One issue that was flagged as particularly important with regard to sustainable development planning for historic districts is the need to prepare strategies that deal with social, cultural and economic equity for the residents of these heritage areas, and measure the success of development action in terms of equitable results achieved. Some case examples raise the question of whether it is reasonable or not to expect property owners to refrain from achieving the full financial potential of redevelopment of privately-owned buildings in order to maintain the sites' public heritage values. Other case examples suggest the creation of funding and investment incentive packages that would mitigate short term economic losses of property owners.

The issue of balance is a common theme raised in the case examples, as is the difficulty of achieving this balance: incorporating multiple disciplines, including history, ecology and sociology, to complement the single-minded approach to development derived from short-term economics. Some case examples express concern over how to design and manage urban areas that function successfully over time for successive generations of both citizens and tourists.

Several of the case examples identify important management strategies for promoting heritage conservation within a developmental context, such as encouraging insurance companies to provide coverage in historic areas, which would then allow building owners in these areas to obtain mortgages. The issue of resilience in post-disaster (e.g. fire or flood) management is also seen in some case examples as an important consideration. Such strategies highlight the array of issues that must be considered in an integrated and holistic planning and management approach to heritage conservation in contemporary urban settings.

Some of the case examples draw attention to the need for historically accurate, culturally correct interpretation, whether it be in the form of visitor centres, museums and historic trails, as these are an important part of telling an authentic story in historic areas, thereby raising appreciation of heritage as a public resource among both visitors and residents.

Data gathering and analysis are often cited in the case examples as important parts of the overall planning process, enabling site-specific strategies to be developed for historic districts, through the identification of the particular characteristics and needs of each area. Site specific strategies replace the need to rely on generic, planning frameworks for urban development, which may not be applicable to the unique characteristics of a particular historic district.

Given the pressures and administrative gaps identified, the case examples explicitly and implicitly call for a mindset change on the part of all of the key stakeholders. In fact, one case called for the need to "look beyond conventional guidelines and engage in dialogue with the residents". Several case examples point to a need for long-term sustainable planning and management. The current narrow focus of the role and responsibility of heritage site managers, whose mandate is limited to solving technical conservation issues, is challenged in some cases examples. These case examples point out the need to provide a wider mandate for management, beyond strictly-defined conservation issues, to involve heritage managers in the development and delivery of memorable and authentic experiences both for residents as well as visitors, as part of a sustainable strategy linking heritage conservation and tourism development. Comprehensive, multi-sectoral management plans are seen as important in incorporating conservation into urban planning and into the provision of utilities and infrastructure. Indeed, in order to achieve an integrated and holistic approach and attain shared objectives, experts in the fields of planning, heritage conservation and tourism must work together to an agreed, common plan.

Chapters 6 and 7 offer detailed case study analyses of two specific urban heritage districts, following which the array of issues and concerns relating to urban heritage planning and management will be further explored in Chapter 8.

6 Place Making in George Town, Malaysia

Neil Khor and Matt Benson

Chapter 3 provided several examples of the planning and management of urban heritage areas and their resources. This chapter describes the experience of George Town, where the government directed a top-down planning exercise, as expected of a World Heritage property. The process had significant government attention and investment, both financial and technical. Chapter 6 is organized around the topics presented in Figure 6.1.

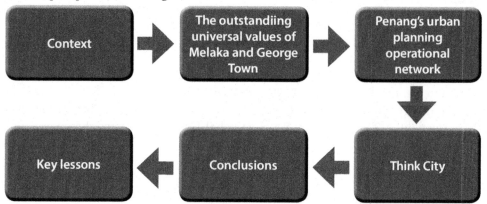

Figure 6.1: Chapter 6 topics

Context

The island of Penang in northern Malaysia (Figure 4.2) has hosted a strong tourism industry since the 1970s when the state government decided to develop the tourism industry to complement local manufacturing, as part of a strategy to generate jobs. This policy resulted in the development of the island's north coast as beachside resorts, which until the mid-1990s made Penang a top tourism destination. This beachside resort model was copied widely throughout Southeast Asia, resulting in competition from neighbouring countries, including Thailand

and Indonesia. Meanwhile, Penang's own appeal was undermined, however, by over-development and pollution.

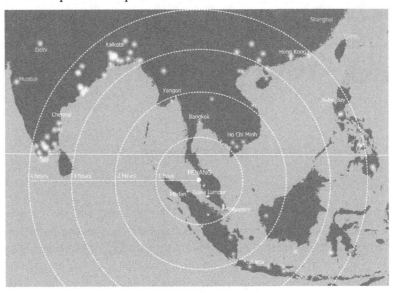

Figure 6.2: Penang

To counter their loss of a competitive advantage in the beach tourism market, the state government diversified its tourism base, through encouraging conventions, exhibitions and medical tourism. This diversification strategy had only marginal impact at first, but became a success following the inscription of Melaka and George Town on the UNESCO World Heritage list in 2008. Visitor growth and diversification has seen heritage tourism in Penang become a key market segment. A 2015 survey by Penang Global Tourism indicated that over a quarter of all tourists visited a heritage attraction during their visit to Penang. Given that as of 2017 Penang was receiving over 6.3 million hotel guests per annum (up from 5.1 million in 2007), it can be inferred that heritage is a drawcard for more than 1.5 million tourists each year (Tourism Malaysia, 2017).

Prior to the inscription of Melaka and George Town as World Heritage in 2008, the development of industrial hubs and suburbs outside the city centre, coupled with a low-income tenant population in the inner city, had led to a hollowed-out heritage core, with dilapidated building stock. A conservation and revitalization strategy, based on the renovation of neglected historic building stock and a reinvigoration of prevailing but threatened traditional trades, formed the basis of the city's World Heritage application. The successful listing provided an opportunity for the conservation and restoration of 5000 heritage buildings in the designated conservation district, as well as investment in new economic activities in the area through adaptive re-use of historic structures.

This strategy led to the introduction of the concept of a 'greater conurbation' planning catchment – as envisaged through the World Heritage inscription process. Taking into account the World Heritage property and its immediate conurbation, two things come into focus: (i) the catalytic effect of using World Heritage inscription of a small area to drive development in a larger area; and (ii) the achievement of growth through land use diversification.

The Greater Penang Conurbation concept became the basis of severerererererherage planning documents, which envision the gradual application of the planning and development principles espoused through the World Heritage Convention (UNESCO World Heritage Committee, 1972) and its operational guidelines throughout greater George Town. This approach is also designed to relieve pressure (both developmental and tourism related) on the World Heritage historic core and channel resources to neighbouring areas. Thus, heritage conservation is a consciously planned driver of development, including diversified and expanded use through visitation and tourism.

As of 2018, many of George Town's heritage assets have been conserved to varying degrees of authenticity and the city of George Town has improved its public amenities, which service both visitors and residents alike. George Town today has a number of heritage-related businesses, including boutique hotels and cafes, and restaurants specializing in local, traditional cuisine. Visitor numbers have grown and, importantly, visitors are now spread across the annual calendar, resulting in less seasonal fluctuation than in the past and fewer hotel vacancies.

As experienced elsewhere, however, UNESCO World Heritage listing has been a double-edged sword. On one hand, it has spurred investment in building conservation; generated new job opportunities for conservation-minded architects, builders and crafts people; and has given rise to a better standard of service in the hospitality industry, as well as innovations in the form of boutique heritage hotels and traditionally-themed restaurants and cafes. On the other hand, the focus on the conservation of built heritage, which became a local political priority after the repeal of rent control and the consequent threat of massive developer-driver urban renewal to replace Penang's characteristic traditional architecture, resulted in higher property prices within the protected World Heritage district and the pricing out of vulnerable communities. As more than 70% of George Town's small businesses and residents had been renting their premises prior to UNESCO listing, they were driven out by property sales, which had a negative impact on living heritage (Geografia, 2010. Thus, while the listing put Penang on the world map, giving a boost to tourism, all of this came at a price to the city's long-time residents.

The integrity of the nominated areas in Melaka and George Town is related to the presence of the elements expressing their outstanding universal value. As of 2018, the properties have largely retained their authenticity, and their listed monuments and sites have been restored with appropriate treatments regarding design, materials, methods and workmanship, and in accordance with conservation guidelines and principles.

6

The outstanding universal values of Melaka and George Town

Melaka and George Town are inscribed on the UNESCO World Heritage list as a serial property under the common title, 'Historic Cities of the Straits of Malacca'. The towns have separate origins and different chronologies, but share analogous histories. Both townships once functioned as entrepots (trading ports), attracting merchants from India, Europe, China and the Middle East. Melaka was founded at the turn of the 15th century by the Srivijayan prince Parameswara and was colonised by the Portuguese, Dutch and British at various points over 450 years. George Town was established a trading port when the Island of Penang was ceded to the English East India Company in 1786 and remained a British port until the first half of the 20th century. Today, these cities' histories are displayed through their multicultural societies, built forms, artisan traditions and crafts, as well as their intangible cultural practices, including religious rituals, local community festivals, languages, oral histories and traditional livelihoods and skills.

Figure 6.3: Aerial view of George Town

In the late-1990s, non-governmental and government agencies formed a group to begin the long process of preparing a UNESCO World Heritage nomination for the two cities. The group identified a 260 hectare (ha) area in George Town that included a core area and a buffer zone (Figure 6.5), and a 288 ha area in Melaka.

Melaka and George Town have both tangible and intangible values. As described in the UNESCO World Heritage inscription document (UNESCO World Heritage Committee, 2008),

"Melaka and George Town, Malaysia, are remarkable examples of historic colonial towns on the Straits of Malacca that demonstrate a succession of historical and cultural influences arising from their former function as trading ports linking East and West. These are the most complete surviving historic city centres on the Straits of Malacca with a multi-cultural living heritage."

Figure 6.4: George Town core and buffer zones

The World Heritage inscription described the site's outstanding universal value as follows (UNESCO World Heritage Committee, 2008):

■ Melaka and George Town represent exceptional examples of multi-cultural trading towns in East and Southeast Asia, forged from the mercantile and exchanges of Malay, Chinese, and Indian cultures and three successive European colonial powers for almost 500 years, each with its imprints on the architecture and urban form, technology and monumental art. Both towns show different stages of development and the successive changes over a long span of time and are thus complementary.

■ Melaka and George Town are living testimony to the multi-cultural heritage and tradition of Asia, and European colonial influences. This multi-cultural tangible and intangible heritage is expressed in the great variety of religious buildings of different faiths, ethnic quarters, the many languages, worship and religious festivals, dances, costumes, art and music, food, and daily life.

■ Melaka and George Town reflect a mixture of influences which have created a unique architecture, culture and townscape without parallel anywhere in East and South Asia. In particular, they demonstrate an exceptional range of shophouses and townhouses. These buildings show many different types and stages of development of the building type, some originating in the Dutch or Portuguese periods.

Penang's urban planning operational framework

Administrative districts

The State of Penang encompasses both the island of Penang and an adjacent area of the mainland (Figure 6.5). Both parts of Penang have their own municipal governments (Penang Island City Council and Seberang Prai Municipal Council), and each municipality is divided into districts. Government agencies manage the cities' infrastructure and deliver urban services at the district level. The capital of Penang is George Town.

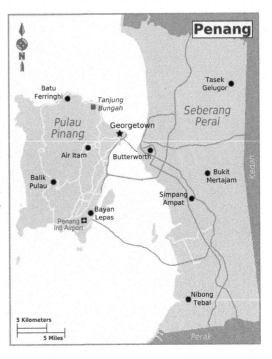

Figure 6.5: Penang administrative boundaries. https://commons.wikimedia.org/w/index.php?curid=31257157

The Malaysian planning system

The safeguarding of heritage values in Penang is embedded within Malaysia's operational framework for urban planning and management. Some of the policies and planning documents shaping the management of the Historic Cities of the Straits of Malacca World Heritage site were in operation prior to the World Heritage inscription, others evolved as a response to the inscription and the requirement for comprehensive safeguarding guarantees.

At the national level in Malaysia, physical planning is informed by five year plans, the national physical plan and various sectoral polices. These, together with state development polices, inform state structure plans, which guide the physical design layout and, ultimately, determine the physical form of cities and larger administrative regions. Land use and development guidelines are prepared at the local government level. Unique areas, such as heritage districts, can be subject to more stringent and detailed 'special area plans' (Malaysian Federal Department of Town and Country Planning, 2010).

National development plans (the 'Malaysia plans')

Melaka and George Town, as a World Heritage site, have been influenced by, and have influenced, the ninth, tenth and eleventh Malaysia plans. The Ninth Malaysia Plan (2006-2010) focused on innovation, and higher value-added and knowledge-based economic activities (Economic Planning Unit, 2005). The Tenth

Malaysia Plan (2011-2015) went a step further by explicitly acknowledging the link between the new economy, talent attraction, economic productivity and the liveability of cities. The Tenth Plan also called for concentrated development and recognised the benefits of agglomeration economies (Economic Planning Unit, 2010). The Eleventh Malaysia Plan (2016-2021) recognises that the nation's past economic success as a low-cost manufacturing centre is no longer viable and that the nation needs to make the transition to become a high value-adding innovator. It also notes that an explicit effort is required to make cities more efficient and competitive (Economic Planning Unit, 2015).

National physical plans

The National Physical Plan 2 (2010-2020) provided a spatial framework for land use, physical development and conservation in peninsular Malaysia, including the island of Penang (Ministry of Housing and Local Government, 2010). The key challenge was how to accommodate an estimated additional 6 million urban residents in Malaysian cities by 2020. The plan recognised the link between live-ability, talent retention and investment. Accordingly, the plan focused development in select centres, integrated through a hierarchy of settlements and linked by an efficient transport system. The plan called for compact, human-scale urban development; better use of brownfield land (previously-developed land that is not currently in use) so as to use existing infrastructure more efficiently; transit-oriented development; and investment in public transport. The National Physical Plan 3 (2020-2040) builds on these ideas, but places greater emphasis on the network of cities and connectivity to regional and rural areas.

Penang State Structure Plan

The Penang State Structure Plan is the overarching planning framework for land development in the state. The plan recognises that there is a hierarchy of urban centres, each with its own specialised function, and acknowledges the benefits of shifting towards a knowledge economy. This transition is supported by improved liveability, not just in the urban core, but in all communities. The plan identifies George Town as a port and transport hub, as well as a focus for heritage tourism activities and investments.

Penang Island Local Area Plan

The incipient Penang Island Local Area Plan will be aligned with federal plan-ning initiatives, but will have state-specific goals. The main emphasis will be on creating a liveable city by 2030 through sustainable development, a high quality living environment, a distinctive urban environment, an effective transportation network and a dynamic and competitive economy.

George Town Special Area Plan

Developed in 2011, the George Town Special Area Plan was officially endorsed in 2016. It is the overarching statutory document that guides the planning and development of the George Town World Heritage property. The plan outlines strategies and sets parameters for the conservation and restoration of key monuments, protection of intangible heritage, improvements to the public realm and upgrades in the areas of traffic, infrastructure and landscaping (George Town World Heritage Incorporated and Penang Island City Council, 2016).

Think City

Introduction

In 2007, the long-term potential of heritage-driven sustainable development in Penang came to the notice of Khazanah Nasional, the Government of Malaysia's investment fund. Khazanah saw the strategic potential of the town's heritage assets not merely as historical curiosity but as an extension of Penang's wider appeal to emerging creative talent. Having enjoyed double-digit growth for most of the 1980s and 1990s, Penang's low-cost manufacturing economy was at that time already stagnating as a result of competition from even lower-cost manufacturing elsewhere in Asia. At the same time, Malaysia's population profile had changed, with a shift towards a younger labour force with higher levels of post-secondary education. Given this shift, the economy required added value and more knowledge-intensive production for it to continue to prosper and expand. To achieve this, new incentives were required to attract highly mobile talent. While capital, talent and technology are capricious elements of production, Penang was an attractive magnet, particularly George Town's heritage core and, by extension, Penang's unique identity.

It was in this context that Khazanah Nasional established 'Think City', a wholly-owned subsidiary that operates as a non-profit, community-focused urban regeneration agency. Established in 2009, shortly after George Town's UNESCO World Heritage listing, Think City sought to develop innovative ways to use heritage assets, and invested in improvements to the urban public realm in George Town and also the Greater Penang Conurbation. The Think City 'approach' combined small grants with larger-scale institutional collaborations, and its investment interventions have included conservation projects, capacity building programmes and place-making initiatives. Think City's experimental and evidence-based approach to urban regeneration in George Town, based on leveraging local community's heritage assets, provides an example that can be replicated or adapted in historic towns and urban districts throughout Asia and beyond.

A key goal for Think City was to revitalise George Town's public and community-held stock of historic buildings, which had been built by successive waves of immigrants to the city and which had degraded over time due to neglect, lack of capital during the period of rent control and a lack of imagination regarding the potential of this built stock for adaptive re-use. Think City leveraged the opportunity to create new ways of thinking about heritage, stimulating both new and traditional forms of economic activity, thereby contributing to improving the liveability of Penang.

Think City's strategic approach, using George Town's heritage assets to drive urban regeneration, and thereby establishing a solid foundation for sustainable development based on historic conservation initiatives, demonstrates how a World Heritage site can become a more attractive, liveable place for local residents, counteracting many of the negatives of gentrification and tourism.

Genesis of Think City

In anticipation of George Town's inscription on the World Heritage List, Khazanah Nasional established an office in Penang, with the aim of transforming the regional economy through knowledge-based added-value activities based on the state's unique cultural heritage assets. The team recognised the link between liveability and economic productivity, and that both needed to be achieved in tandem. They also recognised that the country's experience in city and place making, although limited, had potential, especially in light of the recognition of George Town's World Heritage values. Accordingly, they developed the George Town Transformation Programme (GTTP), which sought to use the island's heritage core as a laboratory in city-making via investment in public amenities, revitalising underutilised physical cultural assets, incubating creative enterprises and crowdsourcing to finance community-based projects.

In 2009, the Malaysian Ministry of Finance allocated 50 million Malaysian ringgit (MYR), approximately 13.5 million United States dollars (USD), to support the Melaka and George Town World Heritage nomination process. For its work on the GTTP, 20 million MYR was entrusted to the Penang Khazanah Nasional team. The team established Think City as a special-purpose vehicle to manage a four-year grants programme to disburse these funds to civil society and the private sector. The 'power of small' and 'catalytic interventions' became the philosophy that would guide its initial approach to place making and the enhancement of George Town as a liveable city.

Think City's team was multi-disciplinary, led by an economist and supported by two programme directors with backgrounds in built heritage and social science. It was supported by an advisory panel of subject experts in 'city making', that is, experienced in the fields of culture, conservation, engineering, planning, transport engineering and city management. The Think City operational team was purposely designed to never exceed six persons, ensuring it did not become a self-perpetuating bureaucracy in its own right, but instead would work to support local government and communities through the mechanism of its small grants programme.

Think City's experimental approach

While the members of the Think City team were mostly local Penang residents, data was needed about the state, so one of Think City's first initiatives was to gain a better understanding of the city, its people and the issues, seeking greater detail using analytical social science frameworks. Efforts were then focused on creating awareness via educational activities and demonstration projects. In parallel, the team sought to build local capacities to underpin wider urban regeneration efforts. Higher level strategies about the role of the George Town World Heritage Site in the wider urban system were also developed, which helped guide key decisions.

Over time, the team developed a unique approach with five stages: discovery, ideation, prototype/pilot, implementation and replication (Figure 6.6). The team also engaged in a continuous process of feedback, iteration and codification, with projects being refined and improved accordingly.

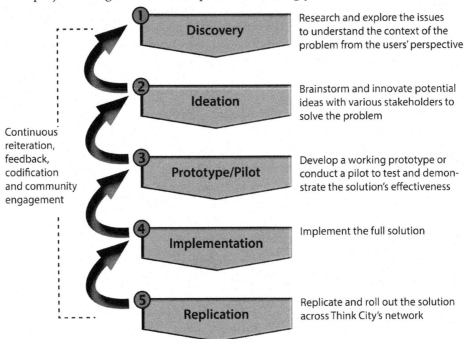

Figure 6.6: Think City's approach

Discovery

Discovery, informed by data collection and analysis, underpinned the evidence-based planning process that is fundamental to Think City's approach.

The first activity undertaken by Think City was a detailed population and land use census of the George Town World Heritage site. The data collected constituted the baseline against which the impacts of Think City's activities were subsequently measured and evaluated.

The baseline mapping method developed by Think City sought to answer fundamental questions such as how many people lived and worked in the heritage area, and how many and what types of businesses were operating in the area. The survey covered every business, residence, association, government agency, hotel, student, street stall and property within the boundaries of the George Town World Heritage site. Data was also gathered on the number of employees, residents, ethnicity, occupation, skills and modes of travel.

The data were used to identify and categorise key stakeholders and to make project implementation strategies participatory. The first survey was carried out in 2009 and a second survey was conducted in 2013, allowing Think City to monitor change. The results of the surveys were used to understand how the city changed in the years after World Heritage inscription, to profile initial urban regeneration interventions and to assess the impact of these interventions. The data gathered during the period of discovery was also used to identify key issues and bring together potential partners. The data gathering and analysis process piloted in George Town has since been used to generate over 400 initiatives in historic centres throughout Malaysia, more than half of them in Penang.

The data from the two surveys indicate that between 2009 and 2013 there was a marked shift in the local economy, from traditional trades and business services towards hospitality and tourism. Furthermore, the number of hotels increased from 61 to nearly 100 during this period (Figure 6.7). The average length of stay declined, and there was an increase in visitors from Asia. There was also a decline in the number of residents. It was from this data that Think City honed its focus on protecting intangible heritage, through supporting traditional trades and residents.

6

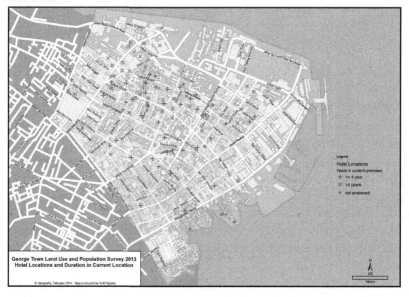

Figure 6.7: Hotels by years in current premises

Ideation: developing a common vision to work towards

Think City's ideation and planning phase involved a robust process of stakeholder engagement and community consultation. This process was facilitated, indeed catalyzed, by George Town's inscription as a World Heritage property, through which the town's outstanding universal values became the basis for the vision espoused by Think City, aligning heritage conservation with sustainable development.

Using stakeholder mapping, the team identified key players and organisations, and graphed their levels of interest versus their levels of influence (Figure 6.8). The team subsequently designed an engagement process to flesh out the key issues and identify possible solutions.

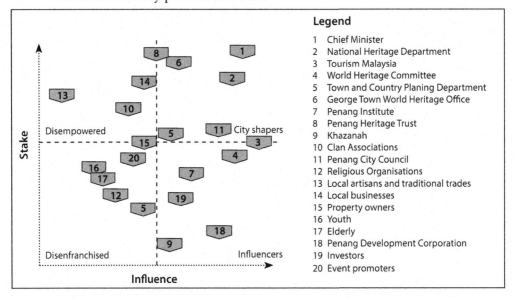

Figure 6.8: George Town stakeholders and spheres of influence

Prototypes and pilot projects

The experimental approach involved sponsoring pop-up events and activities that demonstrated how to rehabilitate and re-use run-down heritage assets and under-utilised public spaces. It also involved giving small grants to organizations to test innovative ideas that leveraged heritage assets for community development purposes. In such projects, small samples were often piloted to test the viability of various techniques. To evaluate these pilot projects, documentation was essential, particularly concerning (i) the efficacy and robustness of community engagement and (ii) the impact in terms of heritage conservation and socio-economic outcomes.

The Think City example illustrates the importance of a data-driven strategy that can track and respond to demographic changes in the community and to the multiple and evolving perspectives of the importance of heritage to community identity and prosperity. The Think City example also highlights the importance of applying best practice in conservation projects. This ensures that investment in public sector amenities, making the city more liveable, is a sustainable undertaking, with well-designed, economically-viable and physically-durable initiatives. Furthermore, the Think City example demonstrates the viability of building an economy based on endogenous cultural development rather than one relying on exogenous mass tourism.

Implementation and replication

Knowing the limitations of its projects in terms of scale and its lack of statutory control, Think City seeks to pursue small and diverse demonstrative projects. The true impact of these initiatives is their impact on local authorities and other organizations with regulatory power. In order for these projects to be replicable and achieve greater impact, it is important that they are documented and transmitted through publications, seminars and partnerships.

The following four examples demonstrate the benefits of the Think City approach.

Armenian Street Affordable Housing project

The Armenian Street Affordable Housing project is an example of how Think City used a process of engagement and collaboration to restore a heritage building and also secure the tenancy of a number of long-term residents in the building. The project began when the Hock Teik Cheng Sin Clan Association applied for a grant to restore ten shop houses on Lebuh Armenian, adjacent to their temple, in the heart of the George Town World Heritage Site. Seven of the shop houses had residential tenants that had been living there for several generations. Given that in the years prior, residents in neighbouring Cannon Square had been forcibly removed and residents in restored buildings near the Lebuh Acheh Malay Mosque had to relocate, the Hock Teik tenants were anxious. The prospect of them being evicted during restoration or paying higher rents was high.

In view of the data collected through the survey, the Think City team was well aware of the declining population and increasing property prices in George Town, so therefore sought a way to avoid the issues of out-migration and gentrification. Think City facilitated a series of meetings between the property owners, tenants and the Asian Coalition for Housing Rights. Through these meetings, a microloan scheme was negotiated through which residents secured long-term, low-cost tenancy arrangements in exchange for a contribution to internal refurbishment of the shop houses. Think City and the Hock Teik Cheng Sin Clan Association financed the repairs to the roofs and structure of the shop houses and the façade improvements.

The success of the project primarily came down to a deep understanding of the city's issues, and a desire to minimise social dislocation. In the words of Khoo Kay Hean, trustee of the Hock Teik Cheng Sin, the arrangement was "a win-win policy because we help them and they help us to maintain the property. It is not just about money, it is also about heritage. If it were just about the money, we would have teamed up with a project partner to turn the place into a hotel or allowed eateries to set up shop."

Armenian Park place-making initiative

Another example of an effective process of community engagement and collaboration was the Armenian Park project. This project, undertaken in partnership with the Penang state government, the local council and the Aga Khan Trust for Culture in 2015 and 2016, was a major place-making initiative in an under-utilised open space in the heart of George Town. It was designed to create a multi-purpose community hub encompassing recreation amenities, pedestrian accessibility, meeting spaces and a museum.

The initiative was part of a city-wide collaboration to enhance the public realm in George Town so as to address a major issue facing many Malaysian historic city centres: population decline, in particular the loss of young families. By investing heavily in the public realm, Think City and its project partners aimed to improve liveability and attract residents back into the World Heritage site. The project sought to catalyze and anchor a wider revitalization of the neighbourhood by improving the quality of life of existing residents.

Following an extensive consultation process, the Armenian Park (Lebuh Armenian/Acheh) precinct improvement project began with enhancing the main public open space. This space was chosen to highlight the communal heritage value of the area, as well as to provide recreation amenities for both residents and visitors. The upgrade included above-compliance universal access principles (e.g. installation of Braille signage and wheelchair-friendly paths), perimeter fencing and shrubbery, lawns, seating, lighting and preservation of existing trees. The subsequent phases of the project included upgrades to the community centre and back lanes, along with the restoration of Syed al-Attas Mansion, adjacent to the site.

Post-construction resident surveys indicate that the project delivered social, economic and environmental benefits to the residents. As a result of the project, residents use the park in greater numbers and for various purposes. Residents also have greater community spirit and are more positive with regard to cleanliness/maintenance, personal safety and noise levels in the neighbourhood. Since completion, the open space has accommodated various community, cultural and sporting events. The Armenian Park upgrade has also spawned economic activity by drawing tourists and visitors to the area, which has benefitted local businesses. As residents are attracted back into the area, they will provide additional customers to local businesses and enhance the vibrancy of the area. Environmental benefits of the project include moderating the inner city's heat island effect, making walking more attractive, and encouraging native fauna into the area (through planting native flora).

The Armenian Park project embodies best-practice planning and place making methods that can be implemented elsewhere. These include using an evidence base to inform planning; ensuring amenity improvements are part of a city-wide public realm improvement plan; community engagement; collaboration; thoughtful design practices that respect local values; ethnical contractor choices; and post-construction place activation methods. The project demonstrates how a detailed and holistic planning process can lead to a marked increase in the community's wellbeing and quality of life.

Fort Cornwallis and the northern seafront rehabilitation

The process of planning for the rehabilitation of Fort Cornwallis and the northern seafront adjacent to the fort is a good example of Think City's approach. The fort – the focal point of George Town's historic World Heritage – is a key national heritage monument. The area described as George Town's northern seafront includes the town's esplanade and a number of prominent public buildings. Covering more than 20 hectares of public space, it is the city's main civic and cultural centre, as well as a popular place for social gatherings. In recent decades, however, the area has been cut off from the rest of the city by a high-speed vehicular artery, which has reduced public access and use of the historic space.

Planning for this project was carried out on multiple levels, from an initial public realm addendum (PRA) of the Special Area Plan, to a detailed conservation management plan for Fort Cornwallis. The community consultation process ensured that the interventions were in keeping with the needs of the local community instead of being tourist-centric.

The rehabilitation project included improving pedestrian movement, landscaping work and a drainage upgrade. Although these initiatives are very much a fixture of contemporary urban design, the underpinning ethos was based on the historical use of the area and historical documents, which allowed for the reinstatement of authentic historic spaces and their uses. For instance, the Kelly Maps of the late 19th century were used to identify recent transformations, and historical photographs were consulted to identify the role played by the area in George Town's socio-cultural life.

The conservation of Fort Cornwallis included the restoration of its original moat, which was filled and had since been covered by a succession of temporary constructions, including a children's playground, a hawker food centre and parking facilities. The restoration of the moat necessitated the relocation of these facilities to avoid conflict between heritage conservation and modern needs. A process of negotiation and the recognition that dimensions of the past could be incorporated into a present-day vision resolved the issue to the satisfaction of all concerned parties. Figure 6.9 provides an impression of the completed northern seafront works.

6

Figure 6.9: Artist's impression of the northern seafront concept

To convey the value of the site to the general public and link the past to current community concerns, the Think City team developed a public archaeology programme in tandem with the conservation project that encouraged community participation in the conservation process.

George Town Festival

Through its small grants programme, Think City developed various community projects involving conservation, capacity building and inter-cultural activities. One example of this is the George Town Festival. It began when Think City provided a small grant to the Penang Heritage Trust to study the feasibility of establishing a traditional performing arts festival. The conclusion of the study was that it would be unwise to unstitch traditional performances from their natural contexts, and that if an arts festival was to be implemented it should instead celebrate the inscription of George Town as a World Heritage property and showcase the outstanding universal values recognised by that inscription. The key ingredient of the festival would be inter-cultural experiences, made possible through the animation of the many unique cultural spaces of George Town.

It was in this spirit that Think City set aside funding to support community participation in the George Town Festival. Starting in 2010, Think City's community partners, particularly in the 'Street of Harmony' (Jalan KapitanKeling), opened their premises and held cultural performances and exhibitions. This led to the establishment of a community-informed 'way-finding system' for George Town. This is a self-guiding heritage trail along which both local residents and visitors alike explore the streets and alleys of historic George Town and discover through their own individual experiences the cultural spaces where the outstanding universal values – both tangible and intangible – of George Town are manifest as part of the life of the city. This initiative was coordinated by the city's World Heritage site management agency, George Town World Heritage Incorporated (GTWHI), which was at the time under the leadership of Maimunah Sharif, who later became the Executive Director of the United Nations Human Settlements Programme (UN-Habitat).

Conclusions and key ideas

The approach modelled by Think City in George Town has proven to be an effective means of aligning conservation and development in a living community whose historic urban landscape is of global World Heritage significance. Some of the key ideas underpinning the Think City approach are as follows:

Leadership and consensus on values

To be an effective and neutral platform to galvanise and widen participation, it was important for Think City to present the big picture objectively and the future vision coherently, with considerable detail. The stakeholder engagement process reached consensus on the idea that the values articulated through the World Heritage nomination and inscription process made George Town unique and served to underpin the city's future place making activities. What stakeholders did not want was a 'pickling' process, in which the city would be preserved like a museum exhibit.

Mainstreaming

Think City recognised that in the context of George Town development planning must be based on both heritage resources and economic realities. The process adopted by Think City involves pulling together the evidence, establishing an effective engagement process and applying lessons from previous initiatives, then combining these with a strong overarching vision, a master plan and onsite monitoring. In keeping with the prototype approach, new or untried methods are tested before widespread implementation. Contractors are monitored through daily meetings. Documentation and codification run in parallel. The process of engagement is continued through high quality hoardings and stakeholder communication. In other words, of the Think City approach is an experimental, but rigorous and iterative process.

Capacity building

Think City has sought to learn lessons from others, as well as to transmit experiential learning through sponsoring courses in urban planning, conservation and place making. For example, Think City, in partnership with the Getty Conservation Institute and Badan Warisan Malaysia, offered a course titled 'Urban Conservation Planning in Malaysia' on three occasions between 2012 and 2015. The course was primarily targeted at mid-career urban planners, with the aim of introducing new conservation methods and tools to their work. The course covered topics such as cultural mapping, conservation master plans, heritage impact assessments, the Burra Charter and the economic arguments for conservation.

As of 2018, Think City and the Getty Conservation Institute are working towards a five-year education programme based in Penang that will establish George Town as a centre of excellence in conservation. Reiteration of the methods in multiple practice examples will enable short-term courses to contribute to

6

sustainable conservation efforts. The course will cover values-based management of a World Heritage property, conservation methods for Southeast Asian shop houses and sustainable management of tourism in historic cities.

George Town laboratory

George Town is a laboratory for an approach to planning, design and management of an urban World Heritage site that is design-driven and knowledge- and community-based. What it illustrates is that the planning process, while often a top-down government-sponsored process, can also be mediated by strong community engagement, and it should be if the result is to enhance the local quality of life and be sustainable.

The key to the success of this planning approach lies in having a well-resourced, knowledge-based, data-savvy, non-partisan organisation such as Think City, with deep roots and acknowledged credibility in the local community to drive its implementation. The approach, in which Think City provided an evidence-based neutral platform, was initiated by a coalition of community stakeholders who leveraged the national and local mechanism of territorial planning, supported by government financial and technical expertise. This approach won over the private sector, particularly businesses and property owners. Without the active support of people, public and private partnerships, the plans would have remained academic. Think City documented its results in reports and publications, which enable the lessons learned to be disseminated and allow others to learn from George Town's conservation and development efforts. Think City's models and initiatives have been applied in a variety of urban planning environments, proving their effectiveness.

Key lessons

Lessons that can be drawn from the Think City approach include the following:

- A successful mix of heritage conservation and tourism requires sufficient funding as well as leaders who understand the need for a thorough process of planning, design and documentation.

- The starting point for bringing key stakeholders together is a vision for the city that clearly articulates its unique features and sense of place. A strong sense of place translates into committed, active participation by citizens in the conservation process.

- A robust database, which can reliably inform decision-making, requires professional and thorough cultural and geographical mapping. Mapping and data collection are best carried out in partnership with the local government to ensure that a single data set is compiled and used by the stakeholders.

- An integrated approach to the planning and implementation of development initiatives in historic areas requires a thorough understanding of the international standards, professional charters, national policies and local planning initiatives that impact upon the areas.

- Avoiding the issues associated with over-tourism requires understanding carrying capacity and the need to set limits of change and enforce those limits.

- Successful programmes require the up-skilling of local professional institutions, practitioners and community operatives to the highest international standards.

- Effective capacity building programmes require engaging qualified local stakeholders in the process.

- Financial support is essential for a successful plan-led approach. For example, the small grants programme was key to winning over businesses and private property owners and to encouraging experimentation with new ideas involving technology and community-led city-making projects.

- The process of ideation must be linked with an ongoing process of testing and feedback. Some projects will not be as successful as others, and it is as important to learn from failures as it is to celebrate successes. Transparency and an open attitude to learning from mistakes are essential.

- Maintaining consensus and resolving conflicts require establishing robust platforms for public participation that include a transparent and incorruptible system of heritage impact assessment that can be applied to all development projects, both public and private, regardless of the source of financing for those projects.

- Documentation is essential. The skills and knowledge gained through pilot projects in urban heritage conservation (lessons learned) must be shared widely and pilot projects upscaled or replicated/adapted elsewhere.

6

References

Economic Planning Unit. (2005). *Ninth Malaysia Plan*, Federal Government of Malaysia, Putrajaya.

Economic Planning Unit. (2010). *Tenth Malaysia Plan*, Federal Government of Malaysia, Putrajaya.

Economic Planning Unit. (2015). *Eleventh Malaysia Plan*, Federal Government of Malaysia, Putrajaya.

Geografia. (2010). *George Town World Heritage Site Baseline Study*, Think City, Penang

Geografia. (2014). *George Town Conurbation Spatial Strategy*, Think City, Penang.

Geografia. (2015). *Fort Cornwallis: Visitor study (draft) 2015*, Think City, Penang.

George Town World Heritage Inc. (2016). *George Town: Historic cities of the straits of Malacca: Special area plan*. George Town, Penang: State Government of Penang.

Malaysian Federal Department of Town and Country Planning. (2018). *National Physical Plan 2 2017*. Ministry of Housing and Local Government.

UNESCO World Heritage Committee. (n.a). *World Heritage Convention*. Retrieved from https://whc.unesco.org/en/convention/

UNESCO World Heritage Committee. (2008). *Melaka and George Town, Historic Cities of the Straits of Malacca*. UNESCO. Retrieved from https://whc.unesco.org/en/list/1223

7 Creative District Bangkok: Changes at the Fringe

Introduction

The George Town case study provided insights into the planning, design and management process for a World Heritage site, which carries with it a series of requirements for authentic development and management. The case study also provided an example of a situation in which significant resources were devoted to the conservation process using what was, at least initially, a top-down approach. In contrast, the Creative District Bangkok case study is a bottom-up approach that drew on scarce financial and human resources. Chapter 7 is organized around a number of topics illustrated in Figure 7.1.

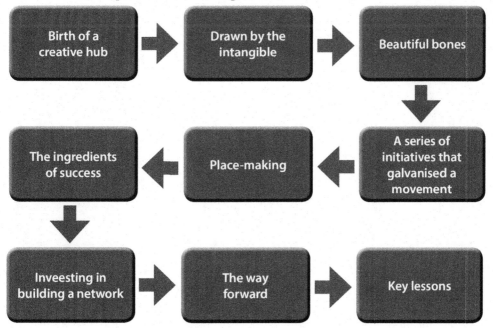

Figure 7.1: Chapter 7 topics

Background

West Bang Rak is a neighbourhood of Bangkok with an area of around 153 acres. It has three main segments. The southern segment is arguably the most vibrant, with two distinct communities creating one of Bangkok's better-known street food hubs. The middle segment, which is much calmer, is a legacy silver and jewellery district that is frequented by contemporary designers, artists and their patrons. The northern segment borders Chinatown and many of its old shop houses are being reclaimed for personal projects. Different as these segments may seem, each has an entrepreneurial spirit that pervades the area and the residents.

Together with many other tangible and intangible elements, the small businesses of West Bang Rak are what make it a diverse and creative district. 'Mom and pop' stores and boutiques dominate the area, with few chain stores. Restaurant owners and street food vendors serve their signature dishes to regular customers throughout the day. Gallery owners showcase exhibits and serve niche clients interested in certain styles and types of artwork. Deeper in the side streets, design shops sell specialised products and services that complement each other. In the evenings, bars with unique themes and characteristics receive guests, both from within the area and elsewhere.

Figure 7.2: Chao Phraya River

Only five years ago, one would have never imagined the vibrancy felt in West Bang Rak today. The area has many things working against it. One of those is its location; it is cut off from the rest of Bangkok by Sri Rat Expressway on its east side, while its southern border is essentially the entire length of the Saphan

Taksin Bridge ramp. Its west side is bounded by the Chao Phraya River, which is considered by Bangkok residents as being on the fringe of the city, while its northern border is far from the main roads leading to the centre of the city. For anyone living in car-reliant Bangkok, West Bang Rak seems an undesirable location for both homes and businesses.

The neighbourhood's layout and state of its street network does not encourage mobility. West Bang Rak has just one arterial road, Charoenkrung Road, and the small street offshoots are not linked with one another. This is a legacy of the city's early ribbon development, which has led to poor traffic flow, encouraged sprawl and created isolated blocks. Charoenkrung Road is considered narrow for a main road and is often congested during rush hour.

Figure 7.3: Traffic conditions in the district

Birth of a creative hub

Despite these challenges, West Bang Rak gradually attracted various new businesses. These did not displace existing enterprises but, in almost all cases, occupied empty properties, and they regularly organized events that brought new people and attention to the area. Seeing this, some older establishments in the area, spurred by this new energy and competition, began to do the same. Several businesses and organizations began to collaborate on activities that promoted places and events, including on social media and in lifestyle publications. Within a few short years, the area was officially dubbed 'the heart of a new creative district'. Against all odds, West Bang Rak overcame its shortcomings and generated its own urban revival.

From an outsider's perspective, West Bang Rak's evolution into a creative hub seems uncoordinated, without any real organization or vision. However, beneath the seemingly disparate residents and businesses lay several networks with a shared vision of building a more vibrant neighbourhood. Various stakeholders had developed plans and together had brought about people-driven change. To understand what occurred, it is necessary to dig deeper and examine the key individuals and events that sparked this change, and to understand the mindsets of the 'first movers', and of those who joined later as well as those who saw an opportunity to bring it all together.

Drawn in by the intangible

In 2006, after years of living abroad, Shane Suvikapakornkul moved back to Bangkok. Upon arriving, he pursued his passion for Asian art books and book publishing. While the book business seemed to be under duress from digitization, Shane saw that the art book sector was relatively stable as customers in this market still required their books in a physical and tactile format. Shane began searching for a place to set up his art book publishing house. A friend recommended that he look at a newly-renovated historic house-turned-retail compound called O.P. Garden in West Bang Rak. He immediately saw the potential of the area and launched Serindia Gallery in 2009 to showcase both books and art.

Figure 7.4: Serindia Gallery and ATTA Gallery

Not long afterwards, Atty Tantivit, a a marine resource management and policy graduate-turned-gallerist, began hunting for a new space for her contemporary jewellery gallery. Following her return from Florence, Italy, she saw a gap in the jewellery market in Bangkok – almost no one was selling wearable contemporary art. Bangkok seemed ready for this kind of enterprise. The plan was to create a space that local and international jewellery artists could use to enter the Thai market. As Atty explored West Bang Rak, she sensed something entirely different from the Bangkok she was accustomed to. Located far from the giant retail outlets on Sukhumvit Road, the area surrounding Charoenkrung Road and its side streets had retained its soul and authenticity. Serindia Gallery's presence provided an important precedent and Atty opened ATTA Gallery at O.P. Garden in 2010.

Graphic designer Lee Anathawat had just graduated from university in Australia and had returned to Bangkok in 2010 when a colleague reached out to her with an interesting proposition – join her company that was renting out an old three-storey shop house as a shared office space. The activities in the area around the office intrigued her. For example, a woman had set up a makeshift restaurant just a few steps away, attracting locals. Down the alley was an elderly man making lanterns and painting them with Chinese characters. Around the corner was a tailor who received orders from across Bangkok. Attracted by this low-key but authentic buzz, Lee went to work in the shop house and, after finding more partners, eventually opened Speedy Grandma on the ground floor of the shop house, a gallery devoted to experimental art.

For years, award-winning architecture firm DBALP had been located in Siam Tower in downtown Bangkok. The firm's founder, Duangrit Bunnag, became aware of an unused warehouse complex on the river bank directly opposite West Bang Rak. He had always harboured a dream of retrofitting a warehouse in Bangkok and this was the first that met his requirements. Despite its remoteness, Duangrit was convinced that the complex would make a great office location. There was a busy public wet market next door and if he or any of his staff needed to cross the river, a small ferry pier was only steps away. The river itself played a major role in influencing his decision. It reminded him of the Thames in London and evoked memories of his time spent in the creative East London. Duangrit and his staff were accustomed to the modern amenities that their location in Siam Tower offered, so the announcement of his intention to move DBALP to the warehouse was met with scepticism. Duangrit overcame the objections, however, and in 2013 they renovated the complex into a compound they called the Jam Factory.

Australian businessman David Robinson left his corporate job in 2002 to volunteer with ActionAid in Southeast Asia. David had fallen for Thailand and decided to stay and call Bangkok his home. Over the years he saw the city evolve and was there to witness a gradual increase in the demand for local contemporary art and culture. He became acquainted with designers who had stationed themselves in West Bang Rak and started frequenting the locale. At the time, the neighbourhood featured a few luxury hotels and some creative establishments but lacked any vitality. From his perspective, the Chao Phraya River was a sadly overlooked and underused asset. In Sydney and London, where he had lived in the past, the waterfronts were well developed and treasured. He frequented the area to enjoy its unique features.

Many others also discovered the area and decided to move there. These new residents and entrepreneurs were drawn to the area for a number of reasons. Some were motivated by the character of the neighbourhood, as expressed through its communities and residents. Others were looking for something different and unique. These first movers to west Bang Rak might not have realized it then, but they subconsciously recognized elements that made the area special. In fact, a common theme among the individuals who saw the potential of the area was that they had all spent some time abroad, for education or work. They had therefore been exposed to different cultures and had experienced life in other major capitals. It is perhaps this experience that encouraged the kind of lateral thinking that allowed them to see West Bang Rak's potential.

Beautiful bones

Many of the first movers were drawn by both the tangible and intangible assets of the district. The beautiful bones had been waiting for the right group of people with the vision to see the potential and put an end to the district's gradual decline.

West Bang Rak's streetscape is fascinating. After the fall of Ayutthaya, the Portuguese were given land (now Talat Noi) directly north of West Bang Rak to settle in. During the reign of Rama III, the growing European community was allowed to base itself in West Bang Rak, resulting in European businesses and consulates being originally grouped in this district, thus creating Bangkok's first unofficial European quarter. This contingent of Europeans later petitioned Rama IV to build a new road parallel to the river, which became Charoenkrung Road, the main arterial road that runs through West Bang Rak. With this act, they became instrumental in introducing roads to the Siamese capital. Thailand's European connection is thus rightfully reflected in the area.

Figure 7.5: Typical shop houses

Almost the entire stretch of Charoenkrung Road is lined with aging shop houses. Joined wall-to-wall, they form a seemingly endless row that is punctuated only by a few side streets and larger buildings. These shop houses are of different eras and are a mix of facades, which architecture and urban planning academics often come to study. They are poorly maintained, but their condition has a sense of elegant decay. With an average of four storeys, the shop houses create a human-scale experience for people exploring the area.

The side streets reveal a wealth of historical buildings that include houses of worship of all the major religions, old Thai houses and several defunct office and commercial spaces that are distinctly European in design and style. A major landmark is the derelict Old Customs House, once Bangkok's gateway for traders bringing goods in and out of the city. It was designed by Joachim Grassi, an Italian architect employed by the royal family during Thailand's modernization period.

Figure 7.6: The Old Customs House

Another key structure is the East Asiatic Company building, which served as the regional headquarters of Hans Niels Andersen, a Danish captain who established a shipping line between Copenhagen and Bangkok. Down at Captain Bush Lane, House No. 1 once served as the office of Societe Francaise des Distilleries de l'Indochine. Other European buildings include Assumption Cathedral and Grand Postal Office Building. Bangkok is not particularly known as a walking city, so West Bang Rak is surprising. It has some of the best sidewalks in the capital. Possibly a legacy of the time before the rise of automobiles, the district's sidewalks are fairly wide and well maintained. Indeed, an assessment of the walkability of Bangkok's districts by GoodWalk, a project by Chulalongkorn University's Urban Development and Design Center, ranked Bang Rak above all other districts. Pedestrians are also encouraged by the open porch running along the front of the shop houses on Charoenkrung Road that shields walkers from the sun and rain.

Figure 7.7: The East Asiatic Company Building

While the history and infrastructure provide compelling visual interest and storytelling potential, it is the communities in the West Bang Rak area that bring life and authenticity. The Baan Ou Mosque and Prince Theatre communities form the heart of the district. Together, they support one of Bangkok's most famed street food hubs where vendors sell diverse dishes throughout the day and evening. It is one of the most competitive food markets in the city, with vendors vying to be the best. A common saying among vendors here is that, 'If your food isn't delicious, your stall won't survive in Bang Rak'.

Figure 7.8: Prince Theatre

A series of initiatives that galvanized a movement

As West Bang Rak gained new tenants, rapid changes occurred. The increasing number of galleries in the area meant more exhibitions and events. One such event was the Embassy of France's 'La Fete' (French Thai cultural festival), which was gradually embraced by West Bang Rak's contingent of galleries, thus giving Bangkokians a reason to walk through the district. 'La Fete' reminded Atty Tantivit of her time as a student in Miami where she would go to the Coral Gables district for 'galleries night'. The welcoming and festive mood at these events allowed her to enter art galleries without feeling intimidated or judged. Inspired by La Fete and her past experience in Miami, she contacted the gallery owners in West Bang Rak, including Shane Suvikapakornkul, Duangrit Bunnag and Lee Ananthawat, and suggested that they create their own galleries nights.

Across the river, Duangrit Bunnag had opened up The Jam Factory Gallery, the Library Cafe, and Candide Books, creating a mixed-use commercial space that would encourage people to linger in the locale. He then launched his first foray into the food world: The Never Ending Summer, a restaurant housed in his riverside warehouse complex. He also started hosting The Knack Market, a monthly art and food fair that offers vendors a lower rental rate for booth space than the average pop-up market in Bangkok. These offerings caused visitors to flock to the area.

The compound effect of these initiatives began to shape the identity of the area. In 2015, David Robinson, observing the activities, invited the individuals he saw shaping the neighbourhood to a meeting. While these key players were familiar with one another's work, they did not know each other personally. Once together, they realized they shared similar values and had a common vision for the area. At the first meeting, it was agreed that they would work together and collaborate to mutually benefit one another while giving back to the area. That meeting was to be a precursor to many public 'town hall meetings'.

Encouraged by this positive outcome, David called for regular meetings, including both one-on-ones and group events. In a matter of months, he managed to bring together artists, entrepreneurs, writers, gallery owners and many others, including design experts. For instance, with the relocation of the headquarters of the Thailand Creative and Design Center (TCDC) to the Grand Postal Office Building in West Bang Rak on the horizon, staff of the TCDC began to participate in the meetings. Staff of the Bangkok Metropolitan Administration (BMA) also began attending. The participation of the BMA was brought about by Yongtanit Pimonsathean, an internationally-known heritage design professional and a professor in the Urban Design Department International (UDDI) at Thammasat University. He recognized David's meetings for what they could become: a citizen-driven project to improve the city, something that Bangkok was lacking at the time, so he encouraged BMA staff to attend the meetings. David held the meetings in several locations in West Bang Rak, encouraging people to experience

7

the area. He facilitated discussions and moved the conversation towards what could be achieved through a coordinated effort.

Figure 7.9: The Grand Postal Office Building

More meetings attracted more people and soon a loose network of individuals was formed. It was during this time that the network formalized a vision: the formation of a creative hub. Rather than creating something out of nothing, the group decided to follow what was organically growing before their eyes and they committed to throwing their support behind a neighbourhood that was clearly becoming a hub for creative work. The group held a workshop that identified 20 potential initiatives to develop the area in the desired direction. Yongtanit suggested that boundaries for the district be drawn to clearly align the government with citizens on what area this experimental movement was focused on. The boundaries, which include West Bang Rak and East Klong San on the opposite side of the river, would come to define the present-day Creative District. The group quickly developed credibility and the loose network of people was recognized with the Wallpaper award in 2015 for 'Design Movement of the Year'. By late 2015, they were unofficially dubbed the Creative District group.

Place making and place branding with street art

The Creative District group began working in earnest toward selecting which of the 20 initiatives to implement first. The group sought projects that would require little time and energy but which would return a relatively high value to the neighbourhood. As the deliberation process went on, the group looked to George Town in Penang, the revival of which was generating a global buzz. Penang's street art, in particular, was being highlighted. The Creative District group decided that street art could be key to 'jumpstarting' the neighbourhood.

Around the same time, Nicolas Dali and Myrtille Tibeyranc were in the planning phase of the second edition of BUKRUK, an urban art festival. The first edition, in 2013, had been a great success, bringing together 30 artists from across Asia and Europe and covering more than 400 square metres of indoor exhibition space in the Bangkok Art and Culture Centre as well as over 1000 square metres of exterior walls. The duo intended to expand the second edition of BUKRUK by moving to a different location and taking it to the streets. Their first choice was Talat Noi, a dense and walkable neighbourhood immediately north of West Bang Rak. The plan was to select walls in the area, paint them and create a walking trail for viewers to appreciate street art.

Figure 7.10: Street art from the BUKRUK Urban Arts Festival

The Creative District group became aware of BUKRUK II and immediately reached out to the team for possible collaboration. The two groups realized that they had a shared vision and agreed to work together. The Creative District group agreed to support BUKRUK II wherever they had gaps and, in exchange, the street art locations would be expanded into West Bang Rak. Yongtanit Pimonsathean stepped in to help connect with representatives of the Crown Property Bureau and to ask for permission to paint on their walls. David Robinson was successful in getting support from Shangri-La Hotel Bangkok, which supported the event as their community project and provided accommodation for the visiting artists. Duangrit Bunnag offered the Jam Factory as the launch party venue. Many others also contributed in ways they could. By the start of 2016, everything was in place for the second urban arts festival to begin.

BUKRUK II was an instant success. Residual interest from the first edition was re-ignited and culture-hungry Bangkokians and tourists flocked to the riverside in January 2016 for ten days of wall art, art exhibitions, artist talks, animation, music nights, visual performances, mapping projections and workshops. Media coverage was extensive and showcased the area. The BUKRUK team was recognized for its hard work in successfully staging an ambitious festival. The Creative District group also benefitted. The street art cemented a visual identity for West Bang Rak as part of the nascent 'creative district'. It also increased foot traffic in the area, bringing more patrons to local businesses. Charoenkrung Road drew pedestrians intent on finding the murals and with time to explore what the area had to offer. Furthermore, BUKRUK II's success supported efforts to promote Bangkok as a cultural capital that offered more than just the traditional arts.

The ingredients of success

Within six months of the launch of their efforts to revive West Bang Rak, the Creative District group had completed one of its initiatives: street art. This had been achieved through supporting and working in collaboration with another group that had a shared vision. The speed at which they achieved their objective took the group by surprise. Sensing a window of opportunity, representatives of the Creative District group began to vigorously promote and 'place brand' the area. Some contacted publications to feature various elements of the locale, while others began giving presentations at key events and institutions discussing design and the city.

The group was often asked why the BUKRUK II project was successful, which prompted the group to reflect on the ingredients of success. They realized that the key factor in the success of BUKRUK II was collaboration. The Creative District group saw that Bangkok was full of organizations, with experience and knowledge in their fields of expertise, working towards fulfilling their particular interests and visions. With a very broad vision of reviving a neighbourhood, the Creative District group was a generalist organization, but by collaborating with the BUKRUK team, a specialist in street art, the Creative District group did not have to learn everything related to street art, they could instead could draw on the BUKRUK team's expertise to help realize one of their objectives. Going forward, the group was cognisant of the need to collaborate with other specialized organizations. Having worked with BUKRUK II, the Creative District group determined its own value proposition: its strong and wide social network and capacity to form partnerships and alliances and to find resources.

The first partnership was successful due to shared values and ethos, and a common vision. Both partners had believed in the positive effects of street art and both believed in responsibly improving the neighbourhood without disrupting the way of life in the area. Both were open to collaborating and sharing resources. Furthermore, both shared the same work ethic and felt the same urgency to deliver results. The Creative District group recognized that partners in any future collaboration must have similar traits and beliefs for projects to be implemented smoothly. With these lessons, the Creative District group developed its working process.

The First Hurdle

As the team moved forward, they recognised that they would need further financial and human resources, which were obtainable through grants. However, to do this required that they go from being a group of loosely affiliated individuals to establishing an official organization. The group realised this in 2016 when a private foundation offered them seed funding to build their infrastructure, but the foundation only worked with registered groups that had official bank accounts. In the same year, the Creative District group received an offer from a company to support the conversion of an abandoned movie theatre into a community centre and arts venue. The donation was part of the company's corporate social responsibility activities, so could only be made to a registered organization. Trust and accountability was understandably an issue. It was at this point that the Creative District group made the decision to register their organization. The group then began a long journey to become a non-profit foundation committed to fostering creativity and using it to develop communities in the West Bang Rak area.

Investing in building a strong network

The approval process for foundations was lengthy and while waiting for the legal green light the offer of funding from the private foundation expired. Likewise, the lease for the movie theatre conversion went to another organization. The group decided to use the waiting time to build relationships and spread its mission and message. This became an important step in their future success. The network that was created at this time could later be instantly activated when the time was right.

The group hosted town hall meetings and small events to connect with new groups and to update the general public on its activities. The group also met with many individuals and organizations working on topics that aligned with the group's ethos and informed them that a support network was being built. Through this process, the Creative District group discovered that active citizenship in Bangkok was well and alive, though not fully embraced by the government and media.

Beyond activist groups, there were many other voices with ideas waiting to be heard and with energy to be redirected to improve the city. Bangkok society had matured and moved beyond a quest for material wealth. Many in the community were pursuing a better quality of life, and not just for some but for all. The problem was a lack of confidence and the general perception that no one cared. The meetings held by the Creative Design group featured more and more expressions of excitement about the future and the advantages the Creative District group network could offer. This built even more confidence among the members of the group in what they were doing.

At the same time as encouraging community voices to be heard, the group proactively connected the various entities in its ever-growing network. With the Creative District group's comprehensive knowledge of the network members' activities, it knew how each member could connect with others to maximize their success. Creatives were connected with event organizers. Companies with activists looking for corporate social responsibility support. Funders to NGOs. Embassies with academic institutions. Through this the group built a reputation as a facilitator, freely and willingly creating relationships to make projects possible and successful, through collaboration and the sharing of resources. The Creative District group, in turn, learned more about how groups and sectors could work together and could challenge how these groups and sectors had previously operated.

Becoming a platform and renewal

In late 2017, the group was notified that its application was successful and it officially became the Creative District Foundation (CDF). Via the many lessons learned during 2016 and 2017, the CDF decided it would no longer lead projects by itself. Rather, it would throw its full weight behind individuals and groups that were working in ways that aligned with the foundation's belief in responsible development of the defined creative district area and the communities in it. The CDF would serve as a node through which to find the resources other groups needed. The CDF thereby became a platform through which to establish critical connections, share resources and find support to achieve objectives.

As soon as it received the notification, the CDF hosted a town hall meeting to announce its new legal status, to update the community on its new operational model and to provide an opportunity for groups to present new initiatives planned in the area. The meeting, which drew 150 attendees, also collected feedback on the proposed initiatives, which CDF later responded to.

The CDF decided that the platform mechanism would work best in a digital format. The online platform, which they will have to build, would serve as both a knowledge repository and a project directory. In this way, the general public could freely access information and also share ideas and submit projects to the foundation. CDF was aware, however, that passive technology would not be sufficient. The foundation therefore decided that it would play an active part in seeking individuals and organizations to join the platform, in facilitating linkages and in providing support to the many voices in favour of the renewal and conservation process in West Bang Rak. In this way, the CDF's role would be to ensure that individuals and organizations met with the right people and were able to do what they wanted to do, while bringing benefits to the Creative District. The CDF would also engage in various initiatives, including community improvement, culture preservation, business development and environmental conservation. The foundation's mechanism would be to encourage organic growth from the community level, and to meet top-down governmental objectives halfway.

The way forward

The way forward for the CDF is filled with hope and opportunities but is also fraught with challenges and risks. While CDF's role has much support, the foundation faces a number of challenges. One such is the sustainability of its operating model. The foundation seeks diverse funding sources rather than the support of one single endowment, as the latter could compromise the foundation's neutrality and independence, which are essential in achieving its vision. The CDF does not wish to become beholden to any other organization's agenda. As such, the foundation intends to include some operational fees in the budgets of initiatives that obtain funding with its support. This should keep the central operations running, but it remains to be seen. The group recognizes the fragility of its financing as it relates to its governance and is actively seeking ways to become more self-reliant.

The focus of CDF, according to several members including David Robinson, Atty Tantivit and Shane Suvarnipakornkul, is the local community and local businesses. Recognizing that threats exist, the CDF has expanded its scope somewhat, in that it seeks to not only support initiatives that benefit the West Bang Rak community but it also seeks to protect the community from displacement, which, due to unregulated development, threatens communities across Bangkok. Every project submitted to the CDF must therefore be community-focused. Project documents must state how they have considered the community and must have a plan of engagement with them, and projects must also ensure they bring ongoing benefits to the community. These benefits could be tangible, such as improved physical infrastructure, or intangible, such as knowledge shared with the right groups of people. This means that anyone wishing to work in the creative district, including the CDF, must first have a deep understanding of the local residents and existing businesses and draw up project plans accordingly. This is important to the CDF because ensuring that the communities in the area benefit from new projects helps to maintain the area's authenticity. Without these communities, the area's authenticity would diminish, and it would become like many others in the modernized Bangkok.

Gentrification of the area is also a major challenge. Lee Ananthawat of Speedy Grandma had already seen some shifts in the area and raised the alarm. Having operated in the area for a number of years, she witnessed changes in her neighbours. Around her, local shop houses were being transformed into working spaces of the creative class. Eateries, galleries and other establishments were joining her in the budding district. While not dramatic, the change was sensed by locals and landlords. The increase in popularity of the area is likely to lead to a rise in rents, which could drive out lower-income earners. As one of the first movers, Lee felt a responsibility to ensure that rents never reach a level where locals are displaced, and therefore sought to raise awareness of the issue. CDF recognizes, however, that controlling the gentrification process is difficult and that efforts to do so have not succeeded elsewhere.

As what the CDF is doing has never been done before in Bangkok, the foundation must carry the burden of a trailblazer. As observed by urbanist Jane Jacobs, a city is "an immense laboratory of trial and error, failure and success, in city building and city design" (Jacobs, 1961), so there is much that can be learned.

The district is now poised to enter a new phase of development and contribute to heritage conservation and to the cultural vitality of Bangkok. As of 2018, the CDF and the community have reached the stage at which more formal planning, management and design strategies are needed. In particular, it is necessary for the CDF to engage directly with the municipal government and secure its cooperation and support, without which new insensitive developments may be approved in the area. Steps must also be taken to enhance awareness of the value of the community's intangible heritage; if this is lost the area will lose much of its significance as a heritage and community resource. The CDF must also engage in planning, to manage the increasing numbers of visitors to the area, which come with increased activity. This requires overcoming issues relating to the transportation network; these issues will become more severe as greater numbers of people visit the area. Therefore, the CDF and other stakeholders need to identify the area's carrying capacity, especially in the traditional market areas and the Muslim quarter.

Key lessons

This case study highlights some of the factors involved in the successful planning and management of heritage areas. The method taken by the Creative District group is an excellent example of a grassroots approach and demonstrates how a small group of people can begin a process of change by engaging a much larger set of interests in the improvement of an area and in maintaining its authenticity. The Creative District group recognized that the authenticity and the history of the area were a major advantage and built on the community's appreciation of those features.

One of the most important lessons from this case study is the value of building of networks. It is important to connect groups and individuals who share a similar vision, values and ethos, and to engage all the stakeholders. Accomplishing shared goals involves harnessing the creativity of multiple talents and guiding them in the same direction.

This case study also illustrates how major changes can be brought about by just a small set of stakeholders. In this case it was a group of citizens who had spent time away from Thailand and had therefore become aware of how other cities had developed and who were able to see value in the West Bang Rak area.

Another interesting aspect of this case study was that many of the new enterprises in West Bang Rak occupied empty properties, and therefore did not displace existing businesses or residents. Furthermore, their enterprises were new activities that brought in additional customers to the area.

Finally, an important aspect of the CDF's urban renewal process was that the local communities have benefited from it and that authenticity has been maintained.

While the CDF and local community face many challenges ahead, the approach that has been taken so far augurs well for the future.

7

Urban Heritage Planning and Management in Asia: An integrated and responsible approach

Walter Jamieson and Richard Engelhardt

The framework for this chapter is presented in Figure 8.1.

Figure 8.1: The framework of Chapter 8

The Asian urban heritage context

The current situation in many urban heritage areas of Asia is one of economic gridlock and social stalemate, as a result of various factors, including weak governance, profit-driven investment, lack of technical knowledge and skills among those responsible for guiding urban development, lack of community engagement, unwillingness to invest in long-term asset augmentation, clashes in planning and management ideologies, numbers-driven mass tourism, lack of effective management mechanisms, the inability of key stakeholders to work together to reach common goals, and inadequate access to financial and human resources.

Urban heritage issues and challenges

As examined in detail in Chapter 2, Asian cities face significant challenges, which stem in large part from the rapid rate of population growth in recent decades. In the past few decades Asian cities have seen remarkable achievements in modern city-building, creating urban magnets that have lured significant numbers of immigrants from the agricultural hinterlands. The consequent urban redevelopment and expansion to provide living and work spaces for this influx of new inhabitants has, however, put at risk the established economic and social equilibrium and stressed the original infrastructure, which was not built to support such large populations or meet modern demands for services such as water, electricity and transport. Furthermore, the attendant economic development, while delivering a measure of profit to select beneficiaries, has intensified inequities between social groups and has led to significant negative environmental impacts.

Those concerned with protecting the legacy of urban cultural heritage in Asia, and the uniquely defining values and traditions embedded in this heritage, have documented, with increasing alarm, in city after city across Asia, an extensive deterioration and loss of physical historic fabric of structures and space, as well as the disappearance of long-established cultural occupations and community practices. Historic urban areas in Asian cities have suffered loss of structural fabric due to not only urban redevelopment but also decay and lack of maintenance, which stems from inadequate knowledge and interest on the part of those responsible, and inadequate financial investment. Investment should – in any reasonably well-managed system of governance – be in sustainable resource management, but has instead been siphoned off into high-cost property development schemes.

Such development has brought with it a dramatic change in the urban environment. As a result of profit-driven investment, residents from long-standing historic communities have been displaced, not only by newer residents, but also by the impersonal infrastructure built to accommodate these new residents. Car-focused urban design has led to extensive road construction and has allowed heavy, uncontrolled traffic and polluting vehicles within and around historic urban areas, posing a serious and immediate threat to the integrity of heritage buildings and neighbourhood spaces. Western-style building design and materials have led to the depletion of artisan skills associated with traditional construction, the disappearance of traditional occupations and the transformation of the traditional economic/residential mix of the community, which once gave urban areas their authentic flavour. Together these factors have resulted in the loss of the 'spirit of place' of many of Asian historic urban areas – a loss that renders the heritage values of these communities unviable as vectors of future development.

The nature of the urban property market presents another significant challenge, which is compounded by the fact that many heritage areas have been designated for higher densities through urban plans and policies, and many of the public officials (i.e policy makers and planners) who are responsible for conservation do not have the required skills and knowledge to manage heritage conservation sustainably. The responsibility for ensuring that urban plans and land use regulations support conservation rests with heritage interests and the affected communities. Furthermore, the dominant urban planning and design models, zoning systems and land-use regulations in Asia derive from outdated Western models that encourage redevelopment rather than retention of a city's heritage. This serves as a formidable obstacle to a responsible approach to city development and, in particular, heritage conservation.

Land-use planning designations and development controls are often not designed to provide for fine-grained zoning that would encourage visitor heritage-appropriate related activities within a heritage area. When zoning and land use policies – which are in most cases legal documents that require regulatory changes to amend them – allow for increased densities or a particular type of land-use, investment decisions are understandably made on the basis of these policies. Land and property owners (including those that own one or two buildings in an historic area – most often their home or business) having purchased land and/or property that has been valued for a high floor area ratio (FAR)[1] are unable or unwilling to justify retention over redevelopment on economic grounds. The likelihood of authorities reducing allowable development is very low given the significant economic loss that property owners would incur if such reductions took place (unless policies and plans offer compensation or the ability to transfer development rights to another site).

With the property market becoming increasingly international, it is often very difficult to convince investors, who have no attachment to a heritage area, that a responsible approach to development must take into consideration the value of traditional uses, which have economic, social, religious, symbolic and political importance. In many situations, policies and plans that could help to compensate the landowner when retention does take place do not exist. Additionally, many design and planning professionals do not have the knowledge and skills to design redevelopment schemes that allow retention to take place while still achieving part, if not all, of the economic value of a property.

Property development and investment stakeholders have had a considerable impact on the nature of Asian cities because the political influence of these property development interests has not been effectively countered by an equally authoritative voice on the behalf of traditional residents and their established interests. A very different outcome would be seen if the interests of local residents

---

1   The floor area ratio is the relationship between the total amount of usable floor area that a building has, or has been permitted to have, and the total area of the lot on which the building stands. https://www.investopedia.com/terms/f/floor-area-ratio.asp#ixzz5OMOGhcBi

and small-scale property owners, including homeowners in heritage areas, were taken into account, and if these stakeholders were given opportunities to influence the nature of urban development.

The case examples and studies in this book have illustrated that, in general, urban development plans and policies have not adequately considered the intangible and tangible cultural dimensions of urban areas. Even when heritage dimensions of urban areas have been valued for their tourism potential, poorly (or un-)managed tourism development has not fully realised this potential and, in too many cases, has resulted in a quick degradation and devaluation of these historic assets.

World-class heritage conservation professionals are, however, working to change the urban development paradigm in Asia and have created excellent inventories of the heritage assets of many of Asia's cities. In some urban areas, heritage conservation plans have been introduced, and heritage professionals are pushing for them to be implemented and mainstreamed into priority development strategies.

Given the important, indeed crucial, role that cities must inevitably play in future human development throughout Asia, there is an obligation for well planned and managed cities that offer increased opportunities for all of their residents. To address the many issues, it is essential to improve planning systems.

Tourism issues in urban heritage areas

Given the power and influence of tourism, positive and negative, as seen in this book, tourism must be considered as a central factor in the overall management of heritage areas.

Tourism is seen by many as an important means of increasing the economic health of urban heritage areas and is often justified in terms of increases in property tax revenue and jobs. For example, it is argued that increased tax revenue will help to fund health and education programmes and new employment opportunities for growing urban populations; programmes and opportunities that would otherwise not be funded due to lack of resources.

Unfortunately, in many instances policies that aim to incentivise mass tourism, including through hotel and infrastructure development, are not sensitive to tangible and intangible heritage conservation. Indeed, uni-dimensional property and other economically-driven development initiatives tend to have negative impacts on heritage. These impacts are further compounded when misguided attempts to package a community's heritage as 'products' for sale to tourists result in de-contextualising the meaning of heritage and degrading the value of the heritage areas for residents, the wider community and visitors. Furthermore, the benefits of tourism often accrue only to property developers and other powerful stakeholders, and the promised investments in employment and social programmes often never eventuate, resulting in declines in the quality of life in

8

urban heritage areas. Moreover, despite the negative impact tourism can have on heritage assets and on residents' quality of life, the economic power of tourism is such that, attempts to limit tourism are often discredited and ignored.

Challenges in managing urban heritage areas

As illustrated by the case examples in this book, many Asian cities lack a coherent vision for heritage management and are deficient in the management structures, mechanisms and mindsets that recognise the necessity of managing heritage areas sustainably. They also lack systems to allow urban heritage and tourism stakeholders to work together and with other interest groups.

Urban heritage areas differ and the management approaches they use must therefore be appropriate to the characteristics of each area. Differences exist in terms of (i) their level of significance and protection; (ii) the level of development pressure; (iii) the type of governance; (iv) municipal legislation and service delivery; (v) demographic nature; (vi) nature of land-use and economic activity; (vii) acceptance of and readiness for tourism; and (viii) size.

The various characteristics are often inter-related. For example, the demographic nature of an area has a significant influence on the type of governance and the ability of the residents to deal with development pressures. The nature of the municipal legislation will very much impact what is possible in terms of governance within the heritage area itself.

Some urban heritage areas experience significant pressures both from development as well as visitation, and are experiencing 'overtourism', while others could benefit from further urban development and tourism, if it is well planned and managed. Some areas may be mixed in terms of institutional, commercial and residential uses activity, while others may be single use areas.

Urban areas also differ in their heritage significance. Some areas of international value are designated as World Heritage sites, some have recognised national historic value, and others have regional or local heritage interest. While World Heritage sites carry with them a set of international expectations and management principles that must be complied with, places of national and local interest are often governed by national policies and standards. These expectations, principles, policies and standards are not always considered in the overall planning and management process, however.

While governments must take responsibility for managing development, in all cases the local community must also be engaged in the process and must benefit from tourism development and heritage management processes. If Asian urban historic areas are to develop in a sustainable manner, the planning and management of these areas must meet the needs of residents while also conserving tangible and intangible heritage. Conservation of the authentic aspects of a city's built heritage and continuation of the traditional cultural practices of its constituent communities must be given priority in both policy and practice, while at the same time allowing urban areas to change, expand and adapt to evolving modern-day expectations, aspirations and standards of environmental excellence.

The way forward – towards a new paradigm for planning Asian urban heritage areas

The issues discussed in this book – when viewed in light of current practices in urban development, planning and management – provide a platform for re-examining the contribution of cultural heritage tourism to socio-economic development. The Sustainable Development Goals and the New Urban Agenda, adopted at the 2018 World Urban Forum, point to integrated, multi-sectoral and knowledge-based approaches to heritage conservation and tourism management as the way to realizing sustainable development. This is based on evidence from many urban areas, including London and New York. In such cities, the responsible management of various inter-related factors – including both tangible and intangible aspects of cultural heritage – has contributed to the overall improvement of the quality of life of residents and the competitive positions of the cities.

An integrated approach is now internationally recognised as an essential condition for achieving responsible heritage area development. In April 2018, the *Barcelona Declaration of Tourism and Cultural Heritage: Better Places to Live Better Places to Visit* made a very strong case for this integration. The declaration refers back to the ICOMOS International Cultural Tourism Charter, approved in 1999, which calls for a closer relationship between the conservation of cultural heritage and the tourism industry. The Barcelona Declaration recognises that making destinations better places to live and visit requires that tourism and cultural heritage stakeholders are at the centre of discussions, and that a multi-stakeholder approach is needed. It considers that cultural heritage is the essence of a place; that it constitutes an inherent value and is one of the main assets of a destination. Moreover, the declaration considers that tourism can provide added value to cultural heritage and can support its long-term conservation. It also recognises that tourism can contribute to responsible social and cultural development. In some cases, also, tourism can help to create a sense of place and pride in a community. The declaration cautions, however, that tourism proponents have a responsibility to ensure a balance between cultural heritage and tourism development. This can be achieved by adhering to five key principles: smart and inclusive management; sense of place and pride; holistic marketing and promotion; balancing place, people and business; and connecting people (NECSTouR, 2018).

The tourism and heritage relationship is also recognised by the United Nations World Tourism Organization (UNWTO), which identifies heritage, both tangible and intangible, as an important element of tourism, and sees tourism as supporting the preservation of culture by generating income and raising the profile of heritage resources (UNWTO, 2018).

8

While an integrated approach is required, heritage conservation advocates are often wary of and unwilling to work in cooperation with tourism initiatives and those responsible for marketing urban cultural heritage assets. Repeated bad experiences with tourism development – experiences in which the heritage profession has invested in conservation only to have this investment expropriated by ill-conceived and poorly-managed development – have estranged many among the heritage profession. The avenue away from the current state of confrontation between heritage conservation and tourism development is through equitably-planned, inclusive and participatory management frameworks. However, those involved in the planning and management of urban heritage areas find it difficult to achieve a comfortable cross-fit between heritage conservation and tourism planning development, and the stakeholders also lack a common vision.

Such conflicts within historic urban areas are the result of different interest groups not taking into consideration the ideological dimensions of their decision-making. Achieving an integrated approach to the development of tourism within historic urban areas requires a willingness to recognise and respect different ideological positions, especially as they relate to the role and influence of public-sector plans and regulations to safeguard heritage. This requires a more nuanced form of planning and management, with its own competencies: a specialised knowledge base in heritage; skill in recognizing and reconciling a variety of stakeholder interests; and recognition of the need for indicators above and beyond the simplistic measures of profit margins and visitor numbers.

An integrated approach will only yield responsible results if the planning and management of urban historic areas incorporates a new understanding of tourism. For the tourism industry, it would not be business as usual. The problems with the present model of tourism, discussed in chapters 1 and 2, indicate a clear need for change. Accordingly, a number of new approaches to tourism development have been proposed by heritage and tourism experts. One of these, by Anna Pollock, provides the most radical rethink of tourism, carrying with it a complete reassessment of the assumptions, beliefs and values that underpin the present tourism operating model. This approach calls for a transformation of the industry 'from a consuming caterpillar to a dancing butterfly' (Pollock, 2012). This transformation requires a realigned set of objectives that would view tourism as a tool for cultural, economic, social and environmental development.

This view is increasingly echoed by international organisations, including the Asian Development Bank (ADB), which positions tourism as a policy and planning tool to meet the overall development objectives of countries and regions (see, for example, ADB, 2013; Jamieson and Schipani, 2014; MTCO, 2017).

Members of the tourism industry are now also recognising the need for a reorientation of tourism. As William Bakker, Chief Strategist of Destination Think! observed, "We can treat our destinations as commodities and consume what we have as fast as we can at the expense of our citizens and our environment, risking our long-term viability. Or we can offer experiences that transform people by creating memories for life, opening people's minds, or simply strengthening bonds with loved ones. All while contributing to the quality of life for our citizens instead of taking it away" (Archer, 2016).

The case examples and studies in this book have demonstrated that if urban heritage is to be conserved and incorporated into the ongoing evolution of local areas, the way forward cannot be 'more of the same'. There is a clear need for a paradigm shift that moves forward from the outdated model of managing heritage as a stand-alone resource, to an integrated approach that incorporates heritage assets into urban planning strategies and management practices. Moving from the old approach to the new one will involve a transition period, which in some instances may require significant effort and time, and will require government regulation and support.

The elements of the paradigm shift are illustrated in Figure 8.2.

Figure 8.2: Paradigm shift

The new paradigm recognises that meeting the needs of residents while also ensuring responsible conservation of heritage areas involves:

- A vision for an integrated approach to urban conservation.
- An agreed set of principles and criteria for responsible heritage area conservation.
- Agreement on the non-partisan, long-term strategic policy dimensions of an integrated approach.
- An understanding of the interface between urban planning, conservation and tourism.
- Adoption of a common set of areas of management concern and a common work plan to guide an integrated planning and implementation approach.
- The identification and discussion of the process-related skills and knowledge required to achieve responsible urban heritage conservation.
- A team of knowledgeable, competent technical professionals, backstopped by a reliable database of information on the urban area, its resources and its demographics.
- A leadership structure committed to implementing and achieving the common vision in a non-partisan, fully-transparent way, which prioritises informed community consent.

Developing a vision for responsible urban area heritage conservation

As noted earlier, the lack of a common vision for responsibly conserving urban heritage areas is a significant obstacle to an integrated approach. A common vision must therefore be developed. Such a vision would need to include the following elements:

- Community heritage assets are valued as an essential element in the provision of a healthy, liveable urban environment.
- Heritage areas are good places to live, work, play, worship, invest and visit.
- Heritage conservation is not an impediment to ongoing urban development but is rather a valued policy and planning dimension.
- Development and management processes must be sustainable.
- The overall planning and management process is based on a community-driven approach that takes into account the needs of the residents and the larger community to achieve liveable, life-enhancing communities.
- The planning and development context is such that heritage resources are used as a lever for cultural, social, economic and responsible urban development and not relegated to an isolated position of backward-looking nostalgia, unrelated to a community's future development, or a concern of only a few elite individuals from vested interest groups.

- There is recognition that while some urban heritage areas are suffering from too many tourists, some communities with lower levels of visitation would welcome well-planned and managed tourism.
- Tourism is realigned to ensure that heritage and tourism are compatible and complementary.

A key consideration underpinning any vision for responsible urban area conservation is a sound understanding of cultural significance, authenticity and integrity. These terms are outlined below.

The *cultural significance* of a place can be defined as the "aesthetic, historic, scientific, social or spiritual value for past, present or future generations" which is "embodied in the place itself, its setting, use, associations, meanings, records, related places and related objects" (ICOMOS, 2013, p. 2). The assessment of cultural significance is the process of studying and understanding the meanings and values of places, objects and collections. It involves three main steps: analysing the object or resource; understanding its history and context; and identifying its value for the communities that created it and/or care for it. Understanding the relative degree of cultural significance of heritage resources is essential if we are to determine which elements must be preserved under any circumstances, which should be preserved under some circumstances, and which, under exceptional circumstances, will be sacrificed. Assessing the degree of significance can be done on the basis of the representativeness, rarity, condition, completeness and integrity, and interpretive potential of a resource.

Authenticity is understood by the conservation profession as a matrix of dimensions: location and setting; form; materials and design; use and function; and 'immaterial' or 'essential' qualities. Together, these form the composite authenticity from which significance derives. Mainstreamed into conservation practice by the nearly-universal adoption of the 1972 UNESCO World Heritage Convention, the importance of the concept of authenticity as underpinning successful conservation practice was reaffirmed in the 1994 Nara Document on Authenticity, which states that authenticity is "the essential qualifying factor concerning values".

Intimately tied to the concept of authenticity, *integrity*, as applied to cultural heritage preservation, is an equally important though less well-defined concept. Similar to authenticity, the concept of integrity can be conceived of as a matrix of dimensions. As a measure of wholeness, intactness and physical coherence, the meaning of integrity can be grasped easily when applied to a single artefact. Artefact conservation typically involves removal of newer accretions, leaving the original fabric intact insofar as possible. When the concept of integrity is applied to a building that has been subject to alterations over time, however, the assessment of the artefact is more relative and is subject to time-dependent measurement. In such situations, conservation practice usually endeavours to preserve the complete picture of a building's history. This conservation approach enables an artefact to retain its 'integrity'. At the urban scale, the changes in the relationship of objects – older and newer – over time become more complex, and they also

8

take on the essential and defining characteristics of a historic area's contemporary authenticity.

The need for a change in mindset

The paradigm shift requires a change in mindset, moving away from the 'silo' – 'it's not my job' – mentality, to informed responsible co-management. This must occur in the public, private and non–profit sectors and at all levels of management.

In the context of this book, the mindset change required is the recognition that heritage resources contribute to the uniqueness of a community, enhance the quality of life of residents in that community, contribute to a unique and authentic brand that can be translated into economic opportunities, increase the confidence and self-worth of the residents, and attract new, unique and diverse types of activity. Heritage resources, when properly planned for and managed well, attract not only visitors, but also skilled residents and investors with resources. For these reasons, heritage conservation interests are wise to work in close cooperation with development initiatives, and specifically tourism initiatives, to develop strategies that are investment oriented without compromising the conservation of the tangible and intangible heritage resources upon which those investments depend.

This mindset change will, of course, be a difficult one. Many would argue that much of the private sector (including the private sector engaged in tourism) will never change of their own free will because their success is measured by maximum returns in the shortest possible timeframes. There are encouraging signs, however, that the private sector is now looking at more responsible investment, and many of the large tourism industry stakeholders, including tourism destinations, are making significant shifts in the way they plan for and manage their tourism operations (Goodwin, 2017). Indeed, visitors are demanding a mindset change given their increased environmental awareness and support for responsible tourism.

It remains the case, however, that property owners and tourism operators who own land and buildings in heritage areas will not willingly forgo the economic returns that the current zoning and land use classifications permit. Therefore, governments, working with the private sector, need to implement compensation measures that recognise the real or potential loss property owners will incur from maintaining heritage, especially in areas where significant development potential can be achieved under existing legislation and land-use regulations. Compensation could include public-sector grants, tax breaks, subsidies, the transfer of development rights, special development bonuses and the creation of urban design strategies that allow for reasonable development within heritage constraints. In cases where compensation measures may not meet the needs of the various stakeholders, the recourse is for heritage interests and residents to seek amendments to unwise zoning and land-use regulations. This must be carried out within the larger urban planning and policy arena.

It will be an equally significant challenge to change the mindset of administrators, given the entrenched nature of many bureaucracies. The bureaucratic challenge is recognised by Charles Landry and Maggie Caust, who call for 'creative bureaucracies' and argue that it is necessary to create in bureaucracies a positive, respectful atmosphere, and an ethos of sharing and helping out. Recognizing that people are at the heart of the system, there must also be a feeling that people's contributions are valued. This approach will result in bureaucracies and organisations that are responsive, adaptive, flexible, outward looking and creative (Landry and Caust, 2017).

Figure 8.3 illustrates how heritage conservation and tourism planning must come together as pieces of a larger urban puzzle, on a base of sound and sustainable urban planning, followed by fine-grained urban heritage conservation that guides tourism development.

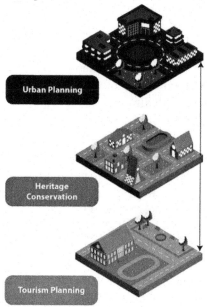

Figure 8.3: The urban planning/conservation/tourism interface

The mindset change will involve adopting collaborative approaches and integrating heritage area conservation into the ongoing planning and development process. Specifically, the mindset change calls for a move away from the following ideas: (i) only those with conservation expertise can determine appropriate conservation strategies and approaches; (ii) only planners are to be entrusted with issues of zoning, land use and regulation; (iii) only the tourism industry is responsible for determining the nature of visitor experiences and how to reach intended markets; (iv) residents are not a central part of the overall development process; (v) the visitor is not central to the overall development of area; (vi) those involved in planning economic development must not consider the value of heritage; and (vii) the only measure of success for a heritage area is the number of international arrivals.

The mindset change will require creating a system of interlinked dimensions and initiatives, which seek to bring about integrated processes that will create balanced, responsible, connected, inclusive, equitable, resilient and data-driven urban heritage development. Most importantly, policy objectives must ensure that this integrated approach produces more liveable, competitive and resilient urban areas. Change needs to be manifested to improve conditions and achieve overall results (Jamieson and Jamieson, 2016).

Making the mindset change happen

Changing mindsets is certainly easier said than done. In the past, heritage and tourism planning were not focused on how change would occur, but assumed that new strategies would lead to automatic change. Furthermore, there was a time when there was little need for people to understand or anticipate change. But today people in every capacity, including urban planning, heritage conservation and tourism planning, need to be primed for change and need to have the ability to influence those changes. Therefore, mindset change requires change management tactics. Such tactics can help to identify the areas that will require the most change, for example the move from working in silos to an integrated approach. Given that stakeholders will differ in their levels of acceptance and understanding of what is required in order to change their mindsets, communication will play a vital role. Planners must engage and work with experts in change management and communications, who will assist in bringing about the desired changes.

For a mindset change to occur there needs to be recognition of the importance of this change throughout an organisation and its employees, as well as among heritage owners, tourism leaders and all other stakeholders. Overall, organisational structures and stakeholder behaviour and systems must be addressed before dynamic and innovative strategies can be created. The implementation of a new strategy, plan or policy is, in essence, the introduction of new ideas into current systems, so such changes will also need to be managed. To influence change, organisations and individuals will need the following attributes: leadership skills, innovation, creativity, team work and problem-solving skills, working in small groups or larger planning teams.

Key strategies for achieving an integrated approach to urban heritage area planning and management at the municipal level

Achieving a more integrated approach must occur at both the national and local (municipal) decision-making levels because most issues related to conserving urban heritage areas are the consequence of policies formulated at these levels. Policies, legislation and regulations must be in keeping with values and dimensions of heritage areas.

The nature of the required changes in legislation and regulations are largely recognised within the heritage community. The challenge is to convince political decision-makers that such change is necessary. This needs to be done on a country-by-country and city-by-city basis. Part of this process will require that heritage stakeholders and urban development and tourism professionals provide better advice and direction to the political sector. Furthermore, public support for urban heritage conservation must be gained. This is because, ultimately, only sufficient public support can bring about the required changes in policies, legislation and regulations.

Given that change must happen soon, in view of the rapid changes in Asia's urban areas, the immediate focus must be on local (municipal) level planning and management, with an emphasis on improving overall organisational and individual capacities, processes and approaches. In order to accomplish this objective, it is necessary to act in five key strategic areas: (i) urban heritage area governance; (ii) planning, design and place making; (iii) community development; (iv) data and knowledge management; and (v) measuring success. These five areas are examined below.

Urban heritage area governance

Urban planners have long recognised that cities are complex systems, with multiple stakeholders. Each stakeholder helps to shape urban areas, and the issues and challenges in these areas clearly illustrate that stakeholders often have opposing visions and goals (Crawford, 2016). Government has an important role in ensuring all views are heard and making certain that outcomes are in the interests of the public.

Governance structures must include inclusive participatory engagement processes, local-level decision-making, risk preparedness, flexibility to respond to changing markets, support to self-help strategies, measures to ensure the safety and security of residents and visitors, and processes where the use of heritage is negotiated, resulting in a sustainable, life enhancing spaces.

The complex urban challenges do not adhere to boundaries set for political or administrative purposes, and policy-makers need to appreciate the complexity of the contexts in which they work and take a leadership role in bringing together the various interest groups.

8

Managing stakeholders

Multiple stakeholders are engaged in planning for and managing urban heritage areas, as Figure 8.4 illustrates. They all affect heritage area development and are also all affected by it, and must therefore be involved in all of the various levels of decision-making.

As seen in the case examples and studies earlier in this book, one of the challenges faced in the planning and management of urban heritage areas is how to engage all stakeholders in an effective way while ensuring that residents are respected and are an integral part of the overall decision-making process.

Figure 8.4: Urban heritage tourism stakeholders

Any effort to ensure communication and coordination between all stakeholders must recognise the imbalance of power, however. Many heritage tourism plans and academic studies assume that by bringing together a wide range of interest groups a synergy will be created resulting in the achievement of responsible sustainable results (for example, Sautter and Leisen, 1999; Landorf, 2009; Curseu and Schruijer, 2017). However, this does not take into account the significant differences in power and influence the various stakeholders bring to the overall tourism development process.

Clearly, large-scale international companies operating in an urban area have a significant impact on the nature of tourism development, especially in terms of the form and quality of private sector development and the branding of a city. Small and medium-sized enterprises are also part of the tourism supply chain and are essential in providing services and contributing to quality visitor experiences, so they also have a significant influence on what the tourist experiences and have the potential to ensure that heritage assets are highlighted and responsibly dealt with.

Governments at all levels can also have a significant influence on tourism development, as they decide what and how urban heritage gets conserved, in part as a result of their legislative powers and influence, and in part by the reality that many political decision-makers are 'influenced' by property and development interests. On the other hand, governments – in their role as custodians of the public good of which cultural heritage is one part – can also be instrumental in helping to guide heritage conservation and management, often with the support of non-governmental cultural heritage professionals and advocacy groups. Governmental regulatory agencies decide what heritage is protected, conserved and how it is used; determine what supporting infrastructure is necessary and what is superfluous or even damaging in an historic setting; have a major role in identity building and therefore branding of a destination; influence the nature and limit the bounds of the visitor experience in their cities; and through planning procedures and subsequent financing mechanisms (taxation and the like), set development policies, and implement and enforce planning decisions.

Residents are clearly central stakeholders, as they live in heritage areas. But they often do not have the opportunity to be engaged in the heritage area development process. This results in the perception, real or imagined, that urban development, including tourism development, represents an intrusion into their daily lives, and is at the root of a host of locally-experienced economic and social ills. Recent protests by residents in key tourism destinations such as Venice and Barcelona (Responsible Tourism Partnership, 2017; Brunton, 2018; Jessop, 2018) are ample evidence that heritage areas that do not take into consideration the needs of the residents will be unsustainable.

A responsible approach to urban development therefore demands that residents are recognised as the key stakeholders and the ultimate decision-makers in conservation area protection, conservation, development planning and use management. Through engagement with residents, the often-cited benefits of jobs and increased quality of life for residents in heritage areas can in fact be realised.

In many planning exercises, citizen involvement is often only lip-service, and does not truly allow residents to influence the decision-making process. One trusted approach to ensuring people within the local community are involved in determining what is best for the community is the work of Arstein on citizen participation. Her work recognises that there are different levels of participation, ranging from tokenism to partnerships and citizen control. The latter is the most favoured form of engagement (Arnstein, 1969).

One of the major challenges in determining what level of tourism activity is best for a community and its heritage is that the various stakeholders can differ significantly in what they perceive constitutes a 'responsible and sustainable' level of tourism. While some stakeholders may see high levels of tourism as a negative phenomenon, others – including businesses and building owners (some of whom are also residents) – may see high levels of tourism activity as having positive (economic) impacts. In addition, some stakeholders may argue that no limit on tourism is necessary in a historic area if proper management techniques are employed. It must be remembered, however, that while carrying capacity levels can be affected by management strategies, there is no doubt that there are absolute limits beyond which resources and systems cease to be sustainable (Meadows et al., 2004).

Governance models

In order to achieve better levels of stakeholder cooperation and coherence, which will support heritage conservation, new governance models are required (Maxim, 2017). In the Asian context, there are many examples of both top-down and laissez-faire hyper-capitalistic planning and management models. These two extremes are not the only choices, however. The approaches presented below work within these two extremes.

The paradigm shift discussed earlier in this chapter supports the concept of 'shared governance', in which everyone is responsible for the planning and management process. This is in keeping with the notion that the government is not the only actor that can plan and manage heritage areas, and represents a shift to a style of governance in which all stakeholders contribute to the planning and management process. Is important to note, however, that the concept of 'shared governance' does not in any way devalue the primary and essential role that the public sector plays in the overall process of conserving urban heritage areas.

A shared governance approach is very much in keeping with the necessity of building of partnerships in heritage, tourism and urban planning. The sharing of responsibilities brings with it a more flexible or adaptable understanding of laws and regulations and moves away from a highly regulated process to one where stakeholders can make use of broader policies and negotiation processes (EENC, 2013). In many cases the private sector prefers more flexible approaches, and working in partnership can achieve creative solutions that meet the needs of all stakeholders, including the heritage interests of residents of historic areas.

There is no one-size-fits-all format for governance given the significant variance in urban heritage areas in terms of their social, political and economic contexts. The governance model appropriate for each heritage area will depend on local land, property and building ownership patterns, along with other factors. Areas with many small landowners, for example, will require a more finely-grained approach than areas with large private sectors and institutional investors and developers. Quite clearly, urban World Heritage sites require different governance models to areas such as that described in the Bangkok case study, which is the product of urban initiatives and the creativity of local stakeholders. The nature of the organisation and the sophistication of the professionals involved will also vary, depending on the scale and nature of activity.

Six governance models will be discussed below. These models, presented in Figure 8.5, are not the only options, but reflect the range of possibilities and the differences in contexts in Asian urban areas.

Figure 8.5: Governance models

Lijiang models of cooperation among stakeholders

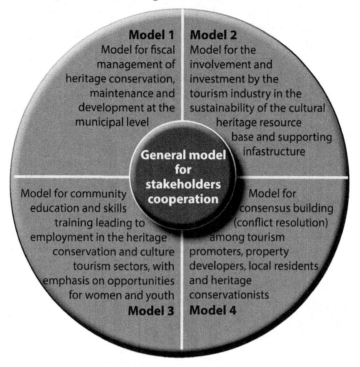

Figure 8.6: Lijiang models for stakeholder cooperation

In 2001, based on the results of an international UNESCO meeting of experts in Lijiang, China, which followed a five-year study of the impact of tourism promotion in medium-sized Asian World Heritage towns, UNESCO developed a series of models for cooperation among stakeholders (UNESCO, 2001). The four interrelated models are illustrated in Figure 8.6. and are described below.

1: This model is for the fiscal capture from tourism for community benefit, based on heritage conservation, maintenance and development at the municipal level. It can be achieved through the identification and implementation of new income-generating mechanisms.

2: This model enables investment by the tourism industry in cultural heritage and supporting infrastructure. It can be achieved through educating tourism operators on the value of heritage and conservation needs, and formulating mechanisms by which the tourism industry can contribute financially and in other ways to preservation activities.

3: This model enables community education and skills training, leading to employment in the heritage conservation and cultural tourism sectors. It can be achieved through identifying new local business and employment opportunities, and designing appropriate training programmes and financial incentives to turn these opportunities into reality.

8

4: This model enables conflict resolution and consensus building between stakeholders, including: tourism promoters, property developers, local residents and heritage conservationists. It can be achieved by providing a mechanism that enables all stakeholders to raise concerns and discuss their situations. It involves empowering local stakeholders and supports joint heritage conservation projects and cultural tourism activities. Model 4 recognises that cultural heritage is a political issue and seeks to make heritage conservation a nonpartisan issue through consensus building (UNESCO and NWHF, 2001).

Heritage areas and districts

The traditional model for the management of historic areas is normally the creation of a heritage district, often established by legislation to control development and encourage conservation within the area. Their mandates are often solely focused on heritage conservation. Heritage districts develop plans dealing with the local heritage attributes and resources to ensure their long-term protection. These districts are typically concerned with understanding their history and evolution, surveying the urban landscape, determining their character, evaluating cultural heritage values, developing a statement of district/area significance and developing recommendations for protection under local or national laws and regulations. Some heritage districts are developed and legally mandated by the municipality while others operate on a voluntary or non-governmental organisation basis.

Main Street program

Figure 8.7: The 'four points' of the Main Street concept. (Main Street America, n.d.)

The Main Street program was created by the National Trust for Historic Preservation in the United States and later evolved in the Canadian context where there was an early recognition of the need for a comprehensive approach to conserving the essence of main streets and revitalising them. The program recognises that conserving main streets requires a proactive approach. This approach is centred around 'transformation strategies', which articulate a "deliberate path to revitalizing or strengthening a downtown or commercial district's economy" (Main Street America, n.d.). Transformation strategies are organised around 'four points': design, promotion, organisation and economic vitality, and are generated by reliable data and inclusive community engagement. Figure 8.7 illustrates the four points.

Destination development management and marketing organisations

Tourism districts and areas are typically managed by destination marketing organisations (DMOs). As their name implies, the mandate of these organisations is largely concerned with marketing the district and its attractions. Recognising that tourism districts must do more than simply market themselves if they want to remain competitive and be sustainable, and must also manage the process of change and improvement, the notion of a 'destination development management and marketing organisation' (DDMMO) has evolved. This concept acknowledges that an integrated approach to management is needed. Possible themes for a DDMMO include: social sustainability, heritage conservation, place making, live-ability and localism, partnerships, new funding approaches, the sharing economy, smart cities, and crisis management and recovery.

Business improvement areas

Many urban areas, and particularly heritage areas, have commercial activities that are crucial to the ongoing vitality of the areas and to finding sustainable uses for heritage buildings. Many have a full-time employee(s) who is responsible for dimensions similar to those in the Main Street approach described above. Typically, a business improvement area would have the following functions: advocate on behalf of the interests of the business improvement area, including the surrounding geographic area; develop streetscape projects that respect the heritage value of the area; oversee the improvement and maintenance of publicly owned spaces and buildings; promote the area as a business, employment, tourist or retail area; deal, when necessary, with problems and issues, under a strategic plan; and undertake safety and security initiatives within the area.

Integrated urban investment, promotion and visitor organisations

8

Many cities have several organisations that promote the various dimensions of the urban areas. This has often resulted in mixed messages, however, and has been an ineffective use of resources. Cities such as New York and London have addressed this issue by bringing together various functions. For example, New York has created 'NYC and Company' while London has created 'London & Partners'. The latter, London & Partners, is an excellent example of an integrated approach to governance. It is a non-profit public-private partnership that promotes London internationally in partnership with the tourism industry, to attract both leisure and business visitors, and showcase the city as a good place to invest, work, study and visit (London & Partners, n.d.).

Adapting heritage area governance models to local contexts

It is not suggested that any one of the above governance models alone would be ideal for the responsible planning and management of urban heritage conservation governance. Each heritage area can, however, draw on the useful dimensions of these models to create an innovative model suited to the local context. Thus, these models can be adapted to the political, social and economic conditions of an urban area. While areas under intense development pressures may require strong heritage areas district commissions largely oriented to controlling development, other areas that need to generate income to support conservation efforts and boost the quality of life of the residents may choose to base their model on the Main Street or DDMMO approaches. Larger urban areas may consider the integrated approach, making heritage the primary concern within the larger development process. The lesson here is to develop models according to local situations.

Planning, design and place making

Planning and design

Traditionally, heritage area planning has been concerned with comprehensive approaches that can take many years and involve designating heritage properties, forming urban heritage committees, developing heritage policy and legislation (and amending them when necessary), creating design guidelines, designing heritage site management plans, and reviewing and assessing plans and development proposals for heritage sites and places. While this lengthy process is taking place, however, urban heritage is being lost.

This heritage area planning process is mostly carried out in isolation from urban planning and tourism planning, except in situations where there are already heritage zoning processes in place, usually in the form of a heritage overlay.[2] If the process of identifying urban heritage area goals and priorities ignores urban planning and tourism planning goals and priorities, however, overall heritage conservation goals can be seriously compromised.

An integrated planning process would employ intersectoral cooperative approaches in and between government departments that are directly or indirectly involved in tourism, culture, urban issues, employment and education. This has been termed 'horizontal planning' (NECSTouR, 2018). An integrated approach would thereby expand heritage area planning to consider visitor activity and determine where capacities might be exceeded and direct visitors to areas that do not receive the same level of visitor attention. Visitors could be redirected not only within the heritage area's boundaries but also to other heritage areas in the larger urban area or the region. This would require all the key stakeholders to work together with the full knowledge of the potential of the region to absorb

---

2   A heritage overlay is essentially a map that identifies heritage resources and areas of significance that must be protected. That map is then laid over a land use map, which identifies heritage resources that must be protected.

tourism in a sustainable manner.

The need for an integrated planning approach is evident given that almost half (46%) of 229 World Heritage sites assessed in 2017 did not have a clearly accessible tourism plan and only 28% of the sites had an extensive level of tourism planning (Becken and Wardle, cited in De Ascaniis et al., 2018, p. 41). In addition, many World Heritage sites often do not have comprehensive strategies for dealing with visitors.

Urban planning, urban conservation planning and tourism planning share common areas of activity including: (i) the identification of issues, goals and objectives, (ii) mapping stakeholder interests, (iii) refining problems, (iv) preparing plans and strategies, (v) holding stakeholder and public meetings, (vi) implementing the results of planning strategy processes and (vii) monitoring and evaluation. Each area of activity has distinct responsibilities and competencies, particularly with regard to methods for collecting and analyzing data and preparing strategies and plans. These common areas demonstrate that the three types of planning can merge for collaborative endeavours.

Planning teams working in urban heritage areas require comprehensive skills and knowledge, including an understanding of the issues and concerns surrounding heritage. While it is not necessary for each team member to be an expert in every area, they must understand the significance of each issue and how the issues are related to the planning of urban heritage areas. The spheres in which issues arise include: infrastructure, land use, zoning, regulations, stakeholder engagement, open space, transportation, safety and security.

The principles underpinning the planning process should include the following:

- Designs and plans should be responsive to authenticity, site and location concerns and land use requirements.

- Contemporary planning efforts must reflect traditional values, patterns and layouts.

- Planning approaches should be multisectoral, considering the relationships between policy areas such as heritage, housing, community development, education, tourism and transportation.

The three key areas of planning that are common to urban, heritage and tourism planning are: place making, tactical planning and planning for carrying capacities, as outlined below.

Place making

Place making is an integrated and holistic approach to planning, design and management that allows the needs of local residents to be met and protects the essence of special places. Place making has been part of design and planning thinking for a considerable period of time, and has been defined as the creative adaptation of given site attributes to meet the needs of all users, not only the visitor (Gunn,

1979). This calls for the retention of the essence of a place. Thus, the concept sounds very much like responsible conservation area planning.

Alan Lew identified different types of place making, which demonstrate the diversity of actions that can contribute to the improvement of a community:

- **Standard place making**: The many incremental changes that may take place over time, often in an uncoordinated manner. For example, the widening of a sidewalk or putting up more signage.
- **Strategic place making**: The creation of a major new addition to a community, requiring new investment. For example, a new open space.
- **Creative place making:** Urban change that incorporates the arts and other creative activities.
- **Tactical place making**: Temporary and experimental initiatives to test new ideas. For example, closing a street to assess the impacts of that street closure (Lew, 2017).

Related to place making is 'place management', which is championed by the Project for Public spaces (PPS). It is an integrated approach that functions naturally at a district/area geographic scale and recognises the interdependence of the many parts of any place or area. The process of place management, as defined by the PPS, involves the following steps: meet with the community and identify the stakeholders; evaluate the spaces and identify issues; develop a place vision; carry out short-term experiments to see what works; carry out ongoing evaluation; and look at long-term improvements. In 1999, the PPS defined 11 principles for creating great community places. These principles serve as a good framework for understanding how to achieve sustainable urban heritage areas: (i) the community is the expert, (ii) create a place, not a design, (iii) look for partners, (iv) you can see a lot just by observing, (v) have a vision, (vi) start with the petunias, (vii) triangulate, (viii) they always say 'it can't be done', (ix) form supports function, (x) money is not the issue and (xi) you are never finished (Project for Public Spaces, 1999).

Tactical planning

Plans and development and planning instruments need to take into account changes in the local contexts, through adaptive and flexible strategies. However, the traditional long-term strategy does not have tactical dimensions. What this has produced is a gap between master plans (or other policy documents) and the actual implementation process. This gap can be bridged by a tactical planning approach.

The tactical approach, which is best described as an approach to planning and activation using short-term, low-cost and scalable policies (Jamieson and Jamieson, 2016), involves a phased method of instigating change, with realistic expectations and low-risk but possibly high-rewards, and which can be implemented with few resources.[3] Tactical plans complement larger-scale and longer-term policy documents, such as master plans, and can be implemented immediately while the larger structural and strategic dimensions of an urban heritage conservation area master or policy plan are put into place. Adopting tactical planning approaches requires a change in mindset for those who are of the opinion that an urban heritage area can only be planned for and managed after a master plan is put into place.

Planning for and managing carrying capacities

The most pressing planning and management issue presently facing many Asian urban heritage areas is most probably overtourism, which was discussed in Chapter 1. The concept of overtourism recognises that there are limits to the acceptable number of tourists in any heritage environment. Research findings indicate that when tourist numbers go beyond a certain level, congestion levels are deemed excessive, living costs go up and access to services is diminished, with the result that resident satisfaction with tourism drops significantly (Coccossis and Mexa, 2004). Furthermore, when tourist numbers become excessive, visitor satisfaction also declines. Large numbers of tourists destroy visitors' enjoyment of heritage environments. Anecdotal accounts from numerous destinations indicate that the physical and psychological capacities of most urban heritage areas have been significantly exceeded. Moreover, protests by residents and complaints by tourists have made it clear that the lack of integrated planning and of strategies for controlling tourist numbers has negatively impacted residents, the visitor experience and the destinations themselves. The various planning and management suggestions that have been put forward to deal with this issue are essentially tied to identifying the limits of acceptable change.

Overtourism in heritage areas indicates that the carrying capacity for tourism has been exceeded in those areas. Concern for carrying capacity dates back to the Club of Rome's 1972 report, *Limits to Growth*, prepared for the first United Nations Conference on the Human Environment, which sparked the global discussion on sustainable development. To mark the 30-year anniversary of its publication, in 2004 the report was updated with additional data, confirming that every resource, area and system has carrying capacity limits (Meadows, et al., 2004).

Carrying capacity measures the level of use that is sustainable. In the case of tourism, it measures how many tourists or visitors can be accommodated without threatening the long-term viability of a site or community. Carrying capacity has five dimensions (physical, social, cultural, psychological and environmental), as shown in Figure 8.8. The physical dimension refers to attributes such as the number of visitors in a particular area, visitor to staff ratios and waiting times to visit facilities. The social/community dimension covers aspects such as the number of

---

3   An example of tactical planning can be found in Landry and Caust's *The Creative Bureaucracy*. This example uses the 90-day project approach, which allows for a process with a specific timeline and series of constraints. Public servants volunteer to work on a project, in a process that cuts across bureaucratic departments.

encounters and the number of people encountered. The cultural dimension refers to aspects such as cultural identity; while the psychological dimension refers to the essential qualities that people seek in their communities and the surrounding environment. The environmental dimension refers to aspects such as ecological capacity and local resources.

Figure 8.8: Carrying capacity dimensions

The tourism industry recognised the overtourism problem in a report titled *Coping with Success* (WTTC, 2017), which outlines a number of strategies to respond to, and possibly extend, the carrying capacity of certain sites. Success of these strategies would require comprehensive data gathering and analysis, long-term planning, and the identification of new sources of funding to mitigate and offset the damage caused by too many tourists. Specific recommendations include: spreading visitors over time, especially in the shoulder seasons; encouraging visits across sites; adjusting pricing to balance supply and demand; regulating accommodation supply and limiting access and activities.

The recommendations assume a certain level of administrative competence and coordination, which is not always the case, however. As Megan Epler Wood, a leading advocate for sustainable tourism, observed, "… if some of the richest municipal governments in the world are struggling with the capacity to analyze, regulate and manage what is known as 'overtourism' what will happen in burgeoning economies where double-digit tourism growth is not uncommon. This is the ticking time bomb." (Wood, 2017) Thus, while the WTTC's suggestions may work in environments with well-developed policy and planning frameworks, they are likely to be less successful in the many Asian cities where imbalances of power and money override the adoption of equitable, sustainable solutions. The WTTC guidelines do, however, provide important directions for policy planners to explore and can be adapted to various political and economic systems, particularly in the management of designated protected historic areas.

Visitor management is based on the idea of establishing limits to acceptable change. It requires an understanding of stakeholders, heritage site and area policies, vision statements by the residents as well as other closely aligned interest groups, and the legislative and regulatory possibilities for managing visitor numbers. By far the most promising strategy is one that calls for dispersing visitors from congested sites to areas with fewer tourists. Conceptually, this idea makes sense. However, convincing visitors not to visit famous sites and to instead visit lesser-known and possibly lesser-value destinations will be difficult.

The major planning issue is where to direct the dispersed tourism and under what conditions. Questions include: Are there other locations with similar attractions and sites of equal attractiveness and value? Are those areas ready for tourism? More work is needed to explore the dispersal concept and to better understand how to measure its impacts and its success in motivating visitors to lesser-known areas. This all involves a regional planning approach. Local policies must be part of much larger decisions on regional planning issues.

Policy and strategy responses to overtourism that have been discussed extensively and can be considered at the local level are presented in Table 8.1.

Policy	Strategy
Restricting access	Area closures especially during periods of cultural and religious activity Limiting group sizes Quotas Charging tourists a daily tariff (e.g. Bhutan) Lotteries Registrations or pre-bookings Barring tourism buses from a neighborhood or area Regulate accommodation supply Raising tourism taxes Limits days that people can rent their homes to tourists Limiting the length of stay
Encouraging off-peak and off-season travel	Price differentiation Responsible marketing and promotion strategies based on data-driven market research
Visitor experience design	Introduce new visitor development programs: circuits, trails, clusters Facilitating visitor journey mapping Use of new technologies and innovation in expanding experiences Develop new experiences

Table 8.1: Policy and strategy responses to overtourism

Community development

An essential element of responsible heritage area development is the principle that residents of these areas should not be economically disadvantaged and, most importantly, their quality of life should be enhanced, not diminished, by activities and initiatives in those areas, including tourism. Community economic development initiatives should adhere to the following principles:

- Develop plans and policies through inclusive planning processes, so that they are inclusive and reflect the diversity of the residents of a heritage area.
- Carefully define and manage carrying capacities.
- Use peaceful and tolerant processes and outcomes.
- Safeguard urban identities.
- Ensure equitable distribution of the benefits of heritage and tourism development.
- Engage in creative and innovative capacity building.
- Introduce innovative financing techniques.

In the planning process, community stakeholders (not just residents but also commercial, hospitality and institutional actors) must make choices regarding what they want to happen within a community. They may need to choose between objectives that are largely related to economic benefits and those with an emphasis on longer-term social benefits, including improvements in quality of life. They may also need to choose the types of uses and the types of visitors they want in a community. Since the financial resources to support conservation activities are often scarce and difficult to access, this calls for both traditional and creative approaches.

Many planners and heritage experts may not always be comfortable with planning for community development. But it is important that socio-economic dimensions are always considered in the process of formulating plans and strategies. Such dimensions include:

- Co-financing mechanisms
- Human and organisational capacity development strategies
- Initiatives supporting the sharing economy
- Community and equity-based economic development policies and programmes
- Programmes to establish community development corporations and cooperatives
- Assistance to provide housing
- Public-private partnerships initiatives
- Revenue capture and recovery mechanisms to finance capital investment
- Small and medium-sized enterprise development programmes
- Supply chain development
- Support for social enterprises
- Sustainable financing for the recurrent costs of asset maintenance
- Community-defined guidelines regarding the maximum use of an area, taking into account in some instances a 24-hour economy, which has activities throughout the day and night.

An important consideration in the preparation of community development strategies is to ensure that the private sector financially supports the provision of the necessary infrastructure to accommodate tourists. Indeed, one of the ongoing conversations in heritage area conservation is what role the private sector (including the tourism industry) should play in the operation and management of individual heritage sites. Too often the tourism industry is seen as a 'free rider'. Their customers make use of free or heavily subsidised attractions and resources, with little recognition that taxpayers are paying for these amenities. The same can be said for heritage conservation costs, which are in some cases absorbed by public authorities and individual property owners. Communities may, in some cases, consider that without a fair contribution to infrastructure costs by the private sector, tourism may not be a viable option in their location, since in some cases tourism can actually cost a community more money than it brings in. On the other hand, with cost-sharing by the private sector, the community may benefit significantly from well-managed tourism (at a scale that suits the local context). A complete impact study is essential if the private sector is to be a full financial partner in tourism development in heritage areas.

One interesting option proposed in India is to make companies responsible for building, operating and maintaining all tourism infrastructure, including amenities and services such as toilets, drinking water, accessibility for the disabled, signage, guides, lighting, food services, cleanliness and security (Johari, 2018). While there is some doubt about the ability of the private sector to maintain sites within the financial structures in which they work, it is an option that can be considered in light of the ongoing financial challenges facing most public authorities responsible for heritage resources.

Increasingly in responsible tourism development the focus has been on better understanding supply chains and how they can be used to generate increased revenue for local businesses and provide new opportunities for residents. While the focus often is on local supply chains that deal with handicrafts, food and local services, supply chains are in fact much larger than local concerns. Sophisticated supply chain management is needed, working in cooperation with local authorities to determine how to maximise the financial and employment-related dimensions of the supply chain. This type of analysis will allow communities to choose economic activities that support heritage conservation and increase quality of life (Hainsworth et al., 2007).

Data and knowledge management

An integrated urban heritage area planning and management approach presents a significant challenge to understanding the nature of an area and its opportunities and challenges. To gain this understanding and ensure decisions are evidence-based, data is required.

8

Data gathering is complex, however, as data must be collected in many areas, including:

- Plans and policies (adopted, implemented and projected)
- Economic activity
- Environmental quality
- Existing and projected demographics
- Human and industry capacity
- Tangible and intangible heritage resources
- Promotion, branding and positioning strategies
- Range and level of influence of stakeholders
- Residents' views of tourism and readiness to accept and support heritage designation
- Tourism-related experiences, services and infrastructure
- Urban services: infrastructure, mobility and access

In larger, complex urban areas it will be necessary to have access to all of this information. While much of this information is already collected in many urban areas of Western economies, this is not the case in many urban areas of Asia. In such cases, data collection and information management is a significant challenge. In cases where the required data is not available, proxies will have to a developed. However, data collection and analysis must be seen as an operational priority. Such data is necessary to establish common, credible and integrated databases for planning and management decision-making (NECSTouR, 2018).[4]

Data collection approaches

Given the complexity of the urban heritage contexts, the planning and management processes require interdisciplinary teams. Multidisciplinary research teams are effective as they can combine their skills and techniques to gain a better understanding of an area. While each discipline may have specific data gathering techniques, various disciplines are today coming together through using what might be seen as 'non-traditional' techniques. Ethnographic approaches, for example, are being used to understand visitor behaviour, which allows for enhanced interpretation and visitor management and, most importantly, better targeting of the types of visitors that will most benefit from an urban heritage area experience. Another example of innovative information gathering, at least within the sphere of heritage and tourism planning, is cultural mapping, which is increasingly being used to understand heritage areas. This was the case in the George Town example in Chapter 6.

An interesting example of cultural mapping in Pembroke Ontario produced a map of the local cultural resources and illustrates the significant resources that can support urban heritage conservation efforts (Figure 8.9).

4 The George Town case study provides an excellent example of comprehensive data gathering, and demonstrates that this is no longer theory but actual practice.

Figure 8.9: Example of cultural mapping: Pembroke, Ontario Canada. Source: City of Pembroke.

Data sharing

In most urban situations, decision-making regarding heritage conservation and the design and the management of visitor experiences is often left to property developers and the tourism industry, even when there is heritage legislation in place. Conservation professionals, heritage interests and communities are rarely involved. This is partly a result of lack of access to information and data regarding the local situation.

To ensure decision-making takes the views of all stakeholders into consideration, data on the various dimensions of a heritage area must be shared with all the stakeholders. This must be done in a user-friendly manner, recognising the interrelated nature of the data. Such data sharing can be achieved through the use of an online 'dashboard'. Using a 'tourism dashboard', for instance, allows stakeholders to see data on the various dimensions of tourism and also assess a destination's 'health'. A sample page from the online Hawaii tourism dashboard is presented in Figure 8.10 (Park and Jamieson, 2009).

8

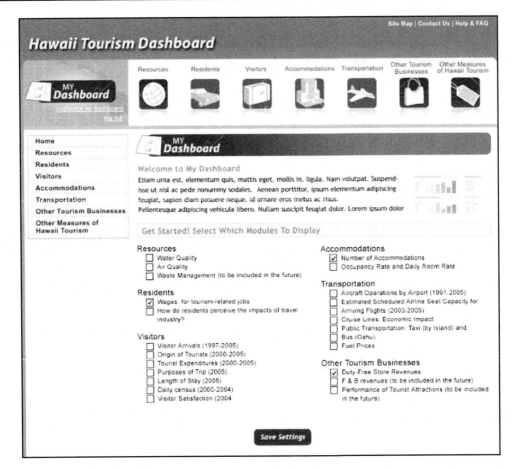

Figure 8.10: The Hawaii tourism dashboard. Source: Park and Jamieson, 2009.

Developing strategic skills and knowledge

As noted above, interdisciplinary teams are essential for planning in complex urban contexts. To plan and implement integrated urban heritage area plans, each planning and management team requires skills and knowledge in the areas listed in Table 8.2. (Part of this table has been adapted from an unpublished, undated UNESCO Bangkok document describing plans to develop a competency framework for cultural heritage management.)

Skills and knowledge in fields such as building conservation, material conservation (stone, wood, plaster, terracotta, modern materials, etc.), documentation processes, value-based management planning, condition assessment, reporting and documentation, and monitoring and evaluation will also continue to be the purview of conservation experts.

The required skills and knowledge can be delivered in various ways, including by distance education, on-the-job learning led by experts, and formal short courses. The method of delivery will depend on the context and location. Detailed course packages with learning objectives and learning content could be developed either nationally or regionally. An example of this method of imparting skill and knowledge sets was the creation of the Alberta Historical Resources Intern Program, which was a joint collaboration between the University of Calgary and the Government of Alberta. It provided people working on historic sites in the province of Alberta with interdisciplinary courses that gave them an overall view and understanding of each component of the historical resource management process (Jamieson and Buchik, 1988).

Table 8.2: Key skill and knowledge areas

Planning and policy dimension	Skill and knowledge areas
Heritage planning and management	Developing conservation plans; condition assessment; recording and documentation; monitoring and evaluation; storytelling surveys; urban revitalisation; urban design; interpretation; review heritage building plans; develop planning and design regulations
Built heritage conservation	Adaptive reuse; a new design and heritage environments; use of traditional materials and techniques; materials conservation, collections management
Management	Project management; site interpretation; community engagement; conflict resolution; visitor management; disaster management; information management; marketing; human resource management
Provision of inclusive, efficient and effective service delivery	Mobility planning and service delivery; provision of housing for residents and visitors; providing safety and security; developing infrastructure especially or peak seasons; ability to communicate with a wide range of stakeholders
Provide for inclusive and equitable economic and community development	Develop the capacity of local people to become involved in the visitor economy; establish investment policies and programs; supply chain management; technical assistance; how to ensure revenue capture and recovery mechanism; ensure that the revenue generated by tourism benefit the local population
Implement visitor management and carrying capacity policies and plans	How to implement carrying capacity policies; provide programming in the form of events and festivals for communities as well as visitors; develop authentic and inclusive visitor experiences; understand how to apply the limits of acceptable change concept

Measuring success

Indicators

As noted in Chapters 1 and 2, success in tourism is often measured in terms of economic growth and tourist numbers, which leads to these factors being prioritised over others. There is therefore a need for more sophisticated indicators of success that go beyond simple quantitative measures.

Examples of indicators can be seen in Table 8.3.

8

Table 8.3: Examples of indicators

Fields	Examples of indicators
Heritage	Compliance with regulations and building codes; current inventory classification of heritage assets; levels of reuse; investments in heritage properties; local involvement in conservation efforts; increased appreciation of heritage values by local people; updated and relevant interpretive systems
Planning	Multiyear heritage area strategy that includes a focus on responsible development, levels of stakeholder participation; partnerships formed and developed, crisis and emergency response plan in place
Carrying capacity	Energy availability at peak seasons; perceptions of crowding on the part of residents; perceptions of crowding on the part of visitors; water availability in peak seasons; levels of congestion
Economic	Levels of consumer spend (local versus visitor); diversity of retail uses; increase in employment levels for local people; number of non-profit and social enterprise visitor businesses; new investment opportunities; number of community owned businesses; level of residential and retail turnover; vacancy in the heritage area
Quality of life	Crime levels availability; quality and cost of housing; have poverty levels been reduced; availability, quality and cost of drinking water; resident satisfaction with the quality of life of the heritage area; regular collection, monitoring and public reporting of data on resident aspirations and satisfaction
Governance	Is the management organisation suited to the size and scale of the area; is the monitoring system reviewed and evaluated periodically; regular monitoring and reporting of visitor expenditure data

Indicators require clear definitions so that all parties clearly understand what is being tracked. Of particular importance from a planning and management perspective is that whatever indicators are chosen they must be able to detect changes that result from a planning or management intervention. To be able to assess the impact of planning interventions within the heritage area, it is necessary to collect baseline data prior to implementing interventions. Comparisons against baseline data will enable the performance of the programme to be measured and can provide evidence for the strategy. Some element of comparability is fundamental to a better understanding of the relative roles, strengths and weaknesses, and the impacts on each other. Indicators need to be easily measurable and must be reliable over time. Moreover, keeping the cost of collecting and measuring indicators to a minimum is essential given that when budgets are cut, monitoring is often the first activity to be eliminated. The data collected will depend on the nature of the heritage area, intended results and expected interim steps. Targets must be set, in cooperation with partners, that reflect the level of investment.

Satisfaction scores

Another way to measure success is using 'satisfaction scores'. These tools must be designed to differentiate between different types of users (residents, local workers, visitors, etc) and how they use the heritage area (retailers, hospitality providers, shoppers, employees, etc.). In the case of a retail heritage area, are the visitors there on a night out, for a quick purchase, for an event or attraction or simply to spend some time socialising with fellow residents? It is important to also ensure the scores identify why residents and visitors are satisfied or dissatisfied.

Paradigm fit

The most important way of measuring success is to evaluate whether or not an urban heritage area has made a paradigm shift of the type described earlier in this chapter. Some of the factors to be examined in assessing a paradigm would include: protection of the vernacular heritage of everyday life; safeguarding of living traditions and intangible cultural practices; presence of immersive cultural experiences for visitors; decentralised local community decision-making (real-time, flexible and adaptive); and sustainable social and economic programmes for the heritage area. Such an evaluation could also include the following questions:

- Has a set of principles and criteria for responsible heritage area conservation been developed and agreed upon?
- Has there been a mindset change (as defined by the planners) on the part of the major stakeholders?
- Is there agreement on the strategic policy dimensions?
- Do stakeholders understand the linkages between urban planning, heritage conservation and tourism?
- Have a common set of areas of management concerns and a common work plan been adopted to guide an integrated planning and implementation approach?
- Have the required process-related skills and knowledge to achieve responsible urban heritage conservation been identified?
- Is there a team of knowledgeable competent technical professionals, back-stopped by effective data collection and a reliable database of information on the city, its resources, and its demographics?
- Is the leadership committed to implementing and achieving the common vision in a non-partisan, fully-transparent way?

Future directions and challenges

The ultimate goal of urban heritage management is the creation of liveable, sustainable communities whose cultural continuum and enduring 'spirit of place' is celebrated and shared with an informed public of residents and visitors alike. The case examples and studies indicate that to achieve such a goal there is a need for a mindset change, leading to a paradigm shift in urban area conservation practice.

Ensuring that urban zoning and land-use regulations protect urban heritage comprehensively and responsibly will require setting in motion a process of change. As things currently stand, this process is likely to be driven by stakeholders in the institutional and private sector, who have significant influence on the urban form and heritage conservation. The process of changing zoning and land use regulations is slow and gradual, so given that urban areas do not have the luxury of time, the focus in the short term must be on improving conservation practices within existing zoning and land-use regulations. Indeed, the emphasis must be on ensuring that the professionals responsible for the conservation process have the structures, tools, skills and knowledge to plan for responsible and sustainable urban heritage conservation.

New structures, tools, skills and knowledge are required at the municipal level, where it can no longer be 'business as usual'. Innovation must become an important part of the urban heritage area conservation process. This will require an integrated approach to planning as well as interdisciplinary team work.

Urban areas in general and urban heritage areas in particular will face a number of challenges in the future as illustrated by Figure 8.11 (drawn from ICLEI, 2018 and WEF, n.d.).

Figure 8.11: Future urban and heritage challenges

Urban heritage area development and planning principles

As a way of defining responsible integrated heritage area conservation so as to help guide urban conservation practice, the authors have developed three sets of principles: (i) overall principles (ii) specific conservation-related principles and (iii) tourism-related principles. These principles are presented in Table 8.4 and discussed below.

Table 8.4: Urban heritage area development and planning principles

Overall principles
The entire historic urban landscape must be conserved. An integrated approach to urban heritage area development and planning is essential. All stakeholders must be engaged in decision-making processes. The creation of partnerships is essential. Planning and policy decisions must be data driven. Heritage area populations must not be displaced. The tourism industry must invest in heritage area infrastructure. Responsible carrying capacity policies must be developed and enforced. Integrated planning processes are key to developing responsible heritage areas. Appropriate governance models must be adopted. Land use & zoning regulations must be updated to conform with the heritage significance of an area.
Conservation-related principles
Conservation-related principles Heritage assets are important. Heritage asset value management is integral to the overall conservation process. Integrated safeguarding of tangible and intangible heritage is essential. Values and shared experiences must be communicated. Heritage monitoring and mitigation are necessary in the heritage area conservation process. Trained and certified professionals must be employed in the conservation process.
Tourism-related principles
Tourism development must support the conservation of local cultural heritage. Tourism development must minimise negative impacts. Tourism development must ensure equitable economic benefits. Tourism development must generate opportunities for quality employment for local people. Tourism development must use visitor management policies and plans.

Overall principles

The entire historic urban landscape must be conserved.

Heritage assets, while valuable individually, have appreciably more value as a collection of tangible and intangible cultural expressions that exist within the physical and cultural space of a community. All stakeholders, collectively, have an obligation to preserve and protect the entirety of the historic urban landscape through all possible means, including legislation, regulation, zoning and the systematic assessment of the heritage impact of all proposed development projects, regardless of sponsor or instigating agency.

An integrated approach to urban heritage area development and planning is essential.

The key stakeholders involved in urban planning, heritage conservation and tourism planning and development must work together to ensure responsible development. This requires a mindset change, in which the various planners (urban, heritage and tourism) reach a common understanding of the needs of the stakeholders and a common vision. It is no longer acceptable that these key players within urban areas do not work together strategically. The staff of municipal

8

authorities, heritage bodies and tourism organisations must develop the skills and knowledge to effectively integrate their objectives, with the ultimate objective of conserving tangible and intangible heritage.

Stakeholders must be effectively engaged in decision-making processes.

All stakeholders need to be engaged in planning processes, as these affect stakeholders' lives and livelihoods. While the residents of urban heritage areas must be respected, the wider common good is paramount, therefore all issues must be considered and all stakeholders included in decision-making processes.

The creation of partnerships is essential.

Partnerships between heritage interests, tourism authorities and the private sector are necessary for sustainable heritage conservation. Cooperation between partners can generate new ideas, vitality and more resources.

Planning and policy decisions must be data driven.

Urban heritage planning and management, including all decisions to develop heritage assets for economic and social gain must be supported by data and integrated analysis designed to safeguard community cultural assets and to equitably benefit the largest number of resident community members possible. Development proposals should be assessed based on their sustainability.

Heritage area populations must not be displaced.

The purpose of the protection and management of a community's heritage assets is to ensure that these assets will be passed with their values intact from one generation to the next. The measure to which this objective is achieved is the inherited transmission of physical property and intangible knowledge across generations. Displacement of traditional residents for profit or political gain is unethical and antithetical to the principles of integrated heritage planning and management.

The tourism industry must invest in heritage area infrastructure.

Infrastructure provides visitors with access to heritage assets, especially to those assets that are associated with a particular place or physical space. External parties wishing to access the heritage assets of a community must accept full financial responsibility for the development and operation of infrastructure that exceeds the needs of the impacted community and of any additional infrastructure required by visitors.

Responsible carrying capacity policies must be developed and enforced.

Exceeding carrying capacity degrades the value of the community's heritage assets, both tangible and intangible, reduces the quality of life of residents and diminishes visitor satisfaction. Visitor carrying capacity limits are real and are easily exceeded, and therefore must be pro-actively managed by local government planners and policy-makers, in cooperation with the tourism industry.

Integrated planning processes are key to developing responsible heritage areas.

Planning processes should be strategic and goal oriented rather than reactive and preventative, and must be designed in cooperation with engaged stakeholders.

This requires linking the heritage and tourism sectors, as well as sectors relating to cultural, socio-economic and infrastructure development. The process must accommodate inputs from heritage interests as well as residents, government and affected interest groups. The process must be purposeful and deliberate, but also flexible so that it can adjust to changing circumstances. The process must also be guided by principles of good management. Where resources are limited and decision-making processes are lengthy, tactical planning approaches are required. These use short-term approaches to conserve tangible and intangible heritage while improving the conditions of local residents. Tactical planning recognises that smaller and modest initiatives can set the stage for big changes, especially when stakeholders are sceptical.

Appropriate governance models must be adopted.

It is important to adopt models that are appropriate to each heritage area. In some cases, a top-down approach may be the most appropriate given the context and the nature of the planning and heritage legislation and structure. In cases where the population has a high level of capacity, self-governance models may be most appropriate.

Land use and zoning regulations must be updated to conform with the heritage significance of an area.

Property development and speculation, whether by members of the community or by outside parties, is an ever-present danger threatening the long-term protection of a community's collective heritage assets and the coherence of the historic urban landscape. Given that planning policies, and zoning and land use regulations determine the development potential of a property or site, and investment decisions, by both outside interests and residents, are made based on the development potential of a site or property, the zoning and land use regulations need to conform with the area's heritage significance. However, given that developers may legally develop property based on the land use zoning and building regulations and conservation measures that were in place at the time of purchase, plans and strategies have to take that into account. If the zoning or land-use regulations are not in keeping with heritage character of an area or if residents desire amendments, these regulations must be changed.

Conservation-related principles

Heritage assets are important.

All communities have unique cultural and natural heritage assets, which are the combined legacy of the efforts of the communities' forebears, transmitted to future generations for care and stewardship. These assets are important and must be protected.

Heritage asset value management is integral to the overall conservation process.

Heritage asset management is an inter-generational public trust, upheld through the application of the best available expertise and know-how. This management allows communities to preserve and, over time, add value to the significance of their cultural and natural heritage assets, by safeguarding both the authenticity and integrity of these assets.

Integrated safeguarding of tangible and intangible heritage is essential.

Heritage assets in a community have both tangible (physical) and intangible (non-physical) dimensions, which must be safeguarded in a holistic, integrated process, recognising that intangible cultural practices – rituals, beliefs, languages, life ways, artistic expressions and occupations – are the well-spring from which arise, over time, tangible physical cultural expressions in the form of buildings, homes, works of art, crafts, food, artefacts, and utensils and other bespoke objects, both permanent and consumable.

Values and shared experiences must be communicated.

Communities must have the opportunity to communicate the inestimable value of their heritage assets to persons from outside their community; to activate these assets for the economic and other benefit of the community, individually and collectively; and thereby to contribute the unique values of their community's heritage values to the common good.

Heritage monitoring and mitigation are necessary in the heritage area conservation process.

Vigilance is a necessary part of responsible heritage asset management. To this end, the community has not only the right but also the responsibility to monitor the state of conservation of its heritage assets, and to demand immediate government intervention to correct any infraction and gain mitigation or restitution as appropriate.

Trained and certified professionals must be employed in the conservation process.

Only trained, certified and experienced conservation professionals should be consulted and employed to undertake repair or restoration work on cultural heritage assets. Their work must be compensated at market rates by the project proponent.

Tourism-related principles

Tourism development must support the conservation of cultural heritage.

The tourism industry must recognise its responsibility to support the conservation of tangible and intangible heritage. It is no longer acceptable that the industry benefit from heritage resources without participating financially in the conservation of those resources.

Tourism development must minimise negative impacts.

All policies and plans must be assessed in terms of their impact on the social, economic and environmental dimensions of a community, with the full intent of ensuring the least possible negative impact on the community's heritage and social systems.

Tourism development must ensure equitable economic benefits.

Tourism must be developed using community-based and social enterprise models, and the developers must ensure that the economic benefits of tourism are shared equitably within the community. Locally-based tourism enterprises must be encouraged and supported to ensure that local people benefit from tourism development.

Tourism development must generate opportunities for quality employment for local people.

An integral part of heritage-related tourism development must be concerned with building the capacities of local people to participate in the tourism economy. This can be achieved through developing skills and knowledge in the local population as well as through implementing hiring practices that prioritise local people. Improving access for disadvantaged sectors of the community is an essential element of responsible tourism development. Employment created through tourism development must provide good quality working environments and conditions.

Tourism development must use visitor management policies and plans.

All stakeholders must ensure that visitor management techniques and plans are an essential part of the overall management process of urban heritage areas. This involves not only ensuring that carrying capacities are respected but also that all visitors have access to the heritage environment, including those with disabilities. Visitor management approaches must encourage respect between tourists and the host community and contribute to building local pride and confidence. The tourism industry must ensure that visitors have access to quality interpretation and presentation.

Epilogue

The mindset change, principles and strategies presented in this book are designed to enable those planning for and managing urban heritage areas to responsibly maintain those areas while ensuring a high quality of life for the residents.

Ignoring the imperative for heritage conservation will not only squander past investments made in an urban area's resources, but will also destabilise the area's long-evolved social equilibrium and place it at a dangerous comparative disadvantage in relation to other competing regional centres of population and development.

A responsible integrated approach is one in which all stakeholders have an equal opportunity to benefit from urban heritage conservation and where all stakeholders understand their roles within a responsible form of development. Such an approach does not exploit the cultural values and heritage assets of a community, but rather respects and validates these values and assets through a sustained programme of conservation and asset-augmentation.

This process is clearly a work in progress, with growing opportunities for collaboration and exchange, towards which all the contributors and authors of this publication will continue to work.

8

References

Archer, D. (2016) 'What does the "M" of DMO mean for your destination?' Destination Think! https://destinationthink.com/m-of-dmo-destination/ (Accessed 3 September 2018.)

Arnstein, S. R. (1969) 'A ladder of citizen participation', *Journal of the American Institute of Planners*, **35**(4), 216-224.

Asian Development Bank (ADB) (2013) Myanmar Tourism Master Plan, Asian Development Bank project TA 46271-001 MYA.

Brunton, J. (2018) Venice poised to segregate tourists as city braces itself for May Day 'invasion', *The Guardian*, 1 May. https://www.theguardian.com/travel/2018/may/01/venice-to-segregate-tourists-in-may-day-overcrowding (Accessed 3 September 2018.)

City of Pembroke (n.d.) Cultural map: Pembroke and the Ottawa Valley. http://www.pembroke.ca/tourism/cultural-mapping/ (Accessed 3 September 2018.)

Coccossis H. & Mexa A., (2002), The coastal zone, in Coccossis, H. (ed) *Man and the Environment in Greece*, Hellenic Ministry for the Environment, Physical Planning and Public Works, Athens.

Crawford, R. (2016) What can complexity theory tell us about urban planning, Research Note 2, April, New Zealand Productivity Commission.

Curseu, P. L. and Schruijer, S. (2017) Stakeholder diversity and the comprehensiveness of sustainability decisions: 'The role of collaboration and conflict', *Current Opinion in Environmental Sustainability*, **28**, 114-120.

De Ascaniis, S., Gravari-Barbas, M. and Cantoni, L. (eds.) (2018) *Tourism Management at UNESCO World Heritage Sites*, Lugano: Università della Svizzera italiana.

European Expert Network on Culture (EENC) (2013) *Challenges and Priorities for Cultural Heritage in Europe: Results of an Expert Consultation*, EECN Paper, September.

Goodwin, H. (2017) WTM Responsible Tourism Awards 2017: Leaders in responsible tourism, http://haroldgoodwin.info/Awards/Report%20-%20WTM%20Responsible%20Tourism%20Awards%202017.pdf (Accessed 3 September 2018.)

Hainsworth, D., Jamieson, W., Noakes, S. and Day, S. (eds.) (2007) *A Toolkit for Monitoring and Managing Community-based Tourism*, Hanoi: SNV Asia Pro-Poor Tourism Network, SNV Vietnam and the University of Hawaii.

ICLEI (2018) *Resilient Cities Report 2018: Tracking local progress on the resilience targets of SDG 11*, Bonn: Local Governments for Sustainability (ICLEI).

ICOMOS (2013) The Burra Charter: The Australia ICOMOS Charter for Places of Cultural Significance. https://www.environment.sa.gov.au/our-places/Heritage/conserving-our-heritage/Burra_Charter (Accessed 10 July 2018.)

Jamieson, W. and Buchik, P. (1988) Training in historic resource management: the development of an approach for Western Canada, *APT Bulletin: The Journal of*

Preservation Technology, **20** (1), 50-61.

Jamieson, W. and Jamieson, M. (2016) Urban destination level tactical tourism planning in developing economies. *Tourism Development Journal*, **14** (1), 1-18.

Jamieson, W. and Schipani, S. (2014) *'Responsible tourism', Myanmar: Unlocking the Potential, Country Diagnostic Study*. Manila: Asian Development Bank.

Jessop, T. (2018) 11 angry tourist hotspots that are best avoided this summer, Culture Trip, 7 February. https://theculturetrip.com/europe/spain/articles/11-angry-tourist-hotspots-that-are-best-avoided-this-summer/ (Accessed 3 September 2018.)

Johari, A. (2018) Adopt a heritage: Should India let private sector companies manage tourism at top monuments?, Scroll.in, 29 March. https://scroll.in/article/873416/adopt-a-heritage-should-india-let-private-companies-manage-tourism-at-top-monuments (Accessed 3 September 2018.)

Landorf, C. (2009) Managing for sustainable tourism: A review of six cultural World Heritage sites, *Journal of Sustainable Tourism*, **17** (1), 53-70.

Landry, C. and Caust, M. (2017) *The Creative Bureaucracy and its Radical Common Sense*, Gloucestershire, UK: Comedia.

Lew, A. A. (2017) Tourism planning and place making: Place-making or placemaking?, *Tourism Geographies*, **19** (3), 448-466.

London & Partners (n.d.) About London & Partners. https://www.londonandpartners.com/about-us (Accessed 3 September 2018.)

Main Street America (n.d.) The Main Street Approach. https://www.mainstreet.org/mainstreetamerica/theapproach (Accessed 3 September 2018.)

Maxim, C. (2017) Challenges faced by world tourism cities - London's perspectives, *Current Issues in Tourism*. https://doi.org/10.1080/13683500.2017.1347609

Meadows, D., Randers, J. and Meadows, D. L. (2004) Limits to Growth: The 30-Year Update, London: Chelsea Green. http://donellameadows.org/archives/a-synopsis-limits-to-growth-the-30-year-update/ (Accessed 11 July 2018.)

Mekong Tourism Coordinating Office (MTCO) (2017) *Greater Mekong Subregion Tourism Sector Strategy 2016-2025*, Asian Development Bank - 49387-001.

Network European Regions for a Sustainable and Competitive Tourism (NECSTouR) (2018) *Barcelona Declaration of Tourism and Cultural Heritage: Better Places to Live Better Places to Visit*, Barcelona.

Park, S. Y. and Jamieson, W. (2009) Developing a tourism destination monitoring system: A case of the Hawaii tourism dashboard, *Asia Pacific Journal of Tourism Research*, **14** (1) 39-57.

Pollock, A. (2012) Are You Serious About Transforming Tourism?, Conscious travel: Signposts towards a new model for tourism, conference proceedings, Second UNWTO Ethics and Tourism Congress: Conscious Tourism for a New Era, 12 September, Quito, Ecuador. https://www.linkedin.com/pulse/you-serious-transforming-tourism-anna-pollock (Accessed 3 September 2018.)

8

Project for Public Spaces (1999) How to turn a place around, New York: Project for Public Spaces.

Responsible Tourism Partnership (2017) 'Anti-tourism protests'. http://responsibletourismpartnership.org/anti-tourism-protests/ (Accessed 3 September 2018.)

Sautter, E. and Leisen, B. (1999) 'Managing stakeholders: A tourism planning model', Annals of Tourism Research, 26 (2), 312-328.

United Nations Educational, Scientific and Cultural Organization (UNESCO) (2001) 'Lijiang Models for Cooperation'. http://www.unescobkk.org/culture/wh/culture-heritage-management-and-tourism-models-for-co-operation-among-stakeholders/lijiang-models-for-cooperation-among-stakeholders/ (Accessed 3 September 2018.)

UNESCO and Nordic World Heritage Foundation (NWHF) (2001) Cultural heritage management and tourism: Models for cooperation among stakeholders, Oslo: NWHF. http://www.unescobkk.org/fileadmin/user_upload/culture/AAHM/Resources/CHMangmtTourism.pdf (Accessed 3 September 2018.)

UNWTO (2018) Tourism and Cultural Synergies, Madrid: UNWTO.

Wood, M. (2017). Saving the Heart and Soul of Tourism Destinations. Huffington Post, May 22. Retrieved from https://www.huffingtonpost.com/entry/saving-the-heart-and-soul-of-tourism-destinations_us_591f4c95e4b0b28a33f62bf1

World Economic Forum (WEF) (n.d.) 'Mapping global transformations.' https://toplink.weforum.org/knowledge/insight/a1Gb0000000LiPhEAK/explore/summary (Accessed 3 September 2018.)

World Travel and Tourism Council (WTTC) (2017) Coping with success: Managing overcrowding in tourism destinations, McKinsey & Company and World Travel & Tourism Council. https://www.wttc.org/-/media/files/reports/policy-research/coping-with-success---managing-overcrowding-in-tourism-destinations-2017.pdf (Accessed 11 July 2018.)

 # Index

Printed in the United States
By Bookmasters